D1336933

0138555976

The Book of 365

The
BOOK *of* 365

ALL THE NUMBERS, NONE OF THE MATHS

Hugh Brazier and Jan McCann

◪ **SQUARE PEG** | London

Published by Square Peg 2014

2 4 6 8 10 9 7 5 3 1

Copyright © Hugh Brazier and
Jan McCann 2014

The authors have asserted their rights
under the Copyright, Designs and
Patents Act 1988 to be identified as
the authors of this work

First published in Great Britain
in 2014 by

Square Peg
Random House, 20 Vauxhall Bridge Road,
London SW1V 2SA

A Penguin Random House Company

Penguin
Random House
UK

A CIP catalogue record for this book
is available from the British Library

ISBN 9780224100823

Printed and bound in Great Britain by
Clays Ltd, St Ives PLC

CONTENTS

365 WORDS OF EXPLANATION

This project started at 199, on the steep steps up to St Mary's
Church in Whitby on the North Yorkshire coast – where, in Bram
Stoker's words, the churchyard hangs over the laneway to the
East Pier. We counted the steps on the way up, and again on the
way back down, and we got the same number each time. Shortly
afterwards – and we're not quite sure how – the idea of numbers,
and things connected to numbers, and writing a book about those
things, took off. All too soon we found ourselves searching out
a topic for every number from 1 to 365 – as well as boring our
friends and relations with questions such as 'Why cloud nine?',
'How many groats in a guinea?', and 'What is a Volkswagen 166
Schwimmwagen, and where can I buy one?'

Although the number of topics in the book matches the
number of days in the year, this is not a calendar book. It isn't
really a book about numbers, either. It's about things, events, and
ideas. We have (of course) tended to write about the topics that
interest us the most – books and bats, music and medicine, food
and feathers, astronomy and art – although a few planes, trains,
and automobiles crept in while our backs were turned, as did a
smattering of matters mildly mathematical. In addition, a few
topics insisted on appearing twice – and how could we turn away
Tristram Shandy or Isambard Kingdom Brunel, when they came
knocking at our door for a second time?

Having started at 199 ourselves, we can hardly insist that
you begin reading at 1 and work your way through, number
by number, until you reach the last page. There is no set order.

You can try it numerically, or alphabetically (via the index), or dip in wherever you like, or you can use the links at the bottom of each page: start anywhere you want, and if you follow the chain of links you will visit every number in the book and end up back where you started without ever retracing your steps.

Finally, please forgive us for including 366 numbers in a book whose title refers to only 365.

TO BEGIN AT THE BEGINNING...

Unlike the platforms at King's Cross station in London, this book does not start with zero, but with 1.

Does that mean a single-celled organism or a one-armed bandit? A jealous god or a unicycle? A whole universe or a solitary hydrogen atom? Perhaps the answer is a unicorn, for a book of this kind surely deserves at least one mythical beast. As Ursula Le Guin observed, 'Children know perfectly well that unicorns aren't real, but they also know that books about unicorns, if they are good books, are true books.'

Through most of human history, adults as well as children treated unicorns not as mythical beasts but as bona fide members of the fauna of far-off lands. They featured not in the myths but in the natural history texts of the Ancient Greeks, they were included in medieval bestiaries, Marco Polo gave a detailed description of one he saw in Java, and a unicorn horn held pride of place among the possessions of Queen Elizabeth I of England.

For those of us who are still not sure on which side of the threshold between myth and reality to place the unicorn, the ideal solution can be found in Lewis Carroll's *Through the Looking-Glass*. The ever-practical Alice finds it hard to believe in the unicorn she meets, having been brought up to think of them as fabulous monsters, but the unicorn is equally perplexed by the sight of a human child, and proposes: 'If you'll believe in me, I'll believe in you. Is that a bargain?'

TO BEGIN AGAIN, TURN TO **89**

2

Pairwise comparisons

'Bullet-headed and with hair like tow', Samneric (Sam and Eric in William Golding's 1954 novel *Lord of the Flies*) are identical twins. They are inseparable and indistinguishable. They breathe together and grin together. Even their names are joined into one breath. If we leave aside the minor problem that they are fictional, they would have been perfect subjects for a twin study.

Twin studies have been an essential tool in behavioural genetics, psychology, and epidemiology for decades. Comparisons of twin and non-twin siblings, monozygotic and dizygotic twins, separated and non-separated twins have all played a part in helping to tease out the differing contributions of heredity and environment in determining how we all turn out.

The first twin study is often credited to the Victorian polymath Francis Galton – but, writing in 1875, he knew nothing of Mendelian inheritance, let alone DNA. Today, what Galton saw as a simple dichotomy of nature versus nurture is increasingly recognised, thanks to the new science of epigenetics, as a complex set of interactions between genotype and environment. Monozygotic twins may start life with matching genes, but those genes soon diverge, subject to subtly different external influences from the moment the fertilised egg splits into two.

In *Lord of the Flies* Samneric function largely as one person, but in real life Sam and Eric would have been two different individuals. Modern science is at last getting closer to recognising – and explaining – what any twin could have told you all along.

THERE IS ANOTHER PAIR OF SIBLINGS (BUT NOT TWINS) AT **289**

3

Tell us a joke

An Englishman, an Irishman, and a Scotsman walk into a bar... Friends, Romans, countrymen... Life, liberty, and the pursuit of happiness... There is something peculiarly appealing about things that come in threes, whether it's a Holy Trinity, three blind mice, or three strikes and you're out. And anyone telling a joke, making a speech, or, for that matter, writing a declaration of independence is likely to use a threefold pattern sooner or later.

Often there is an increase in the number of syllables in the progression from first to third, giving a crescendo-like effect. Alternatively, the first and second items establish a pattern that is broken by a twist in the third. This is the classic structure of many jokes, and an important effect of building up to a climax may also be to make the third item both memorable and irrefutable.

The ancient Greeks included the rule of three, or *tricolon*, in their rules for rhetoric from at least the fifth century BCE. And ever since, from Demosthenes, Isocrates, and Cicero to Abraham Lincoln, Winston Churchill, and Barack Obama, great orators, politicians, and lawyers – not to mention storytellers, comedians, and advertisers – have used threes to make their arguments more persuasive. What we hear in a pattern of three we believe – for it is surely the truth, the whole truth, and nothing but the truth.

YOU'LL FIND A FAMOUS GROUP OF THREE AT **268**

A LEG AT EACH CORNER

In the USA there exists a political boundary that has become something of a tourist destination. The Four Corners Monument marks the only point in the country shared by four states: Arizona, Colorado, New Mexico, and Utah. The monument – maintained and promoted by the Navajo Nation – consists of a granite disc, within which is embedded a smaller disc, made of bronze and inscribed with the words: 'Four states here meet in freedom under God', arranged so that there are two words in each state.

First surveyed by E. N. Darling in 1868 (and again in 1875 by Chandler Robbins, at which time the marker was moved to its current position), it is sometimes reported that the monument is still not in the right location. Indeed, in 2009, a spokesperson for the US National Geodetic Survey agreed that it is placed 551 metres east of where modern surveyors would mark the point. However, once a survey commissioned to establish a boundary has been accepted by the involved parties, the survey markers are legally binding, even if an error is later discovered. And such details do not seem to trouble visitors, whose favourite occupation is to straddle the monument, with a limb in each state.

5

WHY IS A ROSE LIKE A STARFISH?

The answer lies in the number five, because both display penta-radial (five-sided) symmetry. A wild rose has five petals arranged around the centre of the flower, just as a starfish has five identical arms. And that makes the rose a typical plant, but the starfish a very odd animal.

Most of the animals we are familiar with are bilaterally symmetrical, with a head and a tail, a front and a back, a left side and a right. On the whole, animals that do not conform to this pattern are primitive things such as sea anemones and jellyfish, and at first glance a starfish looks rather similar. But in fact starfish and other echinoderms (sea urchins, sea cucumbers, and the like) are surprisingly advanced animals. In terms of their evolution, they are not only bilaterians but also deuterostomes (go and look it up!) – which means that they are more closely related to the vertebrates, including ourselves, than they are to worms or insects, never mind sea anemones. Most starfish larvae are bilaterally symmetrical, and they only develop their strange radial symmetry as they mature.

The number of arms varies among the 2,000 or so starfish species, and one known as *Labidiaster annulatus* can have up to 50. Most, however, including the ceramic and painted specimens commonly seen in bathrooms, have five arms, and fivefold symmetry is very much the rule for all the echinoderms. But precisely why it is five, and not seven, or nine, or seventeen, remains a mystery.

FOR BILATERAL SYMMETRY, CRAWL ON TO **10**

YOU CAN'T HAVE YOUR CAKE...

If the covers of glossy fitness magazines are anything to go by, the rectus abdominis is all the rage. Some people spend hours in the gym every week honing theirs to ripped perfection, while others are content simply to ease theirs into action with the occasional trip from sofa to fridge in search of liquid refreshment.

The rectus abdominis is a long, flat muscle that extends vertically the entire length of the abdomen. We each have two of them, and they flex the vertebral column, drawing the breastbone towards the pubis. The muscles are better known as the 'abs', or 'six-pack', and they give their owner a rock-hard washboard stomach that seems to be universally admired and envied.

The six-pack gets its name from the way the paired rectus abdominis muscles are divided by bands of connective tissue into six distinctive sections, three on each side of the central linea alba (some lucky people have eight sections). And for those men and women who are keen to get the six-pack look, the best gym exercises are the crunch (regular, reverse, oblique, or crossover: take your pick), the knee raise, the seated Russian twist, and the barbell roll-out.

For those who prefer a different kind of six-pack, another trip to the fridge is called for.

These boots are made for…running

Assorted shoes, boots, and slippers make numerous appearances in European fairy tales. Think of Puss in his magnificent thigh-high boots, or the tiny glass slipper that fits Cinderella's equally tiny foot, or those red shoes in which a young girl is forced continually to dance as punishment for her vanity.

Little Thumb or *Hop-o'-my-Thumb* (in French, *Le Petit Poucet*) – written by Charles Perrault (1628–1703) – features the splendidly useful seven-league boots, whose wearer could take massive strides (seven leagues long, in fact) and therefore cover great distances very quickly. The story's eponymous hero is the youngest, smallest, and smartest of seven boys in a poor woodcutter's family. He outwits the ogre, who, while chasing the boys in his seven-league boots, becomes weary and foolishly falls asleep. Little Thumb steals the boots, puts them on his own feet (fortunately, the boots change size to fit the wearer), and saves the day for his whole family.

A league is a unit of measurement with a long and varied history. It was used to describe the distance walked in an hour by an average man, and is now often defined as 3 miles (4.828032 kilometres – though writers of fairy tales are unlikely to have had anything quite so precise in mind).

Incidentally, Perrault, like Little Thumb, was the youngest of seven children.

FOR ANOTHER (MOSTLY) OBSOLETE MEASURE OF DISTANCE, SEE **220**

8

Spinning into the future

In 1768, a small but angry mob broke into the house of James Hargreaves in the village of Stanhill, Lancashire, and destroyed a new-fangled piece of machinery that Hargreaves had recently invented. But why?

For many centuries, wool had been spun into yarn using small spinning wheels that were turned by hand or with a foot pedal, and which were used in people's homes (spinning really was a cottage industry). The story goes that in 1767 Hargreaves' daughter, Jenny, accidentally knocked over the family's spinning wheel. Its spindle continued to turn, and this gave Hargreaves the idea that one wheel clearly had enough power to turn a whole line of spindles. He set to work on building a new machine which had just one wheel but eight spindles – and he named it after his daughter.

Hargreaves patented his Spinning Jenny in 1770, but by this time his idea had already been widely copied, and he made very little money from it. The men who had burst into his house in 1768 were worried that the machine threatened their livelihoods: one person, using the Spinning Jenny, could now do the work previously done by eight. And they were right. Despite their protests, the tide of industrial progress was unstoppable, and by the time of Hargreaves' death in 1778 over 20,000 Spinning Jennies were in use in Britain.

GO TO **32** FOR ANOTHER YARN ABOUT SPINNING

UNTYING THOSE TETHERS

To be on cloud nine is to be in a state of blissful happiness – though quite why is unclear. One explanation arises from Buddhist philosophy, in which cloud nine symbolises the penulti-mate phase of an individual's ten-step progress to enlightenment, and a 'perfect score' of ten perhaps needs to remain always just out of reach. Another possibility is that it originates from the *International Cloud Atlas* of 1896, in which, of the ten cloud types listed, cloud nine, cumulonimbus, was not only the most comfort-able-looking, but also the highest cloud in the atmosphere.

In 1960 the American futurist Richard Buckminster Fuller and the Japanese architect Shoji Sadao created the *Project for Floating Cloud Structures (Cloud Nine)*. This utopian architectural project consisted of geodesic spheres which would, in theory, become airborne by slightly increasing the temperature of the air inside. Fuller and Sadao envisaged that these 'Cloud Nines' would contain mini-cities, and that they could be either tethered in one place, or free-floating so that they could migrate in response to climatic and environmental conditions.

In 1967, for Expo '67 in Montreal, Canada, Fuller and Sadao produced the US Pavilion – a giant dome 60 metres high, designed to look as cloud-like as possible, which lives on as the Montreal Biosphere. Fuller and Sadao are credited with popu-larising geodesic spheres, and their ideas certainly inspired the biomes at the Eden Project in Cornwall, UK. Their 'Cloud Nine' project, however, remained firmly rooted to the drawing board.

FOR SOMETHING ELSE TETHERED, SEE **256**

10

Blots and biases

Rorschach ink blots, and what people see in them, are widely recognised as the archetypal psychological test. They pop up everywhere. Andy Warhol did a series of paintings based on them. There are even online 'Rorschach tests' that you can try out for yourself.

But the real thing is slightly different from the popular image. The official test, as devised by Swiss psychologist Hermann Rorschach (1884–1922), uses just ten specific ink blots. The images are precisely printed, using different colours and complex shading, very different from the crude outlines so commonly seen. The ten ink blots are supposed to be kept secret, to avoid biasing the test results – but now that they are out of copyright they are widely available. There was a storm of protest when Wikipedia published all ten images, along with common responses to them, in 2009.

The official test consists of far more than noting a person's reactions to each of the ten blots. The time taken to respond, questions asked, gestures, many aspects of the behaviour of the subject – all this is taken into account. Nonetheless, some psychologists see the wide availability of the ten ink blots as a problem. Others may see a bigger problem in the continued use of a 93-year-old test that is at best subjective, at worst completely meaningless.

ANOTHER DODGY PSYCHOMETRIC TEST POPS UP AT **180**

11

MAN'S INHUMANITY TO MAN

'The end of the line at the end of the line' – this is the description given to Cell Block 11 at Auschwitz 1, for it was here, during World War Two, that prisoners were brought for punishment for offences such as attempting to escape, or sabotaging the work done in the camp's factories. One of the punishments took place in the four *Stehbunker* ('standing cells') in the basement. They measured just 1.5 square metres, and four men were placed in each cell at once. After spending a night here, without food, water, lighting, heating, or cooling, and standing in their own excrement, the men were forced to do ten hours' work the next day. Not surprisingly, few survived this punishment for long.

On 3 September 1941, Cell Block 11 became the location for what was probably the first mass killing of people using Zyklon-B, a powerful pesticide that, until then, had been used solely to kill the lice in prisoners' clothing. Once exposed to heated air, however, it produced lethal gas. The basement of Cell Block 11 was sealed up, and pellets of Zyklon-B were inserted through vents in the wall. Those inside – some 600 Russian and 250 Polish prisoners – were dead within about twenty minutes. This hideous 'experiment' paved the way for the use of Zyklon-B as a method of mass extermination in specially constructed gas chambers, in which many thousands later died.

GO TO **344** FOR ANOTHER POW CAMP

12

HOW MANY 'GOOD MEN AND TRUE'?

Trial by jury was apparently an Anglo-Saxon invention, established at the end of the tenth century by King Æthelred the Unready, whose Wantage Code (997 CE) stipulated that questions of guilt and innocence in criminal matters should be decided by the 'twelve eldest *thegns*' of each *wapentake* (district). That, at least, is one theory. In truth, the origins of the jury system are rather hazy. Some historians point out that the ancient Greeks had a similar system, while others give the credit to Henry II, during whose reign in the twelfth century the Assize of Clarendon rejected trial by ordeal and trial by combat in favour of what would eventually become trial by jury.

It is commonly believed that a jury consists of twelve people, but this is by no means universally true. In the county courts of England and Wales, for example, the number is eight; in Scotland there are fifteen jurors in criminal trials; and in 1970 the US Supreme Court decided that a jury of six was sufficient.

So a jury need not consist of 'twelve good men and true'. But what about women? In Britain a woman's right to serve on a jury was established in 1919, but in the USA it was not until the 1970s that women became eligible for jury service in all states on exactly the same terms as men.

THE ANGLO-SAXON DOCUMENT AT **139** IS NOT A CODE, BUT A CODEX

13

UNLUCKY FOR SOME

'It was a bright cold day in April, and the clocks were striking thirteen.' The opening sentence of George Orwell's *Nineteen Eighty-Four* (1949) – a disturbing tale about the dangers of totalitarianism – establishes an atmosphere of complete normality; until, that is, we reach the last word. What has happened to the clocks – and therefore, by extension, to society as a whole – to create such a shift in what we think of as normal? Reading on, we discover that this is an imagined future world, and that, although thirteen strikes are utterly strange for us, they are of no consequence at all for the story's protagonist, Winston Smith. The thirteen strikes of the clock have no relevance for the rest of the story: they have done their job in that first sentence.

By contrast, in Philippa Pearce's *Tom's Midnight Garden* (1958), a magical children's fantasy with a happy ending, the thirteenth strike of a clock is central to the plot. It provides the story's hero, Tom, with an escape from boredom and loneliness, for it is a 'portal' into a beautiful garden and into a past where adventures – and a kind of love – are to be found. There (or, rather, then) Tom meets the young orphan Hattie, only to discover that she is not quite what she seems.

Thirteen: unlucky for some, but not for all.

14

The fourteenth Mr Wilson

Until the turn of the twentieth century most British prime ministers were members of the peerage – Viscount So-and-So, the Earl of Somewhere, the Marquess of Elsewhere – and they therefore sat in the House of Lords, not the House of Commons. But over the years the balance of power between Lords and Commons shifted, to give the Commons far greater legislative powers. It therefore became the norm that prime ministers were members of the lower house. When the Marquess of Salisbury resigned as prime minister in July 1902, the tradition of a British government led from the House of Lords came to an end.

But in October 1963 the Conservative prime minister Harold Macmillan unexpectedly resigned, and even more unexpectedly the man who was appointed to succeed him was a peer, the 14th Earl of Home. He quickly disclaimed his title, to become Sir Alec Douglas-Home, and was elected to the Commons in a conveniently timed by-election, but throughout his one-year tenure as prime minister the opposition Labour party under Harold Wilson made much of his aristocratic background. Wilson commented: 'After half a century of democratic advance, of social revolution, of rising expectations, the whole process has ground to a halt with a fourteenth earl.' Sir Alec's riposte is almost the only saying for which he is remembered: 'As far as the fourteenth earl is concerned, I suppose Mr Wilson, when you come to think of it, is the fourteenth Mr Wilson.'

SPONTANEOUS, COHERENT, AND PURPOSEFUL

Can you open your eyes spontaneously? Can you respond coherently when asked your name, where you are, and what day it is? Can you make purposeful movements and obey simple commands? If so (and let's hope you can, if you are reading this book), you score 15 on the Glasgow Coma Scale.

The Glasgow Coma Scale (better known by the acronym GCS) is widely used by doctors and paramedics in the management of head injury, both at the bedside and on the roadside. It is an objective way of recording the level of consciousness, based on three categories of response by the patient: eye opening (E, scored between 1 and 4), verbal response (V, 1–5), and motor response (M, 1–6). The maximum total score is therefore 15, and the minimum is 3. Each of the three categories has a description corresponding to each score. On the verbal subscale, for example, no response scores 1, 'incomprehensible speech' scores 2, 'inappropriate speech' scores 3, 'confused speech' scores 4, and 'oriented speech' scores the full 5. An overall GCS of 8 or less indicates severe brain injury.

The GCS was originally devised at the Institute of Neurological Sciences, Glasgow University, in the 1970s. It is a relatively simple tool, but it has held its own in the increasingly high-tech world of emergency medicine. Although it may now be used alongside a battery of other tests, the GCS remains one of the most widely used scoring systems, with a proven ability to play its part in predicting outcome in traumatic brain injury.

THERE ARE SEVERAL MORE ACRONYMS AT **127**

16

A left-wing sport

The sport of badminton owes its name to Badminton House, Gloucestershire, where it was officially invented in 1873. But children had been batting lightweight feathered projectiles back and forth for centuries, using a variety of bats to try and keep the object airborne for as long as possible. This game, known as battledore and shuttlecock, was taken to British India, from where it returned to England in the nineteenth century – and with the addition of a net and a court of fixed dimensions (and a few rules) the modern sport was born.

One essential piece of equipment is the shuttlecock, or shuttle. The word 'shuttle' (from Old English *sciutil*) refers to something that travels back and forth, like a weaver's shuttle or a shuttle-bus. And so it is with the shuttlecock, hit back and forth across the net.

For a casual game in the back garden a plastic shuttlecock is fine, but serious competition demands a proper feathered shuttle. That means one made with feathers from the left wing of a goose, clipped to length and fastened firmly into a leather-covered cork base. Yes, only the left wing is used – so that the same spin is always imparted to the shuttle.

How many goose feathers do you need to make a feather shuttlecock? It is specified in law 2.2.1 of the Laws of Badminton... Go on, guess.

FOR SOMETHING ELSE THAT FLUTTERS THROUGH THE AIR, SEE **55**

17

FROG JUMPS INTO POND

A haiku has seventeen syllables. Actually, that's not strictly true, for in a traditional Japanese haiku the number 17 refers not to syllables but to *on* (or *morae*), which are not quite the same thing. In any case, whether one is referring to syllables or *on*, this is just one of the rules for the aspiring haiku poet to obey.

Traditional haiku describe the natural world: frogs jumping into ponds, moonlight shining on willow trees, waves breaking on shores. Haiku are written in the present tense, and they describe a brief, everyday event or moment, often combined with a *kigo*, which is a reference to the time of year. There are three phrases, with a pause at the end of the first or second phrase, and a 'cutting word' (or *kireji*) between two images or ideas. The end of the haiku provides a 'light-bulb moment', indicating a sudden flash of clarity for the writer and prompting the reader to feel the same. And haiku are so short that they can be spoken in one breath.

English haiku are written in three lines, in the pattern of 5/7/5 syllables, to correspond with the three phrases of the Japanese tradition. However, in Japanese, haiku are typically written in a single vertical line.

18

KUNG FU MONKS

Founded in the fifth century, the Chán (Zen) Buddhist Shaolin Temple in Henan province, central China, is well known worldwide as a centre of excellence for Chinese martial arts, especially kung fu. In Chinese folklore, the temple is best known for its eighteen bronze monks, the temple's fighting elite, who painted their bodies with bronze paint and who have come to symbolise the exceptionally high reputation maintained by the temple in training its disciples. Initiates could only be considered to have graduated if they could defeat the eighteen bronze monks in combat.

The story of the eighteen bronze monks is still alive and well, and not just in Chinese folklore. Visitors to the 2010 Shanghai World Expo were able to watch a performance by monks from Shaolin who re-enacted the story. Furthermore, the story has helped to establish the huge success of kung fu films worldwide. For example, in *The 18 Bronzemen* (1976) the two heroes undertake kung fu training at Shaolin in order to complete a series of thirty-six taxing tests before being allowed to leave. The last and most demanding test is to defeat the eighteen bronze monks.

FIND ANOTHER TEMPLE AT **46**

19

Cavaliers and Roundheads

A search of the memory for the causes of the English Civil War is likely to lead to a jumble of facts, some half-remembered from school history lessons and some that have sprung half-baked from the pages of *1066 and All That*. Somewhere in the mix, perhaps, will be the divine right of kings, a petition of right, a Catholic queen, ship money, rummage and scroungeage, Cavaliers ('wrong but wromantic') and Roundheads ('right but repulsive'), assorted parliaments (Long, Short, Rump, and Purged), a Star Chamber, eleven years of tyranny, and five birds that had flown (though not necessarily in that order).

Among the immediate causes of the war was a document known as the *Nineteen Propositions*, which was presented to King Charles I by Parliament on 1 June 1642. This list of nineteen proposals was couched in obsequious terms but amounted to a series of uncompromising demands, in effect insisting that Parliament must hold sway over the monarch in virtually every area of government. Parliament, for example, was to be responsible for raising armies, Parliament was to supervise all foreign policy, the king's ministers were to be answerable to Parliament. And strict new laws were to be enforced against Roman Catholics.

Within three weeks, Charles had rejected the *Nineteen Propositions*, leading to open preparation for armed conflict on both sides. The fighting began in earnest with the Battle of Edgehill on 23 October 1642, and eventually ended when Cromwell's forces defeated Charles II at Worcester on 3 September 1651.

20

Counting sheep, and stitches...

Yan, tyan, tethera, methera, pimp, sethera, lethera, hovera, dovera, dick, yan-a-dick, tyan-a-dick, tethera-dick, methera-dick, bumfit, yan-a-bumfit, tyan-a-bumfit, tethera-bumfit, methera-bumfit, giggot.

This method of counting is particularly associated with shepherds in the Lake District. Whether moving their sheep from pasture to pasture, or checking numbers during shearing, shepherds have traditionally counted their flocks using this system.

In the above example, twenty is represented by the word *giggot*, but other regions of the UK use different words: *figgit* (Lincolnshire), *jiggit* (Derbyshire), and the rather different *gun-a-gun* (Rathmell, North Yorkshire). Despite these regional variations, however, each *Yan Tyan Tethera* system of counting is vigesimal: that is, it only goes up to twenty. Counting is therefore done in scores. To count a larger number of sheep, a shepherd would count to twenty using *Yan Tyan Tethera*, and then, in order to keep going, he or she would perhaps drop a pebble in a pocket, or move a thumb down the crook, to represent each twenty counted. At the end of the count, if there were five pebbles in the pocket, or the thumb had moved five notches down the crook, the shepherd would know that 100 sheep (five times twenty) had been counted.

Yan Tyan Tethera is a wonderfully lyrical and rhythmic method of counting, and, perhaps because of this, it was also used by knitters to keep track of their stitches.

THE UNCERTAINTY OF FICTION

A Clockwork Orange, written by Anthony Burgess, was first published in 1962. Burgess claims to have written the book in just three weeks, and – despite occasional controversy regarding its alleged corrupting influence – it is generally regarded as one of the 100 best English-language novels of the twentieth century.

A Clockwork Orange tells the story of teenager Alex – delinquent, rapist, thief – who, in the very last chapter, sees the error of his ways and turns his back on his old life of violence and crime. Or does he?

The British edition of the book is divided into three parts, each of which has seven chapters. The last chapter is Chapter 21, and Alex's metanoia occurs only in this chapter. Yet in the USA, Chapter 21 was entirely omitted from the book. Burgess's American publishers insisted that the story should end on a dark note, believing that this would be more appealing to an American audience. In his 1971 film adaptation, Stanley Kubrick also omitted any reference to the events of the 21st chapter, claiming not to have known of its existence. American editions of the book did not include Chapter 21 until 1986.

Without Chapter 21, not only is the structural balance of *A Clockwork Orange* disrupted, but Alex remains trapped in a disturbing adolescent fug of dead-end hooliganism. Yet readers and critics still argue about which version works best. Leave Alex to his life of crime, or permit him to begin the process of repentance and healing?

THE CLOCK STRIKES AGAIN AT **24**

CONDORS IN CUSTODY

The California condor (*Gymnogyps californianus*) is a New World vulture, a carrion-eating scavenger with a wingspan of up to three metres. It is one of the largest flying birds in the world. It is also one of the world's rarest birds, and it has been the subject of an extraordinary conservation effort.

Condors were once widespread along the western seaboard of North America from British Columbia to Mexico, but hunting, poisoning, contamination by pesticides, ingestion of lead pellets, egg collecting, food scarcity, and habitat destruction led to a steep population decline through the nineteenth and twentieth centuries. By 1937 the species was confined to California, and by 1981 the entire world population was just 22 birds.

Drastic action was taken, and in 1987 the remaining wild birds were captured and taken into protective custody. A condor breeding programme continues to this day at San Diego, Los Angeles, and other American zoos, with captive-bred birds being reintroduced into the wild not only in California and northern Arizona but also across the border in Mexico. Breeding resumed in the wild in 2002. The future of the California condor relies on continued vigilance, particularly to counter the threat of lead poisoning arising from the shot used in hunting. But on the whole this is a conservation success story.

In January 2014 the California condor population stood at 410, including 232 birds in the wild. That's a big improvement on 22.

FOR ONE THAT DIDN'T MAKE IT, SEE **62**

23

INSPIRATION FOR MARCEL DUCHAMP

The photographer Eadweard Muybridge (1830–1904), born in
Kingston upon Thames, was a pioneer of motion photography.
He spent much of his career photographing sequences of moving
bodies – boys playing leapfrog; horses galloping; bison cantering;
pigs trotting; a woman dancing; a man turning somersaults; a
man doffing his straw hat. Perhaps best known is *The Horse in
Motion* of 1878, which proved that, when a horse gallops, all four
feet are off the ground at once for a short time during each stride.

Muybridge's *Woman Walking Downstairs* (1887) was also
extremely influential, but for a very different reason. This
sequence of 23 photographs shows a naked woman descending
a staircase. It was seen by Marcel Duchamp (1887–1968), who,
in his painting *Nude Descending a Staircase No. 2* (1912), sought to
provide a static representation of movement. When Duchamp's
painting was first exhibited, at the New York Armory Show in
1913, it caused a furore; one critic called it 'an explosion in a
shingle factory'. Duchamp openly acknowledged the influence
of Muybridge's photographic sequence.

Muybridge led a colourful life. In 1860 he barely survived
a stagecoach crash in Texas, sustaining serious head injuries.
And in 1872 he murdered his wife's lover but was acquitted on
the grounds of justifiable homicide. Philip Glass, the modern
American composer, was fascinated by the story; the libretto for
his opera *The Photographer* is based in part on court transcripts
of the case.

FOR ANOTHER SEQUENCE OF PHOTOGRAPHS, SEE **222**

A DAY WELL SPENT

If you have 24 hours to spare, you could immerse yourself in an extraordinary video art installation made by Christian Marclay (b.1955) and called *The Clock*. First shown at the White Cube Gallery in London in 2010, *The Clock* consists of a montage of clips, mostly from films but also from some television shows, each of which either provides a glimpse of a clock or a watch, or incorporates snatches of dialogue in which the time of day is mentioned.

There's Peter Fonda in *Easy Rider* at 11.40 a.m., and Gary Cooper at *High Noon*, and there are also plenty of people hurrying for trains, or late for trains, or wondering if it's time for lunch as they glance at their watches. The really clever bit is that the time on *The Clock* exactly matches real time, so that if you look at your own watch while watching it, the times will be identical. Not only does the whole thing act as a real, if rather impractical, clock, but it also provides food for thought on the nature of time – not just on the screen but in life itself.

The Clock has been sold to several art institutions, including New York's Museum of Modern Art (MoMA), the Los Angeles County Museum of Art, London's Tate Gallery, the Israel Museum in Jerusalem, and the Centre Pompidou in Paris. It also regularly goes on tour, so no need to miss a second of it.

KEEP TIME AGAIN AT **82**

25

Something's missing

In 1969 the Parisian novelist Georges Perec (1936–1982) published a novel called *La Disparition*. It has been translated into several languages, and the best-known English version is that by Gilbert Adair, published in 1994 as *A Void*.

The plot concerns a man named Anton Voyl (Vowl in the English translation), whose acquaintances visit his apartment and discover that he is missing. It is a mystery story concerning a disappearance, and it turns out (though it is never stated) that what is really missing is the alphabet's commonest letter. *La Disparition* is not an easy read, but it is a bizarre and remarkable work, illustrating a constrained writing technique known as a lipogram. Excluding those in the author's name, the book does not contain the letter E. The whole thing is written with just 25 letters.

Many reviewers and commentators have tried the same trick in discussing the book, and much that has been written about it has also avoided using the letter E. Doing that in this account would have made it impossible to mention the author's name, so E is not what is missing in this instance. But one letter is omitted, and all 25 others are used – in other words, you are reading not just a lipogram but a pangrammatic lipogram. What is missing here? It's the next best thing to an E.

26

UNFINISHED BUSINESS

From the start, the partition of Ireland was a temporary solution, even in the eyes of the British government. In an effort to find a compromise between the IRA on one side and some very unhappy Unionists on the other, Lloyd George's Government of Ireland Act (1920) split the island into a 6-county Northern Ireland and a 26-county Southern Ireland, but the plan was that both would remain within the United Kingdom, and the way was left open for future reunification – still within the United Kingdom, of course.

In the event, the Anglo-Irish Treaty that ended the Irish War of Independence in 1921 changed the landscape, and another compromise was necessary. Instead of the two parts of Ireland remaining within the UK, they would jointly become the Irish Free State. The Free State formally seceded from the UK in December 1922, and for two days all 32 counties were part of it – until the 6 counties of Northern Ireland opted to rejoin the United Kingdom, leaving a 26-county independent state.

Having originated in a compromise built on a compromise, the Irish Free State in due course became the Republic of Ireland. The Irish constitution of 1937 claimed jurisdiction over the whole island, a claim reflected in the official name of the state, which was (and remains) simply Ireland. That claim was watered down in the Belfast Agreement of 1998, but there is still a sense of unfinished business – often expressed by the use of the phrase 'the 26 counties' to refer to the territory of the Republic of Ireland.

CAN YOU SPARE A DIME?

In the USA, 10 cents won't go far nowadays, but in May 1939 it was enough money to buy the latest issue of *Detective Comics*, a monthly comic book which had been running since 1937. This particular issue – no. 27 – contained the very first appearance of Batman, created by artist Bob Kane and writer Bill Finger.

Batman is the secret identity of billionaire Bruce Wayne, who as a child had witnessed the murder of his parents and swore to take revenge against all criminals. He soon became *Detective Comics'* star, appearing not just in numerous stories but also on its covers and on the cover logo.

Robin (who played Watson to Batman's Sherlock) appeared the following year, in issue no. 38, and Batman's regular foes – including the Penguin, Two-Face, and the Riddler – arrived on the scene in later years. Batwoman was introduced in issue no. 233 in July 1956, allegedly to counter the rumours that Batman and Robin were gay – although this did little to stem a fruitful stream of critical analysis on that theme.

Issue no. 27 of *Detective Comics* has become one of the most valuable comic books of all time. In 2010 a copy sold at auction for well over a million dollars: not a bad result for an initial investment of just a dime.

THE FIRST TO BE EATEN?

When the Imperial Trans-Antarctic Expedition departed Buenos Aires on 26 October 1914, little did its leader, Ernest Shackleton, realise that he had a stowaway on board. Two of the crew – fearing that the *Endurance*, with a crew of 27, was shorthanded – had sneaked a nineteen-year-old Welsh lad, Perce Blackborow, aboard and hid him in a locker. He was discovered on the third day at sea. Shackleton eventually agreed that he could stay, but teased him by saying that 'if anyone has to be eaten, then you will be the first!' And so *Endurance*'s crew of 27 became 28.

On 18 January 1915 pack ice closed tightly around the ship, and eventually she broke up. For nearly two months, the men survived on a nearby ice floe, but they had to take to the lifeboats as the ice began to crack. After five days they arrived at Elephant Island, and Blackborow, now suffering from severe frostbite, was the first to step ashore. Shortly afterwards, all the toes of his left foot had to be amputated. Elephant Island was far from any shipping routes, so Shackleton decided to risk an open-boat journey with four of his men to South Georgia, where there was a manned whaling station. Against all the odds, Shackleton's mission was successful, and the men were eventually rescued.

Young Blackborow spent three months recovering in a Chilean hospital, before returning home to Wales. He received the Bronze Polar Medal for his part in Shackleton's expedition: not eaten after all, but honoured instead!

THERE'S ANOTHER THREAT OF CANNIBALISM AT **86**

29

Florins, farthings, sickles, and knuts

In the good old days, you could exchange your guinea for twenty-one bob, your bob for two tanners, your tanner for six pennies, and your penny for four farthings. Or, if you preferred, you could swap two bob for a florin, or five for a crown. Then along came Decimalisation Day on 15 February 1971, and we gave it all up for something allegedly simpler, but far less poetic.

If you still hanker after the pre-decimal delights of florins and farthings, then pay a visit to Gringotts Wizarding Bank, near the intersection of Knockturn Alley and Diagon Alley, where goblins will usher you through heavy doors into the echoing marble lobby with its long counters. Here you can exchange your bronze knuts, your silver sickles, and your gold galleons, or store them in the bank vaults, which, according to Hagrid, are safer than anywhere else in the world.

There are 29 knuts to the sickle (and 17 sickles, or 493 knuts, to the galleon). Of course, in the wizarding world these strange numbers don't bother anyone, because all calculations can be done with magic. If only we'd thought of that.

AND NOT A STONE WALL AMONG THEM

Sixteen fences, fourteen of which must be jumped twice, makes a total of 30 jumps. It can only be the Grand National, the world's greatest steeplechase, the annual Aintree extravaganza, the ultimate test of horse and jockey – or, depending on your point of view, ritualised animal cruelty on a par with bullfighting.

The annals of horse racing record that the Grand National was first held in 1839, but Aintree had in fact staged jump races in three previous years, and the Liverpool Grand Steeple-Chase of 29 February 1836 should really be recognised as the first of the series. When Captain Martin Becher rode The Duke to victory on that day (three years before he fell into the brook that still bears his name), horse and rider apparently had to clear 42 obstacles. Early steeplechasing was more of a scramble across country than a race along a defined course, however, and contemporary accounts are a little vague concerning the number of fences in subsequent years. It is not clear when that number became the current 30.

We do know, however, that the ploughed fields which the earliest horses had to flounder through were soon grassed over, that a rule saying 'no rider to open a gate or ride through a gateway' was introduced in 1839, and that the stone wall in front of the grandstand was replaced with a water jump in the early 1840s – the first of many changes designed to make the Grand National safer for horses and riders.

TROT BACK TO **23** FOR ANOTHER HORSE IN MOTION

31

SILENT ESSES

If you happened to be wandering along London's South Bank between May and August 2007, you might well have caught sight of one or more of Antony Gormley's figures – life-size casts of the artist's own body – which appeared on prominent buildings, streets, and bridges. There were 31 figures in total (4 made of cast iron and 27 in fibreglass), all the same size and shape, and all simply standing and staring into space.

The installation, which formed part of the exhibition 'Blind Light' at the Hayward Gallery, was titled *Event Horizon*. Gormley, perhaps best known for his *Angel of the North*, which overlooks the A1 in Gateshead, Tyne and Wear, commented: 'Observing the works dispersed over the city, viewers will discover that they are the centre of a concentrated field of silent witnesses: they are surrounded by art that is looking out at space and perhaps also at them. In that time the flow of daily life is momentarily stilled.'

The installation subsequently transferred to New York's Madison Square in 2010, where, as in London, it created a tension between the seen and the unseen, between belonging and alienation, between anonymity and recognition.

AT **9** THERE IS SOMETHING FOR THE SILENT WITNESS TO STARE UP AT

32

GOING FOR A SPIN

It's enough to make mere mortals dizzy – spinning around, on one leg, on the spot, no fewer than 32 times without stopping. But this is what any ballerina worth her salt has to do if she wants to tackle the role of Odile in *Swan Lake*. The spin is called a *fouetté* (from the French for 'whip'), and the first dancer to perform 32 of them, one after the other in quick succession, was the Italian Pierina Legnani (1863–1930). She first achieved this feat in Marius Petipa's *Cinderella* in 1893, and a few years later in *Swan Lake*, in which she thrilled the audience not just with the sheer bravura of her dancing, but also with her masterful interpretation of the resilient and confident character of Odile.

Clearly, the *fouetté* requires great technical ability, for the dancer has to whip herself around on the tippy toes of her standing leg, while the sheer force of her other leg is used to propel her around. Such a move also requires enormous stamina and strength. But just how does a ballerina prevent herself from falling over with dizziness? The answer is 'spotting', which means that she focuses on just one spot, then whips her head around as quickly as possible to return to that centre of focus. Perhaps a little more practice is called for...

YOU CAN PERFORM YOUR *FOUETTÉS* ON (OR UNDER) THE BRIDGE AT **84**

THE NECK BONE'S CONNECTED TO THE...

The human spine normally contains 33 vertebrae. Five of these are fused to form the sacrum, a triangular bone where the spine meets the pelvis, and a further four are fused in the coccyx, our vestigial tail. That leaves 24 articulating (jointed) vertebrae: seven in the neck (the cervical vertebrae, C1–C7), twelve thoracic (T1–T12), and five lumbar vertebrae (L1–L5).

At the tail end, the number of bones in a mammal's spine varies greatly, with long-tailed species having as many as 50 separate bones where we have our fused coccyx. But at the neck end there is remarkable uniformity among mammals of all shapes and sizes. Apart from a small number of sloths and manatees, all mammals have seven cervical vertebrae. Even a giraffe has only seven bones in its neck.

Birds, on the other hand, like their dinosaur ancestors, have a larger, and variable, number of bones in their necks. In spite of its external appearance, a bird such as a robin in fact has a long and flexible neck. Most birds have at least 13 cervical vertebrae, while the long neck of a swan contains 25.

STARS, STRIPES, AND SECESSION

A star and a stripe for each state was the original idea, so the first flag of the USA displayed 13 of each. And then in 1795, with Vermont and Kentucky added to the original number, it became 15 stars and 15 stripes. By 1818 there were 20 states, so that meant 20 stars, but to avoid too much clutter the flag reverted to 13 stripes. And that's the pattern that has been followed ever since: the stripes represent the 13 colonies that declared independence in 1776, and the stars show the current number of states, updated as necessary each 4 July.

In January 1861 Kansas became the 34th state, so the flag was due to be amended to show 34 stars on 4 July that year. But in April the Civil War began, and 11 states broke away to form the Confederate States of America, later claiming two further states. The Confederate flag therefore displayed 13 stars, one for each Southern state. But did that mean a reduction in the number of stars on the Union flag?

No. The Union never recognised the secession of the Southern states, so the number of stars remained at 34. On 4 July 1863, after West Virginia broke away from Virginia to join the Union, it was increased to 35 – and so on, as the number of states has grown, reaching the current number of 50 on 4 July 1960.

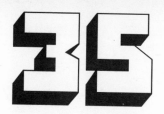

I'M C-C-C-C-COLD

Hypothermia is defined as a state in which the core temperature of the body falls below 35 °C. Not much lower than a normal temperature of 37 °C, but even that two-degree drop can be a serious matter.

Mild hypothermia is characterised by feeling cold, shivering, and numbness in the extremities, but the person can still voluntarily stop shivering. Someone who cannot stop shivering may have progressed to moderate hypothermia, also marked by the 'umbles' – the sufferer mumbles, grumbles, fumbles, stumbles, and tumbles. Below 32 °C we enter the realm of severe hypothermia: shivering stops, unconsciousness is not far off, and without urgent treatment the likely outcome is death.

From time to time we see media reports of people who fall through the ice into a lake, or get lost in the mountains, to be found hours later with a very low core temperature (even as low as 13 °C) and apparently dead – and yet that person survives. Sudden cooling may in fact be protective in certain circumstances. Deep hypothermic circulatory arrest (DHCA), in which the heart is stopped by cooling to 18–20 °C, has been used since the 1950s for some open-heart surgery. Induced hypothermia is also sometimes used as a therapeutic technique to protect the brain from damage when it is starved of oxygen, typically in cases of traumatic brain injury or after a cardiac arrest. Cooling the patient induces a state of 'suspended animation' and may improve the chance of a full recovery.

OBTAIN EMERGENCY HELP FOR A CASE OF HYPOTHERMIA AT **112**

36

ABANDONING THEIR ISLAND HOME

The remote archipelago of St Kilda, 66 kilometres to the west of the Outer Hebrides in the North Atlantic, is a once-in-a-lifetime experience for those who visit by cruise ship or day-trip boat. Visitors marvel at the teeming bird life on the cliffs of Boreray, and explore the old village on Hirta, wondering how the human former inhabitants ever survived a winter there.

Once, St Kilda supported a close-knit community of Gaelic-speaking crofters who relied mainly on catching seabirds – gannets, puffins, and fulmars – for their livelihood, using the birds for food, feathers, and oil. For them, St Kilda represented not a memorable holiday trip but a hard daily grind. It was a truly remarkable subsistence way of life, and it lasted into the twentieth century.

In 1697 about 180 people lived on St Kilda, but by the middle of the eighteenth century, after a visiting ship brought smallpox, the population had fallen to 88, and it scarcely rose above this level for the next 150 years. As contact with the outside world grew ever more frequent, the lifestyle became increasingly unsustainable, and finally, in May 1930, a petition was sent to the Secretary of State for Scotland requesting evacuation. After that, it all happened very quickly. On the morning of 29 August 1930 the remaining 36 islanders boarded HMS *Harebell* and left St Kilda to the seabirds.

ANOTHER REMOTE ISLAND IS FEATURED AT **313**

37

Kittens with cakes

Thirty-seven kittens. How cute! But these particular kittens are perhaps not quite as cuddly as one might wish, for they are most definitely deceased... and stuffed. Some are seated at a large table, piled high with cakes, while some look on and others play croquet. They can be found in a curious – one might say macabre – tableau titled *The Kittens' Tea and Croquet Party*, whose creator, Walter Potter, was a taxidermist. Potter (1835–1918) stuffed his first animal – his pet canary, of all things – when he was just fifteen, and one thing led to another until he had his own show-room in a shed in his father's garden, where he exhibited cuckoos and kittens, butterflies and buntings, squirrels, rabbits, mice, and other assorted creatures, almost all dressed in miniature costumes and doing human things: playing the trombone, sword fighting, dancing, and, of course, taking tea.

After Potter's death, his collection took up residence for a while at Jamaica Inn in Cornwall. But in 2003, the collection was split into lots and sold by Bonhams auctioneers for around £500,000, although it is not clear who now owns the 37 kittens or how much was paid for them. The couple who sold the collection – John and Wendy Watts – sued Bonhams for not accepting an offer of £1 million from the artist Damien Hirst for the entire collection.

ANOTHER POTTER, AND MORE FURRY ANIMALS, CAN BE FOUND AT **270**

MAPPING THE POLITICAL FUTURE

The National Geographic Society was established in 1888 in Washington DC with the objective of promoting the study of world history and culture. Alongside its flagship publication *National Geographic*, the society also produces maps, and in 1945, as World War Two was drawing to a close, one of those maps performed a most unexpected role in the shaping of world history.

In Korea, with tension mounting between the Soviets and the Americans after the Japanese surrender, Colonel Dean Rusk and Colonel Charles Bonesteel were assigned the onerous task of identifying a suitable dividing line between the north (then Soviet-occupied) and the south (US-occupied). They pulled out a National Geographic map of the country but could not find any obvious geographical feature that would make a convenient border. Instead they chose the line of latitude – 38 degrees north, the 38th parallel – that ran across the country. Both sides initially accepted this as the de facto international border. However, tensions continued to increase, resulting in the Korean War, with fighting on a massive scale along the 38th parallel, until – after stalemate and a ceasefire – an armistice was eventually agreed in 1953.

Since then, the dividing line between north and south has been marked by the Korean Demilitarized Zone (DMZ). This only very roughly follows the 38th parallel, and the two countries are still officially at war with each other.

FIND POSSIBLE NORTH KOREAN INFLUENCE AT **279**

BLACK AND WHITE STRIPES

Barcodes started to appear on the packaging of goods for sale in the mid-1970s, and 40 years later virtually everything we buy has a barcode somewhere on it. In the retail industry the standard system is called EAN-13 or UPC/EAN, but there are several other barcode symbologies (*sic*). One common one is known as Code 39 or Code 3-of-9. It is widely used in industry, and it has a number of advantages: it encodes letters as well as numbers, it can be any length, and each character is represented in a straight-forward fashion by one symbol, with no fancy multi-coding and no built-in check digit, so it can be printed from standard word-processing software simply by using a Code 39 font.

But why is it called Code 39? There are two explanations. First, each character is represented by five black bars interspersed with four white spaces, and each of these elements can be either wide or narrow, but in every case 3 of the 9 elements (2 bars and 1 space) are wide – hence, 3 of 9. An alternative explanation is that following these rules results in 40 possible symbols, and reserving one for a start/stop indicator leaves 39 for encoding characters.

The original Code 39 had just 26 letters, 10 digits, and 3 punctuation marks. It has since been extended by using double characters and departing somewhat from the original specification, but the name Code 39 remains.

40

PREVENTION IS BETTER THAN CURE

Quarantine is a common method of border control in which the movement of people and animals is restricted until it is certain that they are not carrying any communicable diseases. The word 'quarantine' originates from the Venetian phrase *quaranta giorni* – meaning 'forty days' – which referred to the late-fourteenth-century requirement that ships and people spend an extended period in isolation before entering port. Quarantine was first used in Dubrovnik, and was soon adopted in the Italian cities of Venice, Reggio, and Genoa, and subsequently even further afield. It was hoped that such measures would prevent the spread of the plague, or Black Death, which had already killed an astonishing 30 per cent of Europe's population.

One person who spent considerably longer than 40 days in quarantine was poor Mary Mallon (1869–1938), better known to posterity as Typhoid Mary, who in 1884 emigrated from County Tyrone in Northern Ireland to New York and worked as a cook. After some years in America, she was identified as a carrier of the pathogen associated with typhoid fever, even though she had no symptoms herself. The US public health authorities considered her to be such a health risk that she was then forced to spend nearly three decades of her life in quarantine, much of it on North Brother Island on New York's East River, where she eventually died – not of typhoid but of pneumonia, after suffering a stroke.

A DIFFERENT FORM OF CUSTODY APPEARS AT **301**

41

No, not the symphony

Wolfgang Amadeus Mozart (1756–1791) wrote his 41st symphony (the 'Jupiter' symphony, in C major) in 1788, at the age of 32. Twenty-one years earlier, at the tender age of eleven, he had completed his Piano Concerto No. 4 (in G major). He composed his first piece when he was just four, and he went on to write over 600 works in his short life. But how to catalogue such a prolific output? Certainly some sort of universal identification system was needed to keep track of so many works.

In 1862, the Austrian scientist Ludwig von Köchel produced a 551-page catalogue (*Verzeichnis*) in which he assigned a number to each of Mozart's compositions (largely arranged in chronological order), and he also provided a short snippet (known as an incipit) of the score for clarification. These numbers came to be known as Köchel numbers (abbreviated to K or KV, for *Köchel-Verzeichnis*), and although there have been several revisions to Köchel's original catalogue, all Mozart's works are still referred to by their Köchel numbers.

Mozart's fourth piano concerto was assigned the number K41. And thanks to Köchel there's no excuse for confusing it with his Symphony No. 41, which is K551.

42

SQUEEZING IN MORE PROFIT

The Gutenberg Bible, of which a few dozen copies survive, was produced in Mainz by Johann Gutenberg some time between 1450 and 1454. It was the first printed book to be produced in the West, and it is also known as the 42-line Bible – because each page has 42 lines of type. But some pages, in some copies, have only 40 lines – although the same pages, in other copies, have 42. Little is known about what went on in Gutenberg's workshop, but three things are clear from this variation in line number.

First, early on in the printing process Gutenberg changed the layout from 40 to 42 lines, presumably because he realised that he would need less paper (and could thereby improve the profit margin) if he closed up the gaps between the lines a little and squeezed in two more lines per page.

Second, after the type for the earliest pages had been broken up, he found that he needed some additional copies of those pages, and for this second printing he used the revised 42-line design. This almost certainly indicates that advance orders for the Bible were coming in faster than anticipated. Gutenberg had a commercial success on his hands.

And third, rather than discard the earlier printed pages, he made the old and new versions of those pages interchangeable by ensuring that each page began and ended at the same point, filling in the extra two lines by using fewer abbreviations.

One beautiful book, three commercial decisions, 42 lines, endless material for bibliographic detectives.

FOR ADVANCES IN PRINTING TECHNOLOGY, SEE **250**

THE DIE IS CAST

If you are a collector of die-cast model cars, you must be well acquainted with the number 43. On the other hand, if you played with toy cars or model railways as a child but have since grown out of it, you are probably not aware of the significance of the number, even though it was always there while you played.

The classic die-cast vehicles of the 1950s and 1960s were manufactured at a scale of 1:43 (i.e. 1 inch on the model equated to 43 inches in real life). Dinky Toys, Corgi Toys, Hornby O-gauge – all 1:43. Or at least approximately so. In practice the scale was somewhat variable, with the cars produced at anything between 1:42 and 1:48 until Dinky Toys standardised at 1:43 in 1964.

The scale used for the cars was originally designed to fit in with the O-gauge train sets, which had been around for much longer. They were in fact built not to a specific scale, but to a gauge (track width) of 32 millimetres. That resulted in a scale of about 7 millimetres to the foot (a nice mixture of units), which was also variously interpreted as 1:43.5, or 1:45, or 1:48. And of course there was no guarantee that any given model was all precisely to the same scale – in fact, it was quite likely that different parts were slightly out of proportion. Endless possibilities for confusion lurk beneath the standard 1:43 scale.

AT **216** YOU'LL FIND THE BIGGEST-SELLING TOY CAR OF ALL TIME

44

DOING YOUR TURNS

Sailboat racing is a very technical sport. That's not because the boats are finely tuned and complex racing machines (though sometimes they are), but because of the complexity of the rules, which in turn leads to complexity in tactics.

Whatever the level of sailing competition, and whatever the class of boat, the sport is governed by the international Racing Rules of Sailing (RRS). Regularly updated, constantly interpreted and reinterpreted, subject to endless discussion and debate on and off the water – every racing sailor needs to be familiar with them, or at least with the basics.

Not surprisingly, some of the most important rules concern situations when two boats meet, and what happens at the marks that delimit the course – which boat has right of way, what the other boat must do to avoid a collision, and so on. And if a boat infringes one of those rules, then Rule 44 may come into play. This rule allows a boat to avoid disqualification by doing penalty turns – one complete turn if it has touched a mark, or two if it has impeded another boat. As soon as possible after the incident, the boat must get clear of others and perform the specified number of turns. Even sailors who merely think they may have broken a rule are seen doing turns, just in case – such is the self-policing nature of the sport.

FOR A FASTER (BUT DRIER) SPORT SEE **107**

MORE THAN AN IRRITANT?

Bedbugs (*Cimex lectularius* and *C. hemipterus*) are flattish brownish bugs, a few millimetres long, that lurk in corners and come out at night to feed on human blood. They do not have many friends, but they are fascinating insects (go and look up 'traumatic insemination', for example), and over the past decade they have apparently become even more fascinating – for there has been a dramatic increase in the number of papers about them published in the medical literature.

The medical interest is driven by the fact that the prevalence of infestations is increasing, and by the suspicion that bedbugs may pose a serious threat to human health. In the medical literature there are reports of 45 different bacteria, fungi, parasites, and viruses that have been found in bedbugs and could plausibly be passed to humans – everything from plague and hepatitis B to rabies and yellow fever.

So far, bedbugs are known to be responsible only for troublesome bites and very occasional anaphylactic reactions. There is as yet no proven case of any of the 45 pathogens being transmitted by a bedbug to a human. But given their lifestyle and the fact that they are becoming more common, there is no guarantee that it will stay that way.

SEE **236** FOR ANOTHER PEST THAT LURKS IN DARK CORNERS

46

$8 + 8 + 17 + 17 = ?$

The Parthenon dominates the Acropolis in Athens and is well known for the ongoing disagreement concerning those marble sculptures that currently reside in the British Museum in London. Equally interesting, but thankfully far less controversial, are the Parthenon's 46 external pillars (8 at the front, 8 at the back, and 17 along each of the sides – yes, that really does add up to 46!). These exhibit a number of refinements that contribute to the building's visually pleasing proportions.

Each pillar is 10.43 metres high and 1.9 metres wide at the base. And each one tapers subtly towards the top, giving the overall building a sense of lightness and elegance that would otherwise be absent. Underneath the pillars is a stone platform (stylobate) that curves up slightly in the centre so that it looks completely flat even though it isn't. This adjustment offsets the strange optical illusion that a long horizontal line that is actually flat appears to sag in the middle. The curve also helps to shed rainwater. Furthermore, the pillars lean slightly inwards in order to counteract the fact that two parallel lines appear to bow, or curve outwards. If you can imagine them extending upwards into the sky, they would meet about 1.6 kilometres above the centre of the Parthenon.

47

THE HOMECOMING OF A GREAT SHIP

Isambard Kingdom Brunel's greatest ship, the SS *Great Britain*, was built in Bristol in 1843, and she made a total of 47 voyages, of which the last one, her return to Bristol to the very same dry dock in which she was built, is the most extraordinary of all. At the time of her construction, the SS *Great Britain* was the largest ship ever built, and also the first steam-powered screw-driven ship. After many years' service – carrying passengers to Australia, and later as a cargo ship – she was badly battered by a storm while rounding the Horn. She limped to the Falkland Islands in the South Atlantic for partial repair, but her seafaring days were over, and she was subsequently used as a floating hulk to store coal and wool.

In 1933, she was scuttled in shallow water in Sparrow Cove in the Falklands, and there she lay abandoned, growing ever rustier as the years passed. Then, in 1970, she was patched up, put onto a huge pontoon, and towed nearly 13,000 kilometres across the Atlantic and back to her home port of Bristol. She arrived on 19 July, witnessed by vast crowds who lined the river to welcome her home, 127 years to the day since she had been launched. Although the SS *Great Britain* can no longer be moved, she has been magnificently restored, and remains a fitting reminder of the genius that designed her, and of the love felt for her by her city.

THERE'S ANOTHER GREAT SHIP AT **104**

48

The humble spud

The tuberous root of *Solanum tuberosum* is sometimes referred to as the 'humble spud'. But that epithet hardly seems fair, in view of the importance of the potato throughout human history. Having been domesticated in the foothills of the Andes some 10,000 years ago, it was imported to Europe by the Spanish in the sixteenth century, and has since become a staple food the world over. Its catastrophic failure to feed the population of Ireland in the 1840s had major social and political consequences, and it even played a minor political role more recently when it was misspelt by an American vice-president.

There is perhaps another reason why we mere humans should look up to the potato. We are used to seeing ourselves as the pinnacle of evolution, the ultimate achievement of millions of years of natural selection, the cleverest, the most advanced, the most complex life-form on the planet. Simpler animals (not to mention plants) have fewer accomplishments, fewer brain cells, fewer of pretty much everything. But not necessarily fewer chromosomes. With our complement of 46 chromosomes, we are certainly better endowed than, for example, fruit flies (which have only eight), but we are also-rans compared with the potato, which has 48. Respect, then, to the not-so-humble spud.

Contrary to popular belief in the UK, Sir Walter Raleigh did not introduce the potato to Europe, but he did do his bit to popularise another New World plant with 48 chromosomes, *Nicotiana tabacum*.

MORE FOOD FROM PERU AT **163**

49

A mug's game?

The UK's national lottery has been running since 1994 – prompting dreams of untold wealth, raising millions for good causes, encouraging irresponsible gambling, imposing a tax on the poor while lining the pockets of its operators, however you prefer to think of it. The principal lottery game, branded as *Lotto* since 2002, involves matching six numbers out of a possible 49.

Why 49? It is a common number in national lotteries, and several other countries – including Canada, Germany, and South Africa – also operate a 6/49 system. Mathematically astute readers can do the sums; others can look it up – either way, the odds of winning the jackpot are 1 in 13,983,816. If 55 million tickets are sold each week, that translates to about four jackpot winners.

Presumably (though they're not telling) the lottery operators have worked out that this encourages people to take part without setting the odds so low that it is possible to game the system. In Ireland, the national lottery started in 1988 as a 6/36 game, thereby offering odds of 1 in rather less than 2 million. One day in 1992, when the jackpot was big enough to make it worth their while, a syndicate attempted to buy all possible combinations of six numbers, at a cost of slightly under half the value of the jackpot. They didn't quite snap up all the combinations before 'unusual activity' was spotted and they were thwarted, but they did make a perfectly legal profit of a few hundred thousand pounds. The Irish lottery is now a 6/45 game.

CALCULATE SOME DIFFERENT ODDS AT **254**

50

Oh zero!

Those who lived through the late 1960s might have forgotten what they got up to at Woodstock in 1969, but perhaps they can dredge up from the addled recesses of their memory the US TV series *Hawaii Five-O*, which first aired in 1968 and continued for another eleven seasons, until 1980. And as the years went by, it frequently ranked among the top 30 TV shows in the USA.

The series is set in Hawaii, and it took its name from the fact that Hawaii is the USA's 50th state – and its most recent, having joined the Union on 21 August 1959. The series' opening sequence (of crashing waves, sweeping views, beautiful women, and glowing sunsets, among other clichés), combined with its equally upbeat soundtrack, has graced TV screens through numerous reruns.

But what about the letter O in its title? It's quite common to use O when we mean zero, and of course 'Hawaii Five-O' trips off the tongue a lot more readily than 'Hawaii Five Zero'. Be that as it may, in 2010 a totally new series – loosely based on the original concept – was aired for the first time. Its title? *Hawaii Five-0*, with a zero.

READ ABOUT A HAWAIIAN INCIDENT AT **353**

NOT IN THE CLUB

When the United Nations was founded in 1945 it had 51 member states, but it did not stay that way for long. There are currently (in 2014) 193 members, accounting for almost all the sovereign states of the world. Only states can be admitted to full membership, but the UN does not itself recognise a state; recognition can only be granted by other states.

There are several states and territories that are not members of the UN, but we have space to mention just a few.

The Republic of China (Taiwan) was one of the UN's founding signatories, but was expelled in favour of the People's Republic of China in 1971. Taiwan has applied several times for separate membership, but this has so far been rejected.

The Turkish Republic of Northern Cyprus is recognised only by Turkey, and its independent status has been explicitly rejected by the UN Security Council. In the Caucasus, Abkhazia and South Ossetia are recognised by a handful of UN member states, while Transnistria (east of Moldova) and Nagorno-Karabakh (an enclave within Azerbaijan) recognise each other, but hardly anyone else does so. Somaliland withdrew from Somalia in 1991, but it is recognised as a sovereign state by nobody.

Kosovo, which declared independence from Serbia in 2008, looks a more likely prospect as the 194th UN member, having been recognised by several UN member states, but its status (so far) remains unresolved.

FOR ANOTHER POSSIBLE MEMBER, SEE **194**

52

One note at a time

A standard piano has 52 white keys. As a beginner you will probably start by playing just these keys, starting at middle C. From this
midpoint, the eight notes C, D, E, F, G, A, B, and C, going either
up or down the keyboard, make up an octave in the key of C.

Pretty soon, however, you'll need to introduce the black keys
that can be found, in groups of two and three, between the white
ones. There are 36 of these, and they enable you to play in other
keys, and before you know it – actually, after years and years of
daily practice – you will, perhaps, be able to find your way around
a Beethoven sonata or even one of those tricky études by Liszt or
Chopin.

Like harpsichords, early pianos had 60 keys in total (five
octaves), but as composers began to write more music for the
piano they persuaded manufacturers to create instruments with
more notes, until, in the late 1880s, Steinway created the 88-key
piano that has become the standard today.

In Jane Campion's 1993 film *The Piano*, love blossoms over the
keys as Ada (played by Holly Hunter) plays the piano for George
Baines (Harvey Keitel). Although the piano originally belonged to
Ada, Baines rescues it from a windswept New Zealand beach and
agrees to trade it back to her, one key at a time, in return for piano
lessons. Ada manages to reduce the terms of the trade to 'just the
black keys', and the 'lessons' turn into a slow sexual seduction,
with Ada playing as George watches. Michael Nyman's score for
the film uses all the keys – white ones as well as black ones.

ANOTHER FILM WITH A FAMOUS SOUNDTRACK APPEARS AT **197**

53

Guardian of the genome

In 1993 the leading scientific journal *Science* awarded the title Molecule of the Year to a little protein called p53. No fewer than six separate groups of scientists, all working independently of one another, had discovered it in 1979 – but some years passed before its real significance began to be understood. And since then it has become one of the most studied and most written-about biological molecules, variously described as the death star, a Swiss Army Knife of cellular regulation, and the guardian of the genome.

The name p53 refers to its molecular mass of 53 (though the true value later turned out to be closer to 44). The manufacture of p53 in our cells is controlled by a gene called *TP53*, and it is a vitally important tumour suppressor. It controls cell division and programmed cell death (apoptosis), which are the very processes that malfunction in cancer. If the *TP53* gene is mutated, either through inheritance or by exposure to something in the environment, the p53 protein may not be produced, or may not work properly, resulting in the growth of a cancer. A wide range of cancers in humans is now known to be linked to mutations in *TP53*. The latest research suggests that p53 may also play a role in non-cancerous ageing processes.

Anyone seeking a cure for cancer could do worse than look at *TP53* and the protein encoded by it. In fact, many laboratories have been doing just that for a few years now.

TURN TO **171** FOR THE DNA THAT ENCODES THE GENOME

54

An interruption from Porlock

In Xanadu did Kubla Khan
A stately pleasure-dome decree . . .

The opening lines of Samuel Taylor Coleridge's *Kubla Khan* are well known, and the poem is among his most discussed works. And yet it stops – rather abruptly – after just 54 lines. Is that it? According to the preface that accompanied it when it was first published, it is a fragment of a much longer poem that had come to Coleridge in an opium-induced dream:

> *On awaking he appeared to himself to have a distinct recollection of the whole, and taking his pen, ink, and paper, instantly and eagerly wrote down the lines that are here preserved. At this moment he was unfortunately called out by a person on business from Porlock . . .*

And so the remainder of *Kubla Khan* was forgotten, and the Person from Porlock became a metaphor for an unwelcome intrusion.

The meaning of *Kubla Khan* remains elusive, and there has also been much discussion of whether the preface is explanation, excuse, or something else entirely. One attractive interpretation sees the poem and its preface together as a single work of art, with the preface functioning as a prose parallel to the poem. On this reading, *Kubla Khan* is a poem about writing poetry, and the pleasure dome, decreed but never built, represents the thwarted creative process. The person from Porlock, then, is not so much an interruption to the work, but rather an integral part of it.

FOR SOMETHING ELSE THAT IS INTERRUPTED, SEE **282**

A NEW BAT

Bats are a vital part of Britain's wildlife, closely monitored not only because of concern for their own wellbeing but also as 'indicator species' of the health of the environment. Surveys of bats are carried out regularly – but anyone who has watched bats flitting around in the dusk, twisting and turning in their pursuit of insects, will know that it can be hard even to see them, let alone identify the species. They are best identified by sound, but there's another problem: the calls they use for echolocation are in the ultrasonic range, too high-pitched for the human ear. An essential piece of equipment, therefore, is the bat detector – a piece of electronic equipment that converts the bats' high-frequency calls to something that we can hear.

In the late 1990s the bat detector brought an unexpected bonus, in the form of an entirely new species of bat. Analysis of the calls of pipistrelles, the most numerous and widespread British bats, revealed that there were two distinct groups, separated by their calls. Some of them used calls of around 45 kHz, while others echolocated at a higher frequency. Subsequent study revealed other differences in appearance, habitat, behaviour, and genetics. And so the world said hello to the soprano pipistrelle (*Pipistrellus pygmaeus*), otherwise known, from the frequency of its calls, as the 55 kHz pipistrelle.

TUNE IN TO A DIFFERENT FREQUENCY AT **198**

TIME PASSES...

56 years. That's how long it took. The link between tobacco smoking and lung cancer was definitively demonstrated in 1950, but it was not until 2006 that the first ban on smoking in public places was introduced in the UK.

Over the first half of the twentieth century, doctors had noted an alarming increase in the number of cases of lung cancer, with the death rate from the disease soaring by a factor of 20. At the same time, rates of smoking were also showing a steep upward trend. Some small-scale studies had suggested a link, but it was far from proven, and most doctors were inclined to attribute the cancers to atmospheric pollution or car exhausts.

The proof came in the form of a study carried out by Richard Doll and Bradford Hill, who compared the smoking habits of cancer patients in 20 London hospitals with those of a control group of patients who were in hospital for other reasons. They found 'a significant and clear relationship between smoking and carcinoma of the lung', and demonstrated that 'the risk of developing carcinoma of the lung increases steadily as the amount smoked increases'.

The results of this ground-breaking study were published in the *British Medical Journal* in September 1950. And 56 years later...

57

Getting the angles right

When Marcel Tolkowsky, diamond cutter and engineer, wrote his book on *Diamond Design* in 1919, his aim was to bring mathematical rigour to what had previously been the imprecise art of cutting and polishing diamonds.

In particular, he specified angles for the so-called brilliant cut. This cutting pattern, based on the octagonal shape of the natural diamond crystal, had been around since the mid-seventeenth century, but Tolkowsky gave it precision and transformed it into by far the most popular diamond cut. He achieved this by working out the best angles and relative dimensions, so that when a ray of light enters the stone, to be reflected and refracted within, as much as possible is returned to the eye of the beholder.

Viewed from above, the brilliant-cut diamond is circular. The widest point is the girdle, and above this is the crown, with 32 triangular facets plus the flat top, which is known as the table. Below the girdle is the pavilion, with 16 triangular facets and 8 diamond-shaped ones, making a total of 57 facets. And very often there is an extra facet called the culet, formed by flattening off the point at the bottom. That would make 58 facets. Oh dear. Maybe we should have done the baked beans after all.

IF YOU PREFER THE BEANZ, YOU MIGHT ALSO LIKE **342**

LONG-LASTING SIDE EFFECTS

Amiodarone is a life-saving antiarrhythmic medication, taken daily to control heart rhythm in conditions such as atrial fibrillation and ventricular tachycardia. It is also one of the drugs used in hospital emergency departments as part of the standard protocol for resuscitating someone who has suffered a cardiac arrest.

It is a powerful drug, but it often has some troubling side effects, including extreme sensitivity to sunlight, a seriously malfunctioning thyroid gland, and deposits on the cornea. It is also notable for having an unusually long elimination half-life of 58 days.

The half-life is a familiar concept in nuclear physics, where it means the time taken for a radioactive substance to lose half of its radioactive atoms. But drugs also have half-lives, referring to the time taken for their concentration in the blood to diminish by half (plasma half-life), or for their effect on the body to be reduced by half (elimination half-life). Most medical drugs have elimination half-lives measured in minutes or hours, such as 90 minutes for the local anaesthetic lidocaine, or 2–4 hours for paracetamol. Amiodarone's half-life of 58 days is way beyond that sort of range. So the drug carries on working for a long time, but so do its side effects. Not every patient experiences all of them, but if they do occur they will likely take weeks to resolve, even if long-term amiodarone therapy is discontinued.

WEARING THE RIGHT BADGE

In 1963, as US President John F. Kennedy signed the Equal Pay Act (EPA), he spoke out against the 'unconscionable practice of paying female employees less wages than male employees for the same job'. At that time, women working full-time could on average only expect to be paid 59 cents for every dollar earned by men.

The 50th anniversary of the EPA was celebrated in 2013, by which time the wage gap had certainly shrunk, but women still earned considerably less than men for the same work – 77 cents for every dollar earned by their male counterparts. And studies of census data suggest that the gap is unlikely to close until 2057, nearly a century after the EPA was passed.

In the 1970s, as the feminist movement gathered momentum, attention was drawn to this gender inequality by the wearing of lapel badges with just the number 59 on them.

In a rather different context, a very similar badge was sported by members of the 59 Club. That badge also had nothing but the number on it – but that's a different story, and it involves motor-cycles and the London Borough of Hackney in 1959.

60

Poles apart

The line of latitude at 60 degrees south runs entirely through the cold and turbulent waters of the Southern Ocean. It crosses nothing but sea, and the only land to the south of it is Antarctica. By contrast, 60 degrees north runs mostly across land. Almost the whole of Alaska, half of Canada, all of Greenland, most of Scandinavia, and the bulk of Russia lie to the north of it.

60 degrees south defines the northern limit of the area covered by the Antarctic Treaty, which came into force in June 1961 and now has 50 signatories. The treaty sets aside disputes over territorial claims and asserts that the continent is to be used for peaceful purposes only, guaranteeing freedom of scientific investigation, promoting international cooperation, protecting the environment, and specifically banning commercial oil, gas, and mineral extraction.

Like the Antarctic, the Arctic is richly endowed, holding perhaps 30 per cent of the planet's undiscovered natural gas and 15 per cent of its oil, and global warming will make these resources ever more accessible. But the Arctic is by no means as well protected as its southern counterpart. With no convenient line of latitude to delineate the area that needs protecting, there is no international agreement – and no likelihood of one – as nations and multinational corporations jostle for position, poised to exploit the area's natural resources.

A DEEPER SHADE OF BLUE

America's Route 66 might be legendary as the road to travel for one's rock'n'roll kicks, but Highway 61 is better by far for the blues. Running 2,300 kilometres from New Orleans to the city of Wyoming, Minnesota, via Memphis, Tennessee, US Route 61 follows the Mississippi River for much of the way, and it passes through a number of places associated with blues musicians. Muddy Waters, 'father of the blues', was born in the Mississippi Delta near Highway 61. 'Mississippi' Fred McDowell wrote the song '61 Highway' in 1964. And Bob Dylan gave his sixth studio album the title *Highway 61 Revisited*.

Route 61 is certainly tinged with a deep shade of blue in places. The 'Empress of the blues' Bessie Smith died after being critically injured in a car accident on the road. And in his 1936 song 'Cross Road Blues', Robert Johnson apparently sold his soul to the devil where Route 61 crosses Route 49, in Clarksdale, Mississippi. A monument consisting of three crossed guitars now marks the spot.

62

No longer the commonest

On plate 62 in what was until recently the most expensive printed book in the world you will find a picture of what was once the commonest bird in the world.

The Birds of America, published between 1827 and 1838, consists of 435 hand-coloured engravings from John James Audubon's paintings, and it is enormous, each page measuring 99 × 72 centimetres. It is also worth a lot of money. About 120 complete copies survive, and a number of them have been sold in recent years for sums in excess of £7 million. After several decades as the world's most expensive book, it was finally knocked off its perch by a seventeenth-century book of psalms in 2013.

Plate 62 in *The Birds of America* contains an image of two passenger pigeons (*Ectopistes migratorius*). Before the arrival of Europeans, the population of this species in the deciduous forests of eastern North America exceeded 5 billion, and in the early nineteenth century Audubon himself saw a single migrating flock that numbered over a billion birds – 'The air was literally filled with pigeons; the light of noonday was obscured as by an eclipse,' he wrote. By then, however, the slaughter had already begun. Through the nineteenth century, the pigeons were hunted on a massive scale, and at the same time the forests on which they depended were cleared to make way for agriculture.

The passenger pigeon was seen no more in the wild after 1900. The last of the species, a bird named Martha, died in Cincinnati Zoo on 1 September 1914.

THERE ARE MORE BEAUTIFUL ILLUSTRATIONS OF BIRDS AT **175**

63

Enough for a bun, but not for a horse

> *Riddle me, riddle me, rot-tot-tote!*
> *A little wee man in a red red coat!*
> *A staff in his hand, and a stone in his throat;*
> *If you'll tell me this riddle, I'll give you a groat.*

This riddle appeared in Beatrix Potter's *The Tale of Squirrel Nutkin*, published in 1903. The groat had already vanished from circulation, so even at that date readers may have found it hard to know if it was worth winning. However, Frances Hodgson Burnett's *A Little Princess*, published two years later, offered a clue when Sarah Crewe, the story's heroine, found one in the street and used it to buy some buns.

The coin that Sarah found, commonly known as a groat, was a four penny piece. In England, groats were first minted in the late thirteenth century. Over the next few hundred years the coin was gradually reduced in weight from its initial four pennyweights – 96 grains (6.2 grams) of sterling silver – to 27 grains (1.9 grams) in 1888, after which it disappeared from circulation.

There were 63 groats to the guinea. That explanation would have been fine in 1903, but today it may be a bit of a puzzle for those who don't make a habit of buying racehorses or cattle.

And in case you were wondering over Squirrel Nutkin's riddle: the answer is a cherry.

64

A TERRIBLE WAY TO PLAY A GREAT GAME

There might well be 204 squares on a chessboard (check this out at 204), but as far as Alexander Yuryevich 'Sasha' Pichushkin was concerned, there were just 64. This was more than enough for his purposes, however, for he planned to kill a total of 64 people – one for each of those squares – and he has become known as 'the chessboard killer'.

Pichushkin was born in Moscow in 1974, and he certainly had a difficult childhood. His first known murder occurred in 1992, when he strangled a school friend and pushed him out of a window. He was finally stopped in 2006, when he murdered a colleague, Marina Moskalyova, but was identified through CCTV footage.

Pichushkin was a keen chess player, and after committing each of the murders he would return home and place a coin on a square of his chessboard. At the time of his arrest, the police found that 63 of the squares had been covered with coins.

However, Pichushkin may have fallen short of his target by more than just one, for he was convicted of 'only' 48 – a fact which prompted him to complain of unfair treatment at his trial in 2007. He also claimed that, given the opportunity, he would have gone on killing indefinitely.

MORE MURDERS AT **187**

65

DAYS TO INSANITY?

The Fall of Math is the 2004 debut album by Sheffield band 65daysofstatic. The band plays 'math rock', which is rhythmically complex music, usually played on guitars. Influenced by music as diverse as the progressive rock of King Crimson and the minimalist style of much of Steve Reich's oeuvre, math rock incorporates odd time signatures, counterpoint, dissonant chords, and irregular stopping and starting.

65daysofstatic is also known as 65dos, or 65days, or even just 65. At its inception it was called 65*daysofstatic, although it's unclear what significance, if any, the asterisk had. But where did that strange name come from in the first place? One theory is that the band was inspired by psychological experiments conducted in the 1950s and 1960s, which concluded that exposure to 65 days of white noise or static would lead to insanity. According to one music critic, 65daysofstatic's debut album provides an 'indescribably wonderful clamour', although how one might feel after 65 days of it is perhaps another matter.

ANOTHER BAND PLAYS AT **182**

ON THE RIGHT TRACK

In St Petersburg it was 60, in the Midwest USA it was 58, on Brunel's Great Western Railway it was just a smidgeon over 84, and in Ireland it is still 63. We're talking railway gauges – and inches, of course. These days more than half the world's railways use the 'standard gauge' track, which is 56½ inches. However, in India, and throughout much of the Indian Subcontinent, the most commonly used gauge is 66 inches. This 'Indian gauge' was first adopted during the days of the British Raj in the 1850s, for it was thought that it would be more stable than standard gauge during the high winds of the monsoons.

In India some of the latest urban tracks – in Bangalore, Mumbai, and Chennai – are being built using standard gauge. And 30-inch narrow gauge has always been used for some of the mountain railways, for example to Shimla and Darjeeling. However, the 66-inch Indian gauge is still most definitely alive and well, with some 55,000 kilometres of route in India alone. And it is also, for reasons unknown, the gauge used for San Francisco's Bay Area Rapid Transit (BART) system.

THIRTEEN SECONDS: LAW AND ORDER RESTORED?

Neil Young's 'Ohio' was written in response to an event that took place on 4 May 1970 at Kent State University, Ohio. On that day, students at the university campus gathered for a mass protest, one of many throughout the country that were staged in response to President Nixon's decision to order an attack on North Vietnamese centres in Cambodia. By this time, US troops were already being sent home from Vietnam, so the invasion of Cambodia was seen by many as a backward step.

The protest at the university began at 11 a.m., but became increasingly tense, and the National Guard were called in. The guardsmen threw tear-gas canisters at the crowd, who simply threw them back. Eventually, the crowd began to disperse, thinking that the conflict had ended. But then, for no apparent reason, the guardsmen opened fire on the students. In just thirteen seconds, 67 bullets from M-1 rifles were fired into the crowd. Four students were killed, and nine others were wounded. More protests and riots occurred across the country in response to the shooting. However, conservatives, and Nixon himself, saw it as a symbol of the maintenance of law and order, and although the guardsmen were brought to trial, they were all acquitted.

Neil Young's song was recorded by Crosby, Stills, Nash and Young, and released as a single in June 1970. It remains one of the best-known protest songs, and has been covered by numerous artists.

68

A loo with a view

Located just to the south of the Thames in London, the Shard
– designed by Italian architect Renzo Piano – is as sharp and
as shiny as a jagged sliver of glass or an upturned icicle. It was
topped out on 30 March 2012, at which time it became Europe's
tallest building, at 309.6 metres. But just a few months later,
in November 2012, it was overtaken by Moscow's Mercury City
Tower, which topped out at 338.8 metres – although whether
Russia can be counted as part of Europe is perhaps open
to debate.

Nonetheless, London's Shard is certainly an impressive
structure – and until the Hermitage Plaza in Paris has been
completed it remains the tallest in the European Union. From its
two viewing platforms the 360-degree panorama over the city
is stunning – and, for vertigo sufferers, not a little unnerving,
although that doesn't bother the base jumpers and abseilers
(some legal, others not) who have already scaled its heights and
thrown themselves off it.

If you get caught short in the Shard, do not panic. Toilets are
provided on the 68th floor, a few floors below the top – and the
view from there, through unobstructed and somewhat discon-
certing floor-to-ceiling glass, is just as good as that from the
official viewing platform one storey above.

FOR SOMETHING ELSE THAT SPARKLES IN THE SUNLIGHT, SEE **57**

69

ONE THING LEADS TO ANOTHER

Having a headache is no excuse for not being able to guess what the topic is here. Of course, a quick Google search on 69 might have inspired some sort of vaguely adequate foreplay in the form of a psalm ('Save me, O God, for the waters have come up to my neck'), or a leisurely London bus route (from Canning Town to Walthamstow Central via West Ham, Stratford, Maryland, Leyton, and Leyton Green), during which there's plenty of time for the imagination to wander away from the city streets to a garden of more earthy delights.

Alternatively, one might perhaps be stimulated to provide an all-too-brief account of thulium (atomic number 69 – good for making high-temperature conductors, apparently), or perhaps to get thoroughly excited about the birth of St Polycarp of Smyrna, who was born in 69 CE but came to a sticky end.

But let's not get too carried away with such matters, however much they might get the heart pumping. For when one really gets down to it, Google is much, much more likely to reach the pinnacle of pleasure with sex. And whichever way you look at it, the 6 and the 9 go together as obviously as yin and yang, day and night, light and dark, female and male, *kama* and *sutra* – and *soixante* and *neuf*, for naturally, in all matters of *l'amour*, the French like to have something to do with it.

NOT SATISFIED YET? TRY **237**

70

A VARIABLE LIFESPAN

'The days of our years are threescore years and ten; and if by reason of strength they be fourscore years, yet is their strength labour and sorrow; for it is soon cut off, and we fly away.' So we're told in Psalm 90 of the King James Bible. And in Shakespeare's *Macbeth*, the 'old man' comments: 'Threescore and ten I can remember well: Within the volume of which time I have seen Hours dreadful and things strange; but this sore night Hath trifled former knowings.'

A score is 20, so threescore and ten adds up to 70, and this figure is often regarded as the normal life expectancy for a human being – in which case Shakespeare's old man must have been rapidly approaching the end.

Nowadays, however, threescore years and ten seems to have lost most of its currency. The expected lifespan of someone living in the developed world today is often considerably longer than 70 (Japan currently tops the list, with 79 for men and 86 for women), while someone in a less developed country may well not live nearly as long as that (in Sierra Leone, life expectancy is just 46 for men and 47 for women).

FOR EXTREME OLD AGE, TOTTER ON TO **157**

CHANCE ENCOUNTERS

A young man walks into a bank, pulls out a revolver, fires on people at random, then shoots himself. A homeless boy eats rubbish as he watches a woman playing ball with a dog. A couple wonder how they will be able to look after their new foster daughter. A man hits ping-pong balls that come shooting out of a machine, over and over and over again.

Such seemingly unrelated fragments of life appear in *71 Fragmente einer Chronologie des Zufalls* ('71 Fragments of a Chronology of Chance'), set in Vienna in 1993, directed by Austrian film-maker Michael Haneke, and released in 1994. The fragments are interspersed with snippets of news reports showing the horrors of war in Bosnia, Somalia, and southern Lebanon (all of which were ongoing while the film was being made), as well as footage of Michael Jackson during the 1993 child sex abuse allegations. Between each fragment is a 'black pause' – a moment of jet-black film during which nothing happens at all.

Haneke's film may well contain 71 fragments, but the key word in its title is in fact *Zufall* (chance), for it explores the random nature of most experience.

A LESS FRAGMENTED FILM CAN BE SEEN AT **74**

72

FAR FROM THE PUTTING GREEN BUT STILL ON PAR

The game of golf has enriched the English language immeasurably, and not just with swear words. Whether or not you concur with Mark Twain that golf is a good walk spoiled, and even if you are a golf widow/widower, you might still make the cut, tee it up, get a hole in one, be par for the course, or be feeling a bit below par, for such phrases are no longer confined to the tee-box, the rough, the fairway, or the putting green.

In golfing circles, 'par for the course' refers to the standard score that a good player should make. Although there is some slight variation, typical eighteen-hole championship golf courses have par values of 72, meaning that players are aiming for a total score of 72.

Each hole also has a par value, and a 72-par course usually has four par-threes, ten par-fours, and four par-fives. Of course, the way will probably be littered with bogeys (one over par) and double bogeys (two over), or, if you're lucky and the wind is blowing in the right direction, birdies (one under), lesser-spotted eagles (two under), extremely rare albatrosses (three under), or virtually extinct condors (four under). As Gary Player remarked, 'the more I practise, the luckier I get.'

73

Variations on black

One of the best-known of the playful typographical devices used by Laurence Sterne in *Tristram Shandy* (published between 1759 and 1767) occurs on page 73 of the first volume. To mourn the death of a character called Parson Yorick, the text on page 72 ends with 'Alas, poor YORICK!' – and on the following page there is nothing but a solid block of black ink.

In 2009, to mark the 250th anniversary of the publication of Sterne's comic novel, an exhibition called 'The Black Page' was staged at Shandy Hall, North Yorkshire, Sterne's one-time home and now a museum. Each of 73 artists was given a piece of hand-laid paper printed with a correctly proportioned outline of the original page and the page number 73, but otherwise blank, and asked to produce an interpretation of the black page, for exhibition and auction. Some exhibitors used ink, others paint, or pencil, or charcoal, or fabric; there were paintings, and drawings, and musical scores, and collages; some were mostly black, some were mostly white, very few had any other colour. All the works were signed, but the signatures were hidden beneath the black mounting board, so bidders did not know whose work they were bidding for. Sterne would have approved.

The auction raised money for roof repairs at Shandy Hall. The bidding for each item in the exhibition started, of course, at £73.

TURN TO **240** FOR SOME SMALLER BLACK RECTANGLES

74

GAME THEORY AT THE OSCARS

The 74th Academy Award ceremony (the Oscars) was held on 24 March 2002 – and it had a particular numerical connection that year, for the Best Picture award went to *A Beautiful Mind*, directed by Ron Howard, starring Russell Crowe, and honouring the work of an American mathematician. The film is adapted from a book of the same name by Sylvia Nasar, and it is loosely based on the life of John Forbes Nash, Jr. Together with John C. Harsanyi and Reinhard Selten, Nash won the Nobel Prize in Economics in 1994 for his work on game theory, differential geometry, and partial differential equations.

Although *A Beautiful Mind* concludes with Nash's Nobel Prize triumph, much of the film focuses on his long struggle with schizophrenia, and its impact on his relationships with women (especially his wife Alicia), friends, and colleagues.

Perhaps, post-9/11, there was something of a more sensitive, thoughtful nature in the air at this 74th award ceremony, for *A Beautiful Mind*, tackling two tricky subjects (schizophrenia and mathematics), won no fewer than four awards (best picture, best director, best supporting actress, and best adapted screenplay), and beat Peter Jackson's *The Lord of the Rings: The Fellowship of the Ring* to the top spot.

THERE'S ANOTHER FILM (BUT NOT AN OSCAR WINNER) AT **152**

BECAUSE IT IS THERE

Everest claims lives: four in 2011, ten in 2012, ten more in 2013, and, at the time of writing, seventeen (all Nepalese) so far in 2014. And the numbers may well rise as more and more people attempt what is still an exceedingly dangerous climb. The cause of death varies: falls are common, as are avalanches, acute mountain sickness, and exposure. Most of the bodies remain on the mountain, for it is simply too difficult and costly to remove them.

On 1 May 1999, American climber Conrad Anker came across a body lying face down and frozen into the surrounding scree at over 8,000 metres on Everest's north face. This was not, however, some recent tragedy, for the body was that of George Mallory. He had lain unnoticed on the mountain for 75 years.

Mallory, along with fellow climber Andrew Irvine, had last been sighted on 9 June 1924, as they climbed towards the summit. The great mystery is whether they actually got there, and died on the descent rather than on the way up. Mallory had taken a photo of his wife with him, which he intended to leave at the top. This was not found on his body, suggesting that he had indeed got to the summit and left it there. Whatever the truth of the matter, theirs was nonetheless a major achievement.

When asked why he wanted to climb Everest, Mallory simply replied: 'Because it is there.'

CLIMB UP TO **356** FOR MORE PROBLEMS AT HIGH ALTITUDE

76

Call and response

Was she worth it? Bingo players certainly believe she was. 'Seven and six' (in old money, seven shillings and sixpence) used to be the cost of a marriage licence, and so the bingo call for 76 – 'Was she worth it?' – elicits the response 'every penny'.

In bingo lingo, the call for 76 can also be 'trombones'. This refers to the signature song from Meredith Willson's 1957 musical *The Music Man*, in which the self-styled 'Professor' Harold Hill uses the song to inspire the good children of River City, Iowa, to play in a marching band. Hill recalls the time when he witnessed the combined forces of several bands: 'Seventy-six trombones led the big parade, with a hundred-and-ten cornets close at hand…'

No doubt the combined noise of all those trombones and cornets would be enough to rouse any bingo player who had momentarily lost concentration, as would the 'fifty mounted cannon' that Professor Hill also remembered. One can certainly think of a few appropriate responses to the ensuing racket.

77

Don't try this at home

At normal atmospheric pressure, nitrogen (which makes up a little over three-quarters of the air around us) becomes a liquid once the temperature drops to 77 kelvins (77 K) – in other words, 77 degrees above absolute zero, or minus 196 °C.

Once you have your nitrogen in liquid form, what can you do with it, apart from creating fog effects in nightclubs and making instant ice cream and super-cooled (but potentially lethal) novelty cocktails? Quite a lot, in fact. Its many medical uses include cryo-therapy for the removal of warts, skin tags, and assorted lumps and bumps, not to mention ticks and other ectoparasites. It can also be employed internally, in cryosurgery or cryoablation – for example to treat prostate and other cancers, and to freeze tissue within the heart that is causing an arrhythmia.

In the laboratory, liquid nitrogen is used in the cryopreserva-tion of biological samples, including sperm, ovarian tissue, and human embryos – and even (though not on the NHS) for the cryonic preservation of whole bodies in the hope of immortality.

78

The tempo is the title

For Dmitri Shostakovich (1906–1975) it is 'Nocturne: Moderato'.
For Béla Bartók (1881–1945) it is 'Andante sostenuto'. For Niccolò
Paganini (1782–1840) it is 'Allegro maestoso – Tempo giusto'.
And for the American composer John Adams (b.1947) it is
'Quarter-note = 78'.

We're talking about first violin concertos – specifically their
first movements – and while Shostakovich, Bartók, and Paganini
all designate the approximate tempo of the piece, Adams is not
only much more prosaic (using straightforward American English,
rather than the traditional Italian), but also much more precise.
His first movement is to be played at a tempo of 78 quarter-notes
(aka crotchets) per minute, and the tempo is also the actual title of
the movement.

John Adams could perhaps best be described as a 'post-
minimalist' composer. He was born a decade after the so-called
'minimalists' Steve Reich, Terry Riley, and Philip Glass, and
although, like them, he often uses repetition as a key modus
operandi, he frequently overlays it with something altogether
more romantic. This is certainly the case with his violin concerto
(written in 1993), in which the solo violin floats ethereally above
what Adams describes as the 'regular heartbeat' of the orchestra –
a heartbeat that was introduced in that first movement at 78 bpm.

FOR MORE ON MUSICAL TEMPO, SEE **208**

79

A legible height

Vehicle registration plates, generally called number plates in the UK and license plates in the USA, have a history almost as long as that of the motor vehicles they adorn. A number of European countries introduced them in the 1890s, and they first appeared in the USA in 1901. In the UK, it has been compulsory to display a registration mark on a motor vehicle since 1 January 1904.

This may come as news to the many devotees of personalised number plates, but the sole purpose of the plates is to identify the vehicle. They must be easy to read at a glance, at a specified distance, and increasingly by automatic number plate recognition (ANPR) systems – not to mention by countless bored children playing number-plate games on long journeys.

The design of the plate, including the lettering, is therefore tightly controlled by regulation. Since September 2001 UK number plates have used a font called Charles Wright, with the height, width, spacing, and every other measurement specified by Statutory Instrument. Among the rules is the stipulation that for all vehicles manufactured since January 1973 (except motor-cycles), the height of the characters is 79 millimetres.

MORE RULES FOR DRIVERS AT **251**

IT'S OBVIOUS

Where do Panama hats originate? How long did the Hundred
Years War last? In which month do Russians celebrate the
October Revolution? After what animal are the Canary Islands
named? What colour is a black box?

Any (or all) of the above might appear in a pub quiz, in a
round of questions with 'obvious' answers that are in fact wrong.
But beware if the quizmaster slips in 'How long was the Eighty
Years War?' – for that would be a double-bluff. The Eighty Years
War, otherwise known as the Dutch War of Independence, did
indeed last 80 years. It started in 1568, when the Seventeen
Provinces of the Netherlands, led by William I of Orange, rebelled
against their Spanish/Habsburg/Holy Roman rulers. The war
came to an end in 1648 when the Peace of Westphalia recognised
the independence of the Dutch Republic, separating the northern
part of the Netherlands from the more southern lands that would
eventually become Belgium.

Oh – and in case you do find yourself taking part in that quiz,
it's Ecuador; 116 years; November; dog; orange.

81

Not for babies

It is at least 3,500 years since humans discovered that chewing on willow bark or sipping a drink made with crushed willow leaves helped to relieve pain, but it was not until the late nineteenth century that the German chemist Felix Hoffmann discovered how to make a synthetic compound that would be metabolised in the body to produce the same pain-relieving substance. That compound is acetylsalicylic acid, better known as aspirin, and it has become the most widely used medicine of all time.

In addition to its impact on pain, inflammation, and fever, aspirin interferes with the blood-clotting mechanism. Anyone who is at risk of stroke or myocardial infarction (heart attack), both of which can be caused by a blood clot, is now routinely put on a long-term course of low-dose aspirin. The low-dose pill is one-quarter the strength of the standard pain-relieving pill, so in the UK it is 75 mg, but in the USA (where it seems everything really is bigger) it is 81 mg, and it is often referred to as a 'baby aspirin'. In spite of that name, and in spite of what can be found on the Internet, it is not suitable for children, nor does it help women conceive (though there is a suggestion that it may help prevent miscarriages).

Strangely enough, if the annual worldwide consumption of aspirin (40,000 tonnes) were expressed in terms of baby aspirins, it would amount to almost exactly 81 low-dose tablets for every man, woman, and child on the planet.

DOES THE ESTABLISHMENT AT **217** SERVE PAIN-RELIEVING WILLOW TEA?

SOMETHING OLD TO SOMEWHERE NEW

On 17 June 2010, American astronaut Shannon Walker arrived at the International Space Station wearing a rather old-fashioned wristwatch. It might have been old, but it was still in good working order, and it was certainly not ordinary, for this watch used to belong to Amelia Earhart. Earhart was the first woman to fly across the Atlantic Ocean – in 1928 as a passenger, and in 1932 as solo pilot – and she had worn the watch on both flights.

The watch is a Longines one-button, two-register chronograph, and Earhart had given the watch to H. Gordon Selfridge Jr., the American-born founder–owner of the London department store. Selfridge had provided Earhart with clothing for all her public appearances after her historic 1932 flight, and they had developed a close friendship. In return for the Longines wristwatch, Selfridge had given Earhart a watch which it is believed she was wearing in 1937 on her last-ever flight, during which she disappeared while attempting to circumnavigate the globe.

The arrival of the Longines watch at the International Space Station was a fitting tribute to Earhart's pioneering spirit, and it occurred 82 years to the day after her first transatlantic flight. The watch has since come back down to earth, and is now on display in the Ninety-Nines Museum of Women Pilots in Oklahoma City.

FOR ANOTHER STRIKING TIMEPIECE, SEE **13**

TIME FOR A SECOND TEENAGE REBELLION?

Most people are familiar with the Jewish coming-of-age rituals known as the Bat Mitzvah (for girls) and the Bar Mitzvah (for boys), which are celebrated at the age of thirteen. At this age, young people are deemed old enough to be accountable for their actions (*mitzvah* means 'commandment' or 'law'), and are also responsible from then on for maintaining Jewish law and tradition. But less commonly known is the concept of the Second Bat (or Bar) Mitzvah, which is celebrated at the age of 83. If the 'normal' lifespan is threescore years and ten (i.e. 70), then an 83-year-old man or woman can be thirteen in a 'second lifetime'.

Quite often, celebrants recite the same portion of the Torah as they did 70 years earlier. Naturally, such a celebration has quite a different feel 'second time around', since not only children but also grandchildren and even perhaps great-grandchildren can be present, and celebrants often assert that they have a far greater appreciation of the ritual at this age than they could possibly have done at thirteen.

GO TO **248** FOR MORE ON THE JEWISH COMMANDMENTS

84

A French cul-de-sac

France's administrative districts, or *départements*, are all numbered, and Vaucluse, in the south-east, is the 84th. Its name derives from the Latin *Vallis Clausis* (closed valley), for its main valley comes to an abrupt end at a cliff face. Its *préfecture* (capital), Avignon, is best known for three things – popes, antipopes, and a bridge.

When Clement V, a Frenchman, was elected pope in 1305 he wanted nothing to do with Rome. He therefore set up court in Avignon, starting a line of seven popes who reigned in Avignon until Gregory XI returned to Rome in 1377. But just a year later Gregory's successor, Urban VI, alienated the French cardinals again, and they retaliated by electing one of their own men as pope. So now there was a pope in Rome and a rival pope (or antipope) in Avignon. This state of affairs – known as the Western Schism – lasted for 40 years, until the Council of Constance reunited the papacy in Rome in 1418.

Avignon's Saint Bénézet bridge was built in the twelfth century, and its 22 arches spanned the Rhône via a small island (the Île de la Barthelasse) in the middle. The bridge is commemorated in the sixteenth-century dancing song 'Sur le pont d'Avignon', although, strictly speaking, it should be 'Sous le pont d'Avignon', for all the dancing was done *under* the bridge, on the Île de la Barthelasse. Centuries of flooding resulted in the loss of an arch here and an arch there, until just four were left standing. They are still there today, stopping abruptly in mid-river – a cul-de-sac, just like the Avignon papacy and the Vaucluse valley itself.

THE BRIDGE AT **324** CROSSES A RAILWAY RATHER THAN A RIVER

HOW LOUD IS TOO LOUD?

Loud noises are bad for you. A single extremely loud burst of sound, such as a gunshot or an explosion (which might measure 150 decibels), can rupture the eardrum or damage the bones of the middle ear. But more insidious damage results from repeated or prolonged exposure to lesser sounds, which gradually destroy the sensory cells (hair cells) in the cochlea of the inner ear. The threshold for this form of noise-induced hearing loss (NIHL) is almost universally set at 85 decibels. That's heavy city traffic, applause in an auditorium, a noisy vacuum cleaner, or a relatively quiet petrol lawnmower. And it's a lot quieter than an ambulance siren, a pneumatic drill, or a rock concert.

Noise at work is a big issue in occupational health and safety, and many countries have laws stating that workers must not be regularly exposed to levels above 85 decibels. In the UK, for instance, the Control of Noise at Work Regulations (2005) stipulate ear protection and regular hearing tests for anyone working in an environment where that level is routinely exceeded.

In the developed world, up to 15 per cent of adults suffer from NIHL, and the problem is growing in developing countries – because, almost universally, industrialisation proceeds at a faster rate than any regulatory framework that could offer protection.

86

Cannibalism for kids?

There were once two brothers named Jacob and Wilhelm. Their father died when they were young boys, and so they worked hard to support their mother and all their brothers and sisters. Jacob and Wilhelm grew up to be fine men, and they devoted their lives to linguistic research and to collecting folk tales.

Jacob and Wilhelm Grimm are of course best known for *Kinder- und Hausmärchen* ('Children's and Household Tales', translated into English as *Grimms' Fairy Tales*). The first volume was published in 1812, and it contained 86 stories, among them old favourites such as 'Hansel and Gretel', 'Rapunzel', and 'Cinderella', as well as less familiar tales including 'The Juniper Tree' and 'The Twelve Huntsmen'.

These stories are packed with just about everything young children require to ignite their imaginations and keep them awake at night: cannibalism, evil stepmothers, beheadings, poisonings, and a generous helping of animals acting like humans.

The 86th, and final, story in the collection is 'The Fox and the Geese', in which a fox threatens to eat a flock of geese. They ask if they can pray first, and, when the fox agrees, the geese start praying, and they pray on and on and on – an elegant open ending to an enduring collection.

ARE YOU SITTING COMFORTABLY? IF NOT, FIND WHAT YOU NEED AT **260**

THE GOVERNMENT OF THE PEOPLE

'Four score and seven years ago our fathers brought forth upon this continent a new nation, conceived in liberty, and dedicated to the proposition that all men are created equal.' So began the Gettysburg Address, given by President Abraham Lincoln on 19 November 1863. Just a few months earlier, the Battle of Gettysburg had resulted in the largest number of casualties in the entire American Civil War, and in the aftermath of that battle, Lincoln's speech marked the dedication of the Soldiers' National Cemetery in Gettysburg.

Lincoln spoke for just over two minutes, yet in that short time he not only affirmed his belief in democracy and in the Union, but he also managed to tie these in with the Declaration of Independence at the start of the American War of Independence 87 years earlier, in 1776. Lincoln's 272-word speech ends with the words: 'That this nation, under God, shall have a new birth of freedom, and that government of the people, by the people, for the people, shall not perish from the earth.'

The Gettysburg Address is fondly recalled – for its brevity, its eloquence, and its sentiment. Lincoln looked back across 87 years of American history, but it would take the passage of more than another 87 years before liberty, equality, and freedom were available to all. Along the way, Susan B. Anthony, Nez Perce, and Martin Luther King used their own gifts of oratory – in 1873, 1877, and 1963 respectively – in the fight to achieve these goals for women, Native Americans, and African-Americans.

MORE ORATORY AT **3**

88

A STAR MAP FOR ANCIENT HUNTERS

It might seem odd to be underground and yet be able to gaze upon the heavens, but at the Lascaux caves in south-western France (or at least in an exact replica of the original caves), you can do just that. Some seventeen millennia ago, early humans painted scenes of hunting on the cave walls, but they also painted what seem to be clusters of stars. The Pleiades appear above the head of a bull with magnificent horns, and similar collections of marks correspond with other familiar star groups.

Many thousands of years later, Claudius Ptolemaeus (*c.*90–168 CE) recorded 48 groupings, or constellations, and over the ensuing centuries others were added to the list, until in 1922 the International Astronomical Union (IAU) changed the rules. Rather than recognising constellations as patterns perceived in the stars, the IAU defined each one as a precisely delineated zone of the heavens. The modern IAU classification divides the entire sky into 88 constellations.

The constellations have inspired generations to look upwards, away from the earthbound present and into the stellar past. One of the most easily recognisable constellations is Orion the Hunter, which is visible throughout the world. With his belt of three stars (Alnitak, Alnilam, and Mintaka), from which hangs his sword (the Orion Nebula, or Messier 42), this hunter has inspired numerous myths and legends. No wonder that the stars also inspired those other hunters, the cave dwellers of Lascaux, who sought to make sense of their place in the mysterious universe.

TURN TO **185** FOR ANOTHER MYSTERY OF THE UNIVERSE

TO BEGIN AT THE BEGINNING (AGAIN)...

...it is night. But Utah Watkins is wide awake and counting sheep.
The sheep jump through a gap in the fence, over a broken stone
wall. One, two, three, four, five...One after another they jump –
some rushing, others strolling. Thirteen, fourteen, fifteen...Lambs
run along at their mothers' sides, mildly panicked. Old ewes
stumble along. On and on they come, twenty-eight, twenty-nine,
thirty...until...until...

High on the hill above Llareggub, sheep farmer Utah counts
wife-faced sheep. Thirty-four, thirty-five, thirty-six, forty-eight,
eighty-nine. He gets no further, and the sheep of his dreams are
smiling and knitting and bleating, just like Mrs Utah Watkins.

Mr and Mrs Watkins appear in Dylan Thomas's radio drama
Under Milk Wood (1954). They live at Salt Lake Farm, a very long
way from the US state of Utah. And counting sheep probably
occupies many of farmer Utah's waking hours too. But if he wakes
in the middle of the night, one can only hope that he doesn't start
counting backwards from 89: this could play havoc with his flock,
although it would find its echo in Llareggub.

COUNT BACK TO **20** FOR MORE ABOUT COUNTING SHEEP

90

A game of two halves

Football (association football, soccer) is a gold mine for the collector of clichés. It's a funny old game that often goes down to the wire, and a player with a cultured left foot may seek out the corridor of uncertainty, leaving the keeper (who is doing his best to keep a clean sheet) in no-man's land, while everyone is hoping not to end the game feeling as sick as a parrot.

Most famously, perhaps, football is a game of two halves. Indeed it is. Each half is 45 minutes, adding up to a match lasting 90 minutes. But how much football is actually played in those 90 minutes? Every time the ball goes out of play for a throw-in or a goal kick, and every time the referee's whistle blows for a foul, the game stops but the clock doesn't. Even with some extra time added for goals, injuries, and substitutions, the net result is that the average 'effective time' of a football match is more like 55 minutes. And in some matches in the English Premier League during the 2010–2011 season, the ball was in play for as little as 44 minutes.

It's a game of two halves all right – one half in which the ball is in play, and one half when no football is taking place.

MORE HALVES AT **58**

A LAST AND A FIRST FOR SPACE EXPLORATION

The official name of NASA's space shuttle programme was the Space Transportation System (STS), and in total it flew 135 missions. Its first lift-off was on 12 April 1981, with space shuttle *Columbia*, and its last was on 8 July 2011, with *Atlantis*.

The programme's 91st flight, STS-91, was flown by space shuttle *Discovery* in June 1998. By this time, shuttle launches had become somewhat routine (barring the tragic loss of *Challenger* shortly after lift-off in 1986), but STS-91 was noteworthy on two counts. It was the last shuttle mission to dock with Russia's Mir Space Station (Mir operated in low earth orbit from 1986 until 2001). And it was the first space mission to carry a prototype of the Alpha Magnetic Spectrometer (AMS), whose job – at the cutting edge of space research – is to search for dark matter in the universe.

Discovery flew more than any other shuttle – 39 successful missions during more than 27 years of service. She took her very last flight on 17 April 2012, riding on the back of a specially modified Boeing 747 from the Kennedy Space Center in Florida to the Smithsonian Institution's National Air and Space Museum in Chantilly, Virginia, where she is now on display.

92

HEADS YOU LOSE

Tom Stoppard's play *Rosencrantz and Guildenstern are Dead* (first performed in 1966) opens with the two title characters betting on the toss of a coin. Again and again, the coin comes down heads, 92 times in succession. Rosencrantz (who is winning) is unconcerned, but Guildenstern worries about what it might mean. Is he willing it? Has time stopped dead, so that a single experience is being repeated 92 times? Is it divine intervention? Is it simply chance? He concludes that probability is not operating, and that they are in the grip of 'un-, sub- or supernatural forces'.

This suspension of the laws of probability opens an absurdist comedy that takes place in the margins of Shakespeare's *Hamlet*. The two principal characters know they have a role to play in that other drama, but here, offstage, waiting in the wings, they are lost, knowing nothing of their own pasts and unable to see a future beyond their role in *Hamlet*.

The fates of Rosencrantz and Guildenstern are sealed before they even appear on stage. They are doomed by the title of the play and by the audience's prior knowledge of *Hamlet*. A world in which a coin comes down heads no matter how many times it is spun is also a world in which Rosencrantz and Guildenstern, no matter how many times the play is performed, will always end up dead.

ROSENCRANTZ AND GUILDENSTERN PLAY THEIR PARTS AGAIN AT **262**

93

Quatrevingt-treize

The year is 1793. In France, the National Convention has abolished the monarchy, declared France a republic, and put the king, Louis XVI, on trial for treason. On 21 January, Louis is beheaded by guillotine at the Place de la Révolution (present-day Place de la Concorde) in Paris. Later that year, Marie-Antoinette suffers the same fate. The counter-revolutionary revolt in the Vendée is brutally suppressed by the Republic. The Terror is in full swing.

This tumultuous year provides the setting for Victor Hugo's last novel, published in 1874 and called *Quatrevingt-treize* ('Ninety-three'). The story focuses on the (ultimately tragic) conflicting values of three protagonists: the royalist Marquis de Lantenac; Gauvain, a commander of Republican troops who has a rather romantic vision of the Republic; and Cimourdain, a committed revolutionary whose sympathies lie with Robespierre.

Victor Hugo (1802–1885) is now much better known for *Notre-Dame de Paris* (*The Hunchback of Notre-Dame*, 1831) and *Les Misérables* (1862), but *Quatrevingt-treize* is regarded by many as his finest achievement. He wrote: '93 was the war of Europe against France, and of France against Paris. And what was the Revolution? It was the victory of France over Europe, and of Paris over France. Hence the immensity of that terrible moment? 93, greater than all the rest of the century.'

MORE TROUBLE IN FRANCE AT **122**

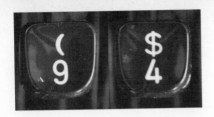

THERE'S LIFE IN THE OLD JOKE YET

The British satirical magazine *Private Eye* is a thoroughly old-fashioned publication. The typewriter, the Letraset, the scissors and paste have long been abandoned in favour of computer typesetting, but you'd barely know it from its appearance. The business model is similarly old-fashioned: a website, a blog, and a Twitter account have come along recently, but the focus is still very much on the printed magazine. What's more, there is relatively little advertising, and the publishers rely mainly on selling copies of the fortnightly publication.

Many of the jokes in the *Eye* are also traditional. Its uncompromising exposure of corruption in British public life takes place against a background of in-jokes and running gags and parodies, many of which have run for decades, and some of which have spread well beyond its covers – 'tired and emotional', 'Ugandan discussions', the *grauniad*, Colemanballs, 'shome mishtake, shurely'. Another running gag revolves around the number 94. Articles frequently stop abruptly, to be continued on the non-existent 'page 94', and 94 is used in many other contexts, for example in relation to someone's age, or to indicate that something has gone on for too long ('BBC crisis: day 94'). It's not as visible as some of the other well-known jokes, but 94 (and variations on it) constitute a constant refrain, to be found at least once or twice in every issue. *Private Eye* itself has been in business since 1961. But it will need to keep going until 2055 before it chalks up its first 94 years.

FOR ANOTHER RECURRING NUMBER, SEE **327**

95

The beginning of the end for indulgences

'As soon as the coin in the coffer rings, the soul from purgatory springs.' These words, attributed to Dominican priest Johann Tetzel, prompted the German priest and professor of theology Martin Luther to nail his *95 Theses* (aka the *Disputation of Martin Luther on the Power and Efficacy of Indulgences*) to the door of All Saints' Church in Wittenberg on 31 October 1517.

In his theses, Luther strongly objected to the sale of indulgences and the veneration of relics (of which All Saints' Church had plenty), which the Catholic Church maintained would allow people to bypass punishment in purgatory. Luther argued that such practices induced a false assurance of peace and led recipients to neglect true repentance. Not surprisingly, Luther was excommunicated from the Church, and a few years later the 1521 Edict of Worms gave permission for anyone to kill him.

Luther went into hiding, but his *95 Theses* spread rapidly across Germany and the rest of Europe – aided by their translation into German, by the recent invention of the printing press, and by the much improved literacy of the populace.

In 1529 the word 'Protestant' became a popular term for supporters of Luther's protests against the Church. Soon the term was applied to all who argued for the Church to be reformed, and to a movement that ultimately led to the Protestant Reformation.

Ninety Six

There are many place names with numerical connections, and a fair few that include numbers, but not so many that consist of nothing but a number. The town of Ninety Six, South Carolina, is one of that select group. It's a small settlement dating from colonial times, situated in Greenwood County about 70 miles (113 kilometres) west of the state capital of Columbia. Just outside the town is the Ninety Six National Historic Site, commemorating the first battle of the American War of Independence in the South, which was fought here in November 1775. The park also contains the remarkably well-preserved remains of a star-shaped fort built a few years later, which was besieged by the Revolutionaries in 1781 – the second battle of the War of Independence to take place at Ninety Six.

The unusual name is most likely a reference to the fact that the settlement grew up beside the 96th milepost on a trail from Keowee, the capital of the Cherokee Nation. But the distance seems to have been at best an approximation, and these days it is hard to check, because in the 1970s Keowee disappeared beneath the waters of a reservoir. Other possible explanations range from the almost-plausible (the 96th stream crossed by the road from somewhere-or-other) to the downright far-fetched (a derivation from the Welsh *nant-sych*, dry stream).

THE TRAIN CRASH THAT INSPIRED A BALLAD – AND A LAWSUIT

The first million-selling record in the USA, recorded by Vernon Dalhart for RCA Victor Records in 1924, was 'The Wreck of the Old 97'. It tells the story of a Southern Railway Fast Mail freight train – the Old 97 – which crashed at Stillhouse Trestle near Danville, Virginia, killing eleven people.

The Old 97 had a reputation for always being on time, but on 27 September 1903 it left Monroe, Virginia, an hour late on its way to Spencer in North Carolina. In order to try and make up time, the driver increased speed, but as the train descended towards Stillhouse Trestle it could not be slowed down, and it soared over the edge into the ravine below. The crash made headline news across the country, and thousands came to gawp at the wreckage.

Vernon Dalhart's 1924 recording of 'The Wreck of the Old 97' was not in fact the first. Virginia musicians G. B. Grayson and Henry Whitter had recorded it in December 1923 for Okeh Records. And the ballad went on to become the subject of a protracted lawsuit concerning the question of copyright: David G. George, who had witnessed the 1903 crash, claimed to have written it. Since then, 'The Wreck of the Old 97' has been recorded many times (by Lonnie Donegan, Boxcar Willie, and Woody Guthrie, among others), and it rivals 'Casey Jones' for the accolade of the USA's best-known railroad song.

THERE'S A CRASH OF A DIFFERENT SORT AT **228**

LIVING THE GOOD LIFE

Question: What do these four women have in common?

Dorothy Height (1912–2010) was a pioneering figure in the US civil rights movement. During the 1950s and '60s she became an advocate for gender equality and the desegregation of the US armed forces.

Etha 'Bea' Fox (1914–2012), from Chicago, was barred from joining the armed forces during World War Two because she was a woman. She went on to become a lawyer, and was a tireless advocate of women in the legal profession.

Nancy Wake (1912–2011) was a British agent during World War Two and saved thousands of Allied lives. She was at the top of the Gestapo's 'most wanted' list, but she survived the war and went on to become one of the Allies' most decorated servicewomen.

Irena Sendler (1910–2008) was a Polish nurse and social worker who smuggled endangered Jewish children out of the Warsaw Ghetto during World War Two, and kept a record of their names and new identities so that they could be reunited with their families after the war.

Answer: They all died at the age of 98.

THERE IS ANOTHER STRONG WOMAN AT **108**

99

A British seaside mystery

The 99, a soft ice cream in a cone with a Cadbury's Flake stuck into it, is as much a part of a summer's day on a British beach as horizontal rain, biting wind, sand-blasted sandwiches, and seawater so cold it could freeze the barnacles off even the most resilient of surfers.

The name '99' for this sort of ice cream has been in existence since 1930, when Cadbury's first produced a shorter version of its Flake bar – called a Flake 99 – specifically for the ice-cream trade. But the origins of the name are something of a mystery, and not even the *Oxford English Dictionary* can shed any light on the matter.

Some say that it is so named because it is 99 millimetres long; others that it used to cost 99 pence. But since the ice cream was in existence well before either metric measurements or decimalisation were introduced to the UK, such notions don't hold water, never mind ice.

Other suggestions, all of them equally suspect, include the idea that the Flake 99 was no. 99 on the order form for Cadbury's products; or that – according to a 1930s advertising campaign – the Flake is made from 99 layers of chocolate; or that there were 99 Flakes in each box; or that the Flake should be stuck into the cone at an angle of precisely 99 degrees; or that it takes 99 seconds to eat. Take your pick.

FIND SOME ICE OF A VERY DIFFERENT KIND AT **75**

100

WE KNOW HOW MANY ACRES — BUT HOW MANY TREES?

If you go down to the New York Public Library, you can visit a Bear of Great Importance and his friends: Winnie-the-Pooh, Piglet, Eeyore, Tigger, and Kanga (but not Roo, who wandered off, never to be seen again). These stuffed toys were the boyhood playmates of Christopher Milne (aka Christopher Robin), and the inspiration for his father A. A. Milne's much-loved books, *Winnie-the-Pooh* (1926) and *The House at Pooh Corner* (1928).

Pooh Bear and friends were donated to the library in 1987, but everyone knows they really belong – with Christopher Robin, Owl, Rabbit, and the occasional Woozle or Heffalump – in the Hundred Acre Wood.

The Hundred Acre Wood is in reality Five Hundred Acre Wood in Ashdown Forest in East Sussex, England. Many features from the stories can be identified with specific locations in the forest, and they were immortalised in the illustrator E. H. Shepard's map at the beginning of *Winnie-the-Pooh* and in numerous illustrations throughout the two books.

The last chapter of *The House at Pooh Corner* is titled 'In which Christopher Robin and Pooh come to an enchanted place, and we leave them there'. The enchanted place is at Galleons Lap, which is 'sixty-something trees' in a circle. Christopher Robin knew it was enchanted because no one had ever been able to count whether it was 63 or 64, 'not even when he tied a piece of string round each tree after he had counted it'.

101

SAMPLING THE SWEETS

In the jargon of confectioners, Quality Street sweets are a 'twist-wrap assortment'. The brand is named after J. M. Barrie's play *Quality Street*, and was first marketed by Mackintosh's of Halifax, Yorkshire, in 1936. In 1969 the company became Rowntree Mackintosh, and in 1988 it was taken over by the multinational Nestlé, but Quality Street sweets are still made in Halifax.

On average, a 1 kilogram tin of Quality Street (the octagonal tin that you hope to get from your granny at Christmas) contains 101 sweets. How do we know this? We bought two tins and counted the contents. One of them contained 100 sweets and the other had 102. And $(100 + 102) / 2 = 101$.

Statisticians might argue with our sample size, but quality control procedures in the factory (not to mention the Weights and Measures Act) will ensure that each tin weighs the same – which, given a consistent mix of the twelve flavours, will produce a very similar number each time. Nonetheless, further research on the statistics of twistwrap assortments might reveal more. Is the ratio of green triangles to toffee pennies constant? Do the coconut éclairs consistently outnumber the orange crunches? Are we the only ones to have noticed a positive correlation between the length of time that a box of Quality Street lies open on the kitchen table and the proportion of its contents that is accounted for by strawberry creams?

Stop press: The 1 kilogram tin has been replaced by one containing just 820 grams of sweets. This calls for more research.

SOMETHING ELSE IS BASED ON A PLAY BY J. M. BARRIE AT **298**

A NUMEROUS MULTIPLICITY

Multitude, numerousness, numerosity, numerality, multiplicity, legion, host, a great or large number, numbers, sight, army…

Thus begins the list of synonyms for multitude (concept number 102) in the first edition of Roget's *Thesaurus* (1852). Peter Mark Roget (1779–1869) was a medical doctor, a writer, a lecturer, a workaholic, and an obsessive list-maker. In 1805 he started making a list of words, grouped by meaning and classified into categories, which he used to enhance his writing, and almost fifty years later he published his personal project as a *thesaurus* ('treasure-house'), containing approximately 15,000 words grouped under 1,000 concepts.

It was such an original and useful idea that Roget's name has become synonymous with his invention – a synonym for synonyms. Since 1852 the *Thesaurus* has grown steadily in extent through a numerosity of editions (both in print and online), has given rise to a multitude of imitations, and has been adapted for a host of other languages and a legion of special topics. And over the years a great number of writers and speakers have consulted (checked, referred to, pored over, studied, perused, scrutinised) its pages.

FOR THE HOURS A WORKAHOLIC WORKS, SEE **247**

103

PUTTING NAMES TO FACES

What do Bill Clinton, Bruce Lee, Marie Curie, Marcel Duchamp, and Mother Teresa have in common? They all appear in an oil painting that first popped up on the Internet in 2009, and which soon went viral. Called *Discussing the Divine Comedy with Dante*, the painting is clearly inspired by Raphael's fresco *The School of Athens* (*c*.1509). Whereas Raphael's fresco contains just 21 figures, this painting is considerably more crowded, with no fewer than 103, and the fun lies in trying to work out not only who's who but also who is watching or chatting to whom.

Some are moderately obvious: Friedrich Nietzsche is talking to Karl Marx, Abraham Lincoln sits next to Mao Zedong, and Charlie Chaplin is crouching on the floor next to Henry Ford. George W. Bush looks through a telescope while Osama Bin Laden stands behind him. And guess who is within Bush's line of vision? Saddam Hussein.

Others are far more obscure – at least to Western eyes. Liu Xiang, the Chinese hurdler who limped out of both the 2008 and the 2012 Summer Olympics, appears in the picture with a winning smile. He may be a bit of a cultural icon in China, but he is unlikely to be widely recognised elsewhere.

In fact, the plethora of Chinese figures provides a clue to the work's origins. The three Chinese men in contemporary dress who survey the crowd from behind a wall in the picture's top right corner are portraits of the work's creators: Chinese/Taiwanese artists Dai Dudu, Li Tiezi, and Zhang Anjiun.

FOR A TRAGIC CASE OF OVERCROWDING, GO TO **133**

104

Ship-rigged and Trafalgar fashion

HMS *Victory*, Nelson's flagship at the Battle of Trafalgar and now a tourist attraction in Portsmouth, is described as a '104-gun first-rate ship of the line'. As so often in nautical matters, there's a lot of jargon packed into very few words there.

104 guns is simple enough, and it was the possession of at least 100 guns, on three decks, that qualified *Victory* as *first-rate* – a term that is now used simply to mean high-quality, but which 200 years ago referred specifically to the largest naval ships. And *ship of the line* means one of the large warships that was used in the *line of battle*, in which the tactic was to manoeuvre a column of ships so that each could discharge a broadside at the enemy.

A more surprising technical term lurking in the first sentence is *ship*. In Nelson's day a ship was not just any old largish boat, but a sailing vessel with a bowsprit and three or more masts, all carrying square-rigged sails. With any other sail plan, the vessel might be a barque or a brigantine (or indeed a brig or a barquentine), or a schooner, a yawl, or a ketch – but she wasn't a ship unless she was ship-rigged, never mind how many guns she carried.

105

ALWAYS A GENTLEMAN

The year 1879 was a turning point in the career of W. G. Grace, the owner of the nineteenth century's most instantly recognisable beard, the man who 'found cricket a country pastime and left it a national institution'.

No, not that career – his other one. In fact, technically, his only one. For on the cricket pitch W. G. remained an amateur throughout his life – always a Gentleman, never a Player. Never mind that he was paid handsomely in the form of expenses, making far more than most professional cricketers of the time. Eyebrows were raised (though the beard was rarely troubled), and in January 1879 Grace survived an inquiry into some 'exorbitant' expenses claimed the previous summer. The year might have been a turning point of a different sort if that inquiry had had a different outcome.

No, the career in question here is his medical one. In 1879, at the age of 31, Grace finally qualified as a doctor after more than ten years of medical studies. And it seems that focusing rather more on his medical studies and rather less on his cricket did have an impact on his performance. For the first time in a decade he failed to reach 1,000 runs in first-class cricket – but he still managed to top the national batting averages and take 105 wickets. Not bad, for an amateur.

SOMEONE ELSE IS STUDYING TO BE A DOCTOR AT **269**

AT THE MERCY OF GEOGRAPHY AND HISTORY

Some political boundaries follow nice straight lines – as in much of the New World, where borders were fixed by simply drawing lines on a map. Boundaries in the Old World, on the other hand, have a habit of wandering hither and thither as dictated by the whims of geography and history – but at least each of the two territories separated by the border generally has the decency to stay on its own side of the line.

Not so in the case of enclaves and exclaves, parcels of land that are cut off from their parent territory. A famous example in Europe is the town of Baarle-Hertog/Baarle-Nassau, where 22 small pieces of Belgium are entirely surrounded by Dutch territory, and in turn contain seven even smaller bits of the Netherlands – a bureaucrat's nightmare but a tourist's delight.

For the ultimate in complexity, however, look at the border where northern Bangladesh meets the Cooch Behar district of India's West Bengal. Here, Bangladesh has 92 enclaves within India, but the prize goes to India, which has no fewer than 106 within Bangladesh. Among numerous enclaves within enclaves, there is one Indian enclave within a Bangladeshi enclave within an Indian enclave. For the inhabitants of these fragments of Cooch Behar, the complicated border has been not a boon to tourism but a source of daily misery, with squalid living conditions and an international border that they are forbidden to cross – though moves are afoot to resolve the situation, as the Indian and Bangladeshi governments work towards a land-swap deal.

MORE FROM INDIA AT **329**

107

Weeded out

Every footballing nation wants to take part in the World Cup; all tennis players aim to play at Wimbledon; all sprinters aspire to be seen on the Olympic stage – so major sporting events impose pre-tournament qualification procedures, using regional competitions, international rankings, or qualifying times to ensure that the paying public sees only the best.

In recent years, Formula 1 motor racing has had a different problem – not too many entrants but too few. It is so expensive to take part that in the 1990s the number of competitors started to fall, and there was a possibility that any car entered, no matter how slow, would be on the starting grid. The qualifying sessions that start each Formula 1 event were being used only to determine positions on the grid, not to weed out the slower competitors – until in 1996 a solution was found in the shape of the 107 per cent rule. This rule states that any car that does not set a qualifying lap time within 107 per cent of the fastest time is not allowed to race – thus preventing slow cars from impeding the fastest, and deterring a team from taking part merely to give its sponsors media coverage.

But nothing stands still for long in Formula 1. The 107 per cent rule was abandoned in 2003 when the qualifying procedure changed, but then reintroduced in 2011 after another change. It now appears to be here for the foreseeable future – unlike some of the teams trying to scrape together the money that will enable them to stay at the races.

THE CAR AT **328** IS PRETTY QUICK, BUT NOT QUITE THE RIGHT SORT

108

THE PATIENT WIFE

Waiting twenty years for your husband to come home from war – not knowing if he is still alive or has been killed in battle – would be more than most people could bear. But in Homer's *Odyssey* Penelope, the long-suffering wife of Odysseus, king of Ithaca, never gave up hope that her husband would eventually return. Odysseus' prolonged absence was spent fighting the Trojans and then, on his way home, getting tangled up in a series of adventures – involving whirlpools and one-eyed monsters, sirens and cannibals – which would surely stretch any wife's patience.

While Odysseus was away, Penelope had to put up with the attentions of 108 suitors, who all presumed Odysseus to be gone for good. She spent her days weaving a shroud for Laertes, Odysseus' father, and her nights unpicking it again, as she fended off her suitors, for she had promised she would make a decision about whom to choose when the shroud was completed. The suitors became increasingly unruly as time went on and still there was no sign of her husband, and still no decision from Penelope.

All ends well for Penelope, for her husband does come home. Things don't go quite so well for the suitors, however, for Odysseus kills all 108 of them.

NOT WEAVING BUT EMBROIDERING AT **202**

THE SPITFIRE'S ADVERSARY

During World War Two, the British had the Spitfire and the Hurricane, and the Americans the P-51 Mustang, but the Germans had the Messerschmitt Bf 109. The Bf 109 was the brainchild of Willy Messerschmitt, who had a reputation to maintain and whose plan was to install the biggest possible engine in the smallest possible frame. The first trials of the Bf 109 took place in October 1935, and the plane entered service in spring 1937.

The Bf 109's top speed was 620 kilometres per hour, and its engine had a fuel injection system that provided a constant flow of fuel even in conditions of negative g, allowing a pilot to dive more quickly and get out of the firing line. Yet its limited range – 600 kilometres – hindered it during the Battle of Britain, when it was deployed to protect bombers but had to scurry home before it ran out of fuel. Nevertheless, the Bf 109 was responsible for shooting down more Allied planes than any other aircraft.

Ironically, the first prototypes of the Bf 109 were powered by a British engine – the Rolls-Royce Kestrel. Rolls-Royce engines – Merlins and, in later marks, the more powerful Griffons – were also fitted into Spitfires. When the operational head of the Luftwaffe was asked by Goering early on in the Battle of Britain what he needed to achieve aerial supremacy, he replied 'a squadron of Spitfires'.

TAKE TO THE AIR AGAIN AT **22**

JUDGING A PERCENTAGE BY ITS COVER

In writing this book, we have both given 110 per cent. We have
kicked no cans down the road (or into the long grass), and we have
left no stone unturned in our search for things to include. Our
capacity for blue-sky thinking has enabled us to push the envelope,
thinking outside the box and casting the net widely in an effort to
put clear blue water between this book and others.

We have done our utmost to avoid picking the low-hanging
fruit, even though we have sometimes compared apples and pears.
We have arranged all our ducks in a row, and we have addressed
the elephant in the room by eating it one bite at a time.

In a nutshell, we have relied on teamwork (no 'I' there),
singing from the same hymn sheet, though at the end of the day
we have from time to time agreed to disagree. Each of us has had
to step up to the plate, and we have not been backward in coming
forward to ensure that neither of us has been left to shoulder the
burden of the lion's share of the labour of Hercules.

Going forward, we anticipate a win–win situation. The book
will sell like hot cakes, and we are 110 per cent confident that it
will not be judged by its cover (though we do like the cover, very
much).

Across the piece, we have avoided clichés like the plague – and
we also recognise an impossible percentage when we see one.

LET'S GIVE YOU A HEADS UP THAT YOU CAN ALSO TOUCH BASE AT **90**

111

A birthday fellowship

Any self-respecting fan of J. R. R. Tolkien's trilogy *The Lord of the Rings* should celebrate 22 September each year, for this is Hobbit Day, when both Bilbo Baggins and his nephew Frodo were born – Bilbo in the year 2890 and Frodo in the year 2968 in the Third Age – although discrepancies between the Shire calendar and the Gregorian calendar apparently mean that there is some uncertainty about the exact date. *The Fellowship of the Ring* – the first volume of the trilogy – opens shortly before the joint birthday celebrations in the year 3001. Frodo is about to become 33, and Bilbo a very respectable 111 years old: in his own words, it's not his one-hundred-and-eleventh birthday, but his eleventy-first. The long-expected party will take place at the Party Tree, which stands proudly at the centre of the Party Field in Hobbiton. Gandalf the Grey will provide the fireworks, and there will be a luxurious supper for all the guests (a gross of them: 33 + 111).

And then...well, there's a ring, and some kind of dark lord, and elves and dwarves and goblins – not to mention oliphants and nazgûls and a balrog – and a true heir to the throne, and remarkably few damsels (in distress or otherwise). At the end of the whole affair, Frodo's faithful companion Sam Gamgee returns to the Shire to find that the Party Tree has been felled and lies abandoned in the middle of the field. In his films of the trilogy, director Peter Jackson preferred to overlook not just that particular detail but the whole of Tolkien's far darker ending. Jackson did, however, give Bilbo's eleventy-first birthday all the attention it deserved.

TO FIND OUT WHAT HAPPENED ON HOBBIT DAY IN 1877, TURN TO **148**

112

Dialling in the dark

The idea of dialling 999 in an emergency is pretty well ingrained in Britain and Ireland. After all, the system has been in operation since 1937, and everyone has had plenty of time to get used to it.

Are we all set for the big change, then? The deadline is 31 December 1996. When that date comes, we will all be using 112 instead of 999. Yes, 31 December 1996. That was the date set by the European Union in 1991 for full implementation of the new single European emergency call number in all member states.

In the early 1990s there was no uniformity, and many European countries (even if they had a national system) used different numbers for police, fire service, and ambulance. A single Europe-wide number would bring obvious benefits.

In the event, pushing 112 out across Europe took just a little longer than anticipated. There were technical issues involving coordination among emergency services and telephone networks, but above all there was the issue of awareness. For a few years now, 112 has been operational in all EU states, often (as in the UK) alongside the old national number. Many other countries have also adopted it, and in 2012 the International Telecommunication Union decreed that 112 and 911 should be the two standard emergency phone numbers for the whole world. But no one seems to know about it. In spite of publicity campaigns run by the likes of the European Emergency Number Association and the 112 Foundation, a survey in 2013 found that 73 per cent of European citizens were still in the dark.

DIAL AGAIN AT **290**

A RECIPE FOR CONFUSION

The number 113 appears in cookery books more frequently than seems either plausible or necessary. That's because 113 grams is the equivalent of 4 ounces, and in the 1970s, when British publishers of cookery books wanted to bring their products up to date and ensure that they were in tune with Europe (Britain had just joined what was then the EEC), they started translating imperial measurements into metric ones. So a Victoria sponge cake no longer called for 4 ounces of this, that, and the other but 113 grams of sugar, 113 grams of butter, and 113 grams of flour (but still 2 eggs).

Forty years later, it is unfinished business. Although most recipe books (except of course American ones) do now specify quantities in round numbers of grams and litres, the old habit of starting with imperial quantities and translating them into the oddest numbers is far from dead.

And it's not just recipes. Why, in Britain, do you buy a pint of milk but 250 grams of butter, while in Ireland milk is sold in litres and butter comes in packs of 8 ounces?

MORE MEASUREMENTS AT **224**

114

CHAPTER AND VERSE

The Qur'an is divided into 114 *suras* (chapters), and each *sura* is divided into a number of *ayat* (verses). The *suras* vary greatly in length: the longest one (*Al-Bagara*) has 286 *ayat*, while the shortest (*Al-Kawthar*) has just three.

The Qur'an is not arranged chronologically or thematically; instead, it is (roughly) arranged in order of the length of the *suras*, with the longest at the beginning and the shortest towards the end. With just one exception (the *At-Tawba*), all of the *suras* start with the *Bismillah*: 'In the name of God, the Merciful, the Compassionate'.

The word *Qur'an* means 'the recitation', and Muslims believe that it was revealed verbally to Muhammad through the angel Gabriel (or *Jibril*) over approximately 23 years, from 609 to 632 CE. During the Islamic month of Ramadan, one of the traditional practices is the *Tarawih* (night prayers), during which people meet to recite the whole of the Qur'an. This is quite a feat, as the Qur'an contains a total of 6,236 *ayat*. An even more impressive accomplishment is to memorise the entire Qur'an, which usually takes between three and six years. Someone who achieves this is honoured with the title of *hafiz*.

PEOPLE GATHER AGAIN, BUT FOR A DIFFERENT PURPOSE, AT **349**

115

GONE IN MILLISECONDS

In the *Call of Duty* series of video games, element 115 (ununpentium) appears in the Zombies back-story. It is harvested from meteorites and is used to create zombies, as one of its effects is to reanimate dead cells. The Nazis' dastardly plan is to use the zombies as super-soldiers, but (will they never learn?) it turns out that zombies are rather hard to control and threaten the very existence of mankind – unless you can just get your hands on the Focusing Stone, a floating rock packed with element 115…

Meanwhile, back in the real world, ununpentium is one of about twenty synthetic elements that have so far been created in the laboratory. It was first synthesised by nuclear fusion in Russia in 2003, and just a few dozen atoms have so far been observed. The name is a temporary one, referring (via Latin and Greek) to its atomic number, which is 115. That means it has 115 protons in its nucleus, 23 more than the heaviest element that occurs naturally on earth, uranium. Like all heavy elements, ununpentium is unstable, subject to radioactive decay.

Ununpentium has a half-life of less than a fifth of a second. Don't blink while you're trying to reanimate that corpse, or you'll miss it.

116

THE SNIPER'S WEAPON OF CHOICE IN SPACE

On board the Starship *Enterprise* was a hand-held weapon called the TR-116 Projectile Rifle. The TR-116 was the weapon of choice for a sniper, since it could precisely target people at long range, and it could even shoot through solid matter. It had been developed by Starfleet Security to be used where conventional-energy weapons (basic phasers) were of no use, especially in dampening fields (in which an energy field interferes with power emissions, blocking sensor readings).

The TR-116 first appeared in 'Field of Fire', which was the 163rd episode of the television series *Star Trek: Deep Space Nine*. Here it was used by Science Officer Chu'lak to murder three Star-fleet officers; Chu'lak modified the rifle with a micro-transporter, which enabled him to beam the rifle's titanium bullet into another room just a few centimetres from its target. Chu'lak – a Vulcan – claimed that he committed murder because 'logic demanded it'. His victims were chosen because they all possessed photographs of people showing emotion, and for Chu'lak this was clearly a sign of extreme personal weakness – hence unforgivable.

It all ended as it should in that episode, but the TR-116 was just one among numerous weapons deployed by the crew of the *Enterprise*. There were isokinetic, plasma, and transphasic torpedoes; pulse cannon and phased polaron cannon; Ferengi energy whips; Varon-T disruptors; and all manner of biological, chemical, and radioactive weapons. And that's to say nothing of the myriad weapons used by Starfleet's enemies.

MEANWHILE, IN AMERICA

There was quite a lot going on in July 1942. In Europe, the deportation of Jews from the Warsaw Ghetto began, Anne Frank and her family were forced into hiding in Amsterdam, and the Germans gave the Messerschmitt Me-262 its first test flight.

Meanwhile, on the other side of the Atlantic, Irving Berlin's musical *This is the Army* premiered in New York, Cary Grant got married, Dmitri Shostakovich appeared on the cover of *Time* magazine...and in Washington DC the National Gallery of Art hosted the 'Art Exhibition by Men of the Armed Forces'. The exhibition showed 117 works – in oil, watercolour, tempera, pencil, and crayon – selected from over 1,500 entries for an art competition sponsored by *Life* magazine and open to all US Armed Forces personnel. After a month-long stay in the capital, the exhibition went on tour in the USA, visiting Syracuse, Baltimore, and Saint Paul.

The USA became involved in World War Two after its naval base at Pearl Harbor was bombed by the Japanese on 7 December 1941. But on American soil life went on much as it had before, and musicals, weddings, magazine covers, and displays of art still occupied the daily lives of Americans. Yet as those 117 works of art toured the country, they helped to bring home the reality of warfare for those directly involved in it, since the sole condition of entry was that all the artworks had to depict scenes or events connected to the artists' own experiences while on active duty.

A MUCH SHORTER WAR IS FOUGHT AT **258**

118

DEVASTATION

The top of the Beaufort wind force scale in common use is force 12, hurricane-force, representing winds of 118 kilometres per hour and above.

The scale was devised by Francis Beaufort (1774–1857) in 1805. At first it was just for his own personal use, but in 1829 Beaufort was appointed Hydrographer of the Navy, and two years later he commissioned the second voyage of HMS *Beagle* – an expedition that is notable not only for having Charles Darwin on board but also for the first official use of Beaufort's scale to record conditions during the voyage. Then in 1838 the Admiralty issued a memorandum ordering that it should henceforth be used to record wind speed in all naval ships' logs.

In the nineteenth century the Beaufort scale was defined by the amount of sail that a warship could carry, with force 12 described as 'that which no canvas could withstand', but the development of steamships made this meaningless, so in 1906 the descriptions were amended to refer to the state of the sea. The standard description of force 12 at sea today is that the air is filled with foam and spray, the sea is completely white with driving spray, and visibility is very seriously affected. On land, the effect of a wind of 118 kilometres per hour is often described in a single word: devastation.

THE EFFECTS OF A HURRICANE ARE DESCRIBED AT **193**

119

FACE TO FACE WITH JUPITER

America's first transcontinental railroad was completed on 10 May 1869, when the Union Pacific and Central Pacific Railroads joined their tracks at Promontory Summit, 106 kilometres north-west of Salt Lake City, not far from the Great Salt Lake in Utah. Large crowds gathered, and there was much waving of flags as Union Pacific's *No. 119* locomotive met Central Pacific's *Jupiter* face to face, and the last spike – a specially crafted and engraved Golden Spike – was driven home as east met west.

After the excitement of that day, Pacific's *No. 119* continued working as a freight locomotive, until it was scrapped in 1903. It was not until several decades later that its historical significance began to be recognised. In 1948 a re-enactment of the Golden Spike ceremony took place at the Chicago Railroad Fair, and in 1975 the National Park Service decided to reinstate part of the original track (which had long since been bypassed) at Promontory Summit and commission replicas of both the *No. 119* and the *Jupiter*.

Since 10 May 1979 (exactly 110 years after the first Golden Spike ceremony), visitors to Promontory Summit have been enjoying the sight of *No. 119* face to face with *Jupiter*, as the last spike is driven home in regular re-enactments. The original Golden Spike now lives behind glass in the Cantor Arts Center at Stanford University in California.

120

THAT 'PILE OF BRICKS'

What to do with 120 firebricks? The American minimalist artist Carl Andre (b.1935) arranged them in a straightforward rectangle – two bricks high, six bricks wide, and ten bricks long – and laid them out on the floor of the Tate Gallery, London, in 1974. Two years later, the *Sunday Times* published an article about recent additions to the Tate's collection, and included an illustration of Andre's sculpture. The article provoked uproar, and the Tate was ridiculed by many for appearing to buy nothing more than a pile of bricks: indeed, the work soon became popularly known simply as *The Bricks*. (Its actual title is *Equivalent VIII*, and it is the last in a series of eight sculptures, all of which have the same height, mass, and volume, and are therefore 'equivalent' to each other.) Yet those who defended the work recognised Andre's significant contribution to ground-breaking art and to the exploration of the dynamic relationship between artworks and their audiences.

The work has continued to be a catalyst for lively debate. As a result of public and press interest, it has been exhibited many times since, and continues to capture the imagination of the public, becoming one of the best-known works of modern art in the Tate's collection.

FOR ANOTHER PILE OF BRICKS, SEE **201**

STERILISATION HEAT

Being well aware that an army marches on its stomach, Napoleon was keen to find a way of preserving food so that his military campaigns could be extended beyond the season when fresh food was available, and he must have been pleased when a French confectioner named Nicolas Appert came up with a viable way of achieving this in 1810 – by inventing canned food.

From its Napoleonic origins, the food canning industry developed through the nineteenth century, becoming increasingly mechanised and sophisticated. And today it is a very sophisticated business indeed, relying on all sorts of automated processes, protocols, and even mathematical modelling. Before being sealed in the can, most food is heat-treated to kill off bacteria and other microorganisms that might spoil the food or poison the consumer, and it is important to determine the effectiveness of the heat sterilisation techniques. So food microbiologists test hypotheses, draw graphs, and discuss decimal reduction times, z-values, and F-values.

One important concept is the thermal death time (TDT) for each microorganism, which is the time required at a specific temperature to effectively kill the organism. Although the actual time and temperature used will vary with the type of food, the standard temperature at which TDT is measured is 121 °C. In 1812, Napoleon's army might have appreciated just a little of that heat in Russia.

122

THE CONFUSION OF BATTLE

In 1944, in the weeks after D-Day, there were two different Battles of Hill 122 in Normandy.

The first is also known as the Battle of Mont Castre and le Plessis-Lastelle. It took place just east of La-Haye-du-Puits on the Cotentin Peninsula between 3 and 12 July 1944. The American 358th and 359th Regiments were pushing south against determined German resistance, but progress across the small fields and dense hedgerows of the *bocage* countryside was slow and bloody, with exceptionally heavy casualties on both sides.

A few days later another Battle of Hill 122 was fought, by different troops in a different place. The hill was a key defensive position overlooking the town of Saint-Lô. On 15 and 16 July 1944, the American 134th Infantry Regiment stormed and took Hill 122, opening the way for the liberation of the town. Again, casualties were heavy.

Having two battles with the same name is confusing enough, and the confusion is compounded by the better-known Battle of Hill 112, which also took place in Normandy at very much the same time. This hill was a key objective during the Allied assault on Caen, and the site of fierce fighting between British and German forces from late June to early August 1944.

All of these hills, like many other military objectives in World War Two, were named for their heights above sea level in metres – presumably by an Allied commander jabbing his finger at a spot height on a map.

FOR ANOTHER SPOT HEIGHT ON A MAP, SEE **307**

123

Easy-peasy lemon squeezy

In Denmark it's as easy as scratching one's neck. In China and Indonesia it's like turning your hand over. In Romania it's understandable to a hedgehog, while in Japan it's as simple as lying on one's back and eating rice cakes. Although their origins are often obscure, these phrases all mean the same thing: doing something that is very easy.

The English-speaking corners of the world have a particularly well-documented number of such expressions: undertaking a simple task is 'as easy as' falling off a log/ABC/123/pie/shooting fish in a barrel/taking candy from a baby. Or, if you prefer, it's a piece of cake, or a walk in the park, or child's play.

'As easy as 123' is an especially common phrase. Everyone can count that far, can't they? In the mid-1980s a shareware spreadsheet that was developed for MS-DOS was called As Easy As – a somewhat oblique reference to the name of the dominant spreadsheet of the day, Lotus 1-2-3. It was a good marketing ploy. Any fool could use it. So simple, but best not muddle up the fish in the barrel with the pieces of cake, or mistake the hedgehog for the pie.

FOR MORE CHILD'S PLAY, GO TO **325**

124

RED DIESEL, GREEN DIESEL

Regardless of whether it's a red lorry, yellow lorry, or any other tongue-twisting truck, the fuel in its tank had better be neither red nor yellow, or the driver will be in trouble with the law.

Solvent Yellow 124 (SY124), otherwise known as Euromarker, is a marker that is added to diesel fuel intended for off-road use. In most countries, fuel for agricultural machinery, construction vehicles, and boats is taxed at a lower rate than road fuel, and SY124 is added to deter its illegal use in road vehicles.

Since 2002, EU countries have been obliged to mark non-road fuels with 6 milligrams of SY124 per litre of fuel. It is often used in conjunction with other dyes, resulting in different colours in different countries. In the UK, for example, off-road diesel is red, while in Ireland it is green.

Given colourful fuel, it seems only appropriate that there should be a black market for the stuff. SY124 and the other modern additives may be more difficult to remove than some earlier dyes, but the diesel-laundering business is apparently thriving, especially on both sides of the Irish border, where it costs the taxpayer millions in lost revenue every year.

MORE PETROCHEMICALS AT **205**

125

From joy to freedom

Beethoven's Symphony No. 9 in D Minor, Opus 125, premiered in Vienna on 7 May 1824 and broke new ground for several reasons. It was extraordinarily long (over an hour); its orchestra was exceptionally large, with double the usual number of wind and brass instruments; and its last movement – which incorporates Beethoven's setting of Friedrich Schiller's *'An die Freude'* ('Ode to Joy') – includes the most unusual addition of a full chorus and vocal soloists.

The symphony makes an appearance in the soundtrack of Stanley Kubrick's film *A Clockwork Orange* (along with Gene Kelly's 'Singing in the Rain' and bits of Rossini's *The Thieving Magpie*). It also turns up in Peter Weir's *Dead Poets Society* (along with The Cadets' 'Stranded in the Jungle' and Jimmie Driftwood's 'The Battle of New Orleans'). And some of it is now the Anthem of the European Union.

It was played on Christmas Day 1989 in Berlin, just a few weeks after the demolition of the Wall. During that performance, in the final movement's 'Ode to Joy' the word *Freude* (joy) was altered to *Freiheit* (freedom).

THE EU'S ACHIEVEMENTS ARE CELEBRATED AGAIN AT **261**

126

The ultimate in photographic convenience

February 1963. Welcome to the future of photography. Kodak introduces a totally new camera, the Instamatic. Inexpensive, well-made, and easy to use. Ideal for the amateur photographer. And with it comes a new film format, the 126 cartridge. Forget fiddly spools of film. Forget threading the film over the sprockets. Forget rewinding. The 126 film is safely locked away in a plastic cartridge. Just open the back of the camera, drop in the cartridge, click the camera shut, and get snapping.

The combination of Instamatic camera and 126 film – coinciding with the arrival of affordable colour photography – was a real breakthrough. The first Instamatics were very simple indeed, with a fixed-focus lens and just two exposure settings (sun and cloud). Later models were a little more sophisticated, but Instamatic remained a byword for simple mass-market photography, with over 50 million of the cameras sold in the first seven years. The smaller-format Pocket Instamatic appeared in 1972. The last of the Instamatics went on sale in 1988.

The 126 cartridge film format was launched by Kodak (under the brand name Kodapak) in response to complaints about the complications of loading and unloading roll film. The name 126 referred to the 26×26 millimetre frame size – the characteristic square snapshots of the 1960s and 1970s. The last of the 126 film cartridges disappeared from the shops in around 1999.

MORE BREAKTHROUGH TECHNOLOGY AT **286**

DELETE, ELEGANTLY

It is said that there are only 10 types of people in the world – those who understand binary and those who do not. And the first group will immediately appreciate that the number 127 is much prettier in binary notation, as 1111111.

Apart from its elegance, 127 has an important place in the history of computing, as the highest possible number in a seven-bit coding system. When you are using a code with seven bits (binary digits) per character, each of the seven can be either a 1 or a 0, so your set of codes runs from 0 (0000000) to 127 (1111111).

The ASCII (American Standard Code for Information Interchange) character set uses this seven-bit code to represent the numbers 0–9 and the letters A–Z and a–z, plus a variety of punctuation marks and control symbols, and although it is rather long in the tooth (having originated with telegraphs and teleprinters in the early 1960s), ASCII is still the foundation for modern computer character sets. So whether you're reading a word-processed document or a webpage, and whether it uses CP1252, UCS, UTF-7, UTF-8, UTF-16, Unicode, ISO 8859, or any other extended character coding system, underneath it all lurks good old ASCII.

As the highest value in the system, 127 in ASCII has a special meaning – it is not a character but the code for 'delete'.

128

Beige-box computing

The earliest personal computers were sold in kit form, designed to appeal to technophiles who enjoyed technology for the sake of technology. The first Apple computer (the Apple I, 1976) was no exception – a naked circuit board, with no monitor and no keyboard.

Later Apple machines were less off-putting, but the big breakthrough came in January 1984 when Apple launched the Macintosh computer, bringing GUI, WIMP, and WYSIWYG to the mass market and packaging it all up in a neat beige plastic box. It had 128 kB of random-access memory (RAM), and in September 1984 (when a more powerful 512 kB version was introduced) the original was renamed the Macintosh 128K.

The Macintosh was a computer not for technophiles but for people who just wanted to get the job done. This was black-box computing, in the sense that the user cared only about inputs and outputs, and did not have to understand what went on inside the box. To this day, that is the Apple approach: the closed architecture may be an issue, but if it does what you want, it's just what you want.

The Macintosh was also a breakthrough in design. The clean lines and the simple beige box set the standard for later Apple products, which continue to be sold at premium prices at least partly because they look so beautiful. From the start, the Macintosh has offered black-box computing in a handsome beige box.

FIND A TWO-DIMENSIONAL BLACK BOX AT **73**

AN AIRSHIP TO REMEMBER

Luftschiff Zeppelin 129 is better known as the *Hindenburg*, a rigid airship launched by the German Zeppelin Company in 1936. Rigid lighter-than-air aircraft had been developed in the late nineteenth century, and had been used for military and commercial purposes since the start of the twentieth. *Hindenburg* was the biggest, best, and most advanced of the commercial craft, building on the outstanding success of its predecessor the *Graf Zeppelin*. It was the first airliner to provide a regular scheduled transatlantic service, the fastest and most comfortable way to cross the ocean.

But it all went up in smoke on 6 May 1937, when LZ-129 *Hindenburg* exploded in full view of the newsreel cameras while landing at Lakehurst, New Jersey, killing 35 of the 97 people on board and one person on the ground.

The *Hindenburg* disaster effectively brought an end to the era of transcontinental airship travel. The only puzzle is why it hadn't ended some years earlier – for there had already been many airship disasters, such as the loss of the British *R-101* in 1930 and the USS *Akron* in 1933, both of which killed more people than *Hindenburg*. By 1937 Germany was the only country still using what was clearly an unsafe mode of transport. Its days were already numbered.

ANOTHER TRANSATLANTIC DISASTER IS COMMEMORATED AT **337**

130

The swoosh of a steel blade

Between 1853 and 1870, Baron Georges-Eugène Haussmann tidied up large swathes of Paris, knocking down the old, narrow streets and replacing them with wide, leafy boulevards. But some vestiges of the old streets remain, and one of these – the Cours du Commerce – can be found tucked behind 130 Boulevard St Germain.

It was here, in 1792, that Dr Joseph Ignace Guillotin undertook a series of experiments that involved chopping the heads off live sheep. But the sheep were just guinea pigs, for Guillotin really wanted to find a more humane method of execution for human beings. A quick, clean decapitation was certainly less barbaric than the usual method at that time, which involved tying the condemned prisoner's four limbs to four oxen, and driving the oxen in four different directions.

Although beheading devices already existed, Guillotin made a number of important refinements, including using a diagonal blade which, when dropped from a height of about four metres, did the job nicely. Guillotin's contraption forged a name for itself by cutting off the heads of kings, queens, and numerous others until 1977, when the last such execution took place.

Today, if you wander from 130 Boulevard St Germain into the Cours du Commerce, you will most likely hear the cheery clatter of wine glasses and coffee cups. But listen very carefully, and you may just catch the echo of an altogether more sinister sound: the swoosh of a falling metal blade.

131

Kill or cure?

Iodine 131 is the best known of the 36 radioactive isotopes of iodine, and it is the kind of chemical that would send certain sections of the British popular press into a spin. Does it cause cancer, or is it a cure for cancer?

On the one hand, iodine 131, as a fission product of uranium, is a feared component of fallout from nuclear warfare, nuclear testing, or an accident at a nuclear power plant. The main effect of exposure to it is cancer of the thyroid, because the thyroid gland eagerly absorbs iodine (which is essential for the manufacture of thyroid hormones) and does not distinguish between stable, non-radioactive iodine and the radioactive stuff.

On the other hand, iodine 131 is a valuable tool in medicine. It has been used in radiotherapy since the 1940s, and in this context it is often referred to as radioactive iodine (RAI) or radioiodine. One of its main uses is in the treatment of thyroid cancers, including cancers that have spread from the thyroid to other parts of the body. A high dose of iodine 131 is delivered in a drink, from which it is rapidly absorbed by those cells, wherever they are. As long as the dose of iodine 131 is high enough, the cancerous cells are killed, while relatively little damage is done to the surrounding tissues.

FOR A SOURCE OF IODINE, GO TO **235**

132

REBELS WITHOUT A CAUSE?

In the run-up to the Mexican presidential election of July 2012, Enrique Peña Nieto, candidate for the Partido Revolucionario Institucional (PRI), gave a speech at the Universidad Ibero-americana (UIA). Inevitably, there was a student protest, but the country's main television network, Televisa – which has a long history of alleged political bias in favour of the PRI – reported that the protestors had been brought in from outside the university. The students responded in a YouTube video in which 131 of those who had protested held up their UIA student cards and gave their names and ID numbers.

Immediately, others started tweeting '#YoSoy132' (I am number 132), and the protest movement Yo Soy 132 was born. It flourished briefly in the second half of 2012 as a movement promoting 'true democracy', and parallels were drawn with the Arab Spring and the Occupy movement. Social media were used to spread the word, and support was pledged from across the world.

Peña Nieto went on to win the election, and in the autumn of 2012 Yo Soy 132 staged a few marches and protests in Mexico and beyond – but that was about it. Although the movement still runs a number of websites, and is represented by several accounts on Facebook and Twitter, there is little sign of activity and Yo Soy 132 seems to have lost sight of any particular agenda. In the age of social media, it is easy to spread the word, but perhaps not so easy to work out what exactly that word should be.

ALLEGIANCE TO A CAUSE IS ALSO ON DISPLAY AT **59**

133

WHY WASTE GOOD METAL?

In the Museum of Fine Arts in Boston, Massachusetts, is an oil painting by J. M. W. Turner, dated 1841 and titled *Slavers Throwing overboard the Dead and Dying – Typhoon coming on* (more commonly known simply as *The Slave Ship*). Turner painted it after reading *The History and Abolition of the Slave Trade* by Thomas Clarkson, who was a key figure in the British abolitionist movement.

Turner's painting depicts the *Zong* Massacre. In 1781, the *Zong*, a slave ship, was on the way to Jamaica with her manacled and cruelly overcrowded cargo when she was becalmed in the Doldrums. The slaves began to suffer from scurvy and dysentery, and some died. The ship's captain, Luke Collingwood, feared that he would arrive in Jamaica with a ship full of dead bodies. Figuring that the insurance would cover the loss, he decided simply to jettison them. Estimates vary, but it is thought that 133 slaves – many of them women and children – were unshackled (why waste good metal?) and thrown overboard.

Once the *Zong* was back home in Liverpool, James Gregson, the ship's owner, made a claim of £4,000 for his lost cargo. The case went to court – but not for the murder of 133 people; the issue to be settled was the question of who was liable for the costs.

RACISM REAPPEARS AT **311**

SIGN ON THE DOTTED LINE

When you 'sign the Official Secrets Act' in the United Kingdom you may find yourself doing so on MOD Form 134.

There are at least three possible misunderstandings here. First, there is not one Official Secrets Act but four, as the Acts of 1911, 1920, 1939, and 1989 are all still in force. Second, it is not one of the Acts that is signed, just a form stating that you are aware of them. And third, signing the form actually makes no difference at all, as the provisions of the Official Secrets Acts apply regardless of whether a person has signed a piece of paper.

Nonetheless, anyone employed in a government job that gives access to state secrets or other sensitive information is likely to have to complete and sign a form declaring that 'I am aware of the Official Secrets Acts and that I am subject to them…' For Ministry of Defence employees the relevant form is MOD Form 134.

Whether the Official Secrets Acts themselves provide an effective defence for the security of the nation is another matter. In 1985, Clive Ponting was accused of revealing secret information about the sinking of the *Belgrano* in the Falklands War, but was acquitted by the jury on the grounds that disclosure was in the public interest. A few years later the system was the subject of further scrutiny – not to mention ridicule – in the *Spycatcher* affair. And to this day any attempt to make the Acts stick runs the constant risk of merely drawing attention to the very thing that the authorities are trying to hush up.

FOLLOW OTHER RULES AT **44**

135

Bewildered by a whale

Between 'Call me Ishmael' in Chapter 1 and the 'great shroud of the sea' that engulfs all at the end of Chapter 135 there is a whale of a tale. Herman Melville's *The Whale* was published in London in October 1851, and a month later an American edition came out under the now more familiar title of *Moby-Dick*. The change of title was just one of many differences between the two editions – due partly to Melville's own last-minute changes and partly to publishers' whims and printers' errors – and the result is a text riddled with uncertainty that has bewildered scholars ever since.

Moby-Dick, indeed, has bewildered readers of all sorts. Even though it is now counted as one of the great American novels, many of those who read it (or try to read it) today would probably agree with some of the early reviewers, who described it in terms such as 'a strange, wild work', and 'an odd book, professing to be a novel; wantonly eccentric; outrageously bombastic'.

Among the most bewildered of all were the reviewers of the first English edition in 1851, some of whom complained that Melville had cheated by using a first-person narrative for a tale that ended with no survivors. They had in fact been misled by an egregious error in the English edition, which ended with Chapter 135 and the death of Ahab and all his crew, and omitted the Epilogue, in which the narrator Ishmael explains how he himself survived the wreck.

BETTER LISTEN TO MARGE

At what weight is a person so obese that he or she is classified as
disabled? Real-life social security departments might have trouble
working this out, but for Homer Simpson the magic number is
136 kilograms (300 pounds). In the episode of *The Simpsons* called
'King-Size Homer', which was first aired in the USA in 1995,
this is the weight at which Homer will be able not only to opt out
of the new calisthenics programme at the Springfield Nuclear
Power Plant but also to work from home. Ignoring Marge and
Lisa's repeated warnings, Homer eats and eats until he reaches his
target. But his life begins to fall apart when he is refused a seat at
the cinema because of his size, people make jokes at his expense,
and he is too fat to drive – let alone ride a skateboard, which splits
in half under his weight. Of course, everything works out fine in
the end. Homer averts certain disaster at the nuclear power plant
by wedging his butt into an exploding gas tank, turning a potential Chernobyl into a 'mere' Three Mile Island.

At 136 kilograms, Homer's body mass index (BMI) would be
well over 40. This is most definitely on the wrong side of obese (a
BMI greater than 25 is overweight), and it would almost certainly
cause other health issues (such as respiratory, cardiovascular, or
musculoskeletal impairments) that could have earned him the
'disabled' label.

137

Islands, islets, atolls, and reefs

'No man is an Iland', as John Donne observed in 1623. But what exactly constitutes an island? The usual definition is 'any piece of land smaller than a continent and surrounded by water', but just where would we draw the line? Should we perhaps rule out those that only appear at low tide? Or maybe those too small to appear on a map?

According to official statistics, the state of Hawaii has 137 islands. This figure includes the obvious eight major islands (Hawai'i, Maui, Kaho'olawe, Lāna'i, Moloka'i, O'ahu, Kaua'i, and Ni'ihau), plus a whole heap of smaller islets, atolls, and reefs. But any Internet trawl will quickly dredge up several other figures (Wikipedia, for example, has 152), suggesting that 137 is at best a guesstimate.

The Hawaiian islands were formed where the Pacific Plate moved over a 'hot spot' in the earth's mantle, creating undersea volcanoes, some of which broke through the ocean's surface to form the islands we see today. In time, as the plate moved, so the islands were left behind, and the hot spot is now about 32 kilometres to the south-east of the island of Hawai'i in an area called the Lō'ihi Seamount. This will be the site of the next Hawaiian island if geologic processes continue as they have for millions of years, so sometime in the dim and distant future the official count of 137 will certainly have to be revised.

SURF BACK TO **50** FOR MORE ON HAWAII

138

Ink pots, chamber pots, cockle pots

The Victoria and Albert Museum in London describes itself as 'the world's greatest museum of art and design', and it attracts over 3 million visitors a year. But let us take you past the throngs of tourists, up to the sixth floor where the crowds are thinner, and there, among the ceramics study galleries, to Room 138.

Here you will find a collection of British and Irish pottery from the fourteenth to the nineteenth centuries, some 450 items in a labelled display and at least 3,000 more in 'visible storage' – on view but unlabelled, a profusion of familiar and unfamiliar objects. Feast your eyes on salt-glazed stoneware, lead-glazed earthenware, slipware, creamware, and pearlware, from London, Liverpool, Bristol, Dublin, Staffordshire, and all points in between. Gaze at goblets, bottles, tiles, trays, tureens, butter dishes, sugar bowls, wassail bowls, slop bowls, candlesticks, knife handles, miniature figures, loving cups, lemonade cups, tea canisters, teapots, coffee pots, mustard pots, bulb pots, ink pots, chamber pots, cockle pots, posset pots, punch pots, porringers, piggins, storage jars, tobacco jars, scent bottles, sauce boats, gin flasks, beer mugs, beer jugs, cream jugs, hunting jugs, toby jugs – and a button.

Perhaps most intriguing is a collection of eighteenth-century puzzle jugs, which were used in inns as a drinking challenge. A puzzle jug looks like an ordinary jug, but its neck is riddled with holes, making it impossible to pour from it without spilling most of the contents. Or so it seems. Discover their secret – and many more secrets – by visiting Room 138 in the V&A.

TRY ANOTHER PUZZLE AT **204**

139

Eadfrith's illuminations

'*Quoniam quidem multi conati sunt ordinare narrationem.*' These are the opening words of the Gospel of Luke (in translation: 'Forasmuch as many have taken in hand to set forth in order'), and they appear on Folio 139 recto of the Lindisfarne Gospels, an illuminated codex (a manuscript whose pages are bound together in book form) now held in the British Library.

The Lindisfarne Gospels were produced on the small island of Lindisfarne just off the coast of Northumbria in north-east England. The manuscript contains all four of the Gospels of the Bible, and it was probably produced by just one monk, Eadfrith, who was Bishop of Lindisfarne from 698 to 721.

Folio 139 is an especially beautiful page, and it clearly cost a great deal in terms of materials, time, and sheer patience. It is a work of art in its own right, for its colours still dazzle and the bravura of its design is as clear today as it was in the eighth century: spirals, circles, and knots are elaborately interwoven with herons, snakes, and cats. Eadfrith blended native Celtic and Anglo-Saxon elements with those of Rome and the East to create a unified vision, and Folio 139 is one of his most elegant illuminations.

FOR MORE FINE CALLIGRAPHY, SEE **354**

140

Characters in search of a purpose

Twitter, the online microblogging service, has taken off in a big way since its launch in July 2006. The tweet is limited to 140 characters, which is just about the right length if you want to plug your latest book, drum up support for your latest cause, or let off steam about what your local politician is doing or not doing, or if you are a troll and you enjoy being nasty to complete strangers.

But why the 140-character maximum? The explanation can be found in the capabilities of the standard mobile-phone text messaging system, SMS, which has a limit of 160 characters per message. Any text longer than this is split into two or more messages. Twitter was designed for use on mobile phones as much as on computers, so to avoid any 'tweet-splitting' a limit of 140 characters was set, leaving 20 for the sender's username.

Twitter is currently one of the ten most-visited websites – it's too soon to tell how long it will survive before it is dropped in favour of the next passing fad – and in 2012 it had 500 million registered users, who between them managed to post 340 million tweets per day. Almost anyone who is anyone posts regular tweets, since the need to see and be seen holds sway in the online world just as much as in the real world – although whether the world leaders, bishops, cardinals, pop icons, and sports stars actually write their own tweets is open to speculation.

THE SMART PHONE AT **332** IS NOT SO WELL EQUIPPED FOR TWEETING

141

The cartoonist's art

On 28 January 1829, William Burke was publicly hanged in
Edinburgh. His crime, with his accomplice William Hare, had
been to supply the anatomist Dr Robert Knox with cadavers
by the simple expedient of murdering seventeen people. The
notoriety of the case was such that 'burke' enjoyed a brief
sojourn in the English language as a verb meaning to murder
by smothering.

Meanwhile, in London, the Roman Catholic Relief Bill was
about to be passed into law, completing the process of Catholic
emancipation in Britain and Ireland and – from an extreme
Tory viewpoint – threatening the very fabric of British society
by undoing all that had been achieved 141 years earlier in the
Glorious Revolution of 1688.

Hence a curious satirical cartoon that is held in the prints
and drawings collection in the British Museum. It is by William
Heath, and it is entitled 'Burking Poor Old Mrs Constitution,
Aged 141'. The cartoon was published in March 1829, and it
shows the Duke of Wellington (the prime minister) and Sir Robert
Peel (the home secretary) smothering an old woman, while behind
a door lurks a Roman Catholic priest representing Robert Knox.

As a cartoonist, William Heath is overshadowed by his
contemporary George Cruikshank, but this work is a good early
example of what is still a standard cartoonist's device: commenting
on one topical issue by using imagery referring to another.

THERE ARE THREE PRIME MINISTERS AT **14**

142

A BUS TO NOWHERE

An abandoned 1946 International Harvester K-5 bus rusts quietly away down the Stampede Trail, 64 kilometres west of Healy, Alaska. The bus had previously been used as a temporary shelter for construction company workers, and it bears the number 142 on its side, together with the words 'Fairbanks City Transit System'.

For several months in 1992 it was the home of Christopher McCandless, a young man who hitchhiked to Alaska to fulfil a dream of living in the wild. On 6 September that year a local hunter discovered McCandless's severely malnourished body in his sleeping bag inside the bus. The cause of death is uncertain: perhaps he had eaten toxic seeds; perhaps he had simply died of starvation and hypothermia. In any event, why had he not sought help?

Whether McCandless was a counterculture hero, or whether he was merely a woefully ill-prepared misfit, who can judge? But his story undoubtedly struck a chord, inspiring a book – *Into the Wild*, by John Krakauer – in 1996, and a film of the same title in 2007, directed by Sean Penn.

As for the bus, it has become a magnet not only for those who wish to remember McCandless, but also, perhaps inevitably, for trophy hunters: the steering wheel and dashboard have gone, and perhaps it won't be too long before the whole rusting hulk disappears. But, for now at least, the number 142 is still clearly visible among the flaking paintwork.

MORE WILDERNESS AT **348**

143

A CHINK IN APARTHEID'S ARMOUR

In 1988, 143 men from various cities around South Africa staged a press conference in which they simultaneously declared that they would not serve in the South African Defence Force (SADF). Labelled 'the 143', their protests were just the latest in the ongoing End Conscription Campaign (ECC), which had started in 1983.

In the 1970s those who objected to conscription did so for religious and/or pacifist reasons, but in the early 1980s the first political objectors appeared. At the time, South Africa was still in the midst of apartheid, and any kind of dissent – including that posed by the ECC – was seen as a threat to the stability of the country. Anyone who refused to obey the call-up faced a lengthy stint in jail.

Support for the ECC gradually increased, despite the risk of imprisonment and serious harassment, and in 1985 its 'Troops out of the Townships' rally attracted thousands of supporters. In the same year it hosted a peace conference in Johannesburg, and branches were soon established in other cities – among them Port Elizabeth, Pretoria, Stellenbosch, and Pietermaritzburg.

The ECC was banned in 1988, with the minister for law and order, Adriaan Vlok, declaring that it was part of the 'revolutionary onslaught against South Africa'. But the willingness of 'the 143' to state their objections in such a public manner helped to open the floodgates of protest and to provoke division in the wider white community. Conscription eventually came to an end in 1993, and apartheid collapsed just a year later.

MARCH BACK TO **132** FOR MORE POLITICAL PROTEST

144

In and out of sync

It is 1972. Luxembourg's Vicky Leandros wins the Eurovision Song Contest with the mawkish 'Après toi'; Harry Nilsson's equally schmaltzy 'Without you' is the singles chart-topper in the UK; and the overly emotional *Jesus Christ Superstar* opens in London's West End. Meanwhile, in New York, the experimental composer Steve Reich (b.1936) has been working on something rather different: namely, *Clapping Music*. This requires nothing more than two performers (with four hands between them), an extraordinary degree of concentration, and a total absence of schmaltz. Both performers clap out a one-bar rhythm, then one performer shifts it 'out of sync' by one beat, and keeps doing so, for no fewer than 144 bars, until the two performers are once again playing the same rhythm. And so it continues. The concept is so simple, yet the result is astonishingly varied, setting up a veritable garden of rhythmic delight.

Much of Reich's music from this period involves repeating patterns that gradually change, beat by beat or bar by bar, tricking the listener into thinking they are listening to something far more complicated than is actually the case. Reich went on to produce many other compositions that use repeating patterns, but *Clapping Music* remains one of his best-known and most intriguing works: 144 bars, and not a whiff of the mawkish.

EVEN MORE MINIMAL MUSIC AT **273**

COULD DO BETTER?

'Disobedient.' 'Obstinate.' 'Slow.' As far as his teachers were concerned, Richard Trevithick (1771–1833) could definitely have done better. Once his schooldays were over, Trevithick worked as a steam-engine repairman in Cornwall's mines. He remained virtually illiterate and he died in poverty. Yet Trevithick was a key figure in the technological advances that characterised the Industrial Revolution.

Always an enthusiastic tinkerer and experimenter, Trevithick's greatest legacy is his invention of a steam-powered locomotive, which he named *Puffing Devil*. *Puffing Devil* used 'strong steam'. At 145 pounds per square inch (psi), this was considerably more powerful than the 5 psi steam used in James Watt's earlier stationary engine. It also eliminated the need for a condenser and could use a much smaller cylinder, thus making significant savings in terms of weight and size.

On Christmas Eve 1801, Trevithick and six of his friends climbed aboard *Puffing Devil* for a steam-driven trip up Camborne Hill in Cornwall. A few days later the locomotive overheated, caught fire, and was destroyed. Trevithick went back to the drawing board many times, further refining his ideas. But his recognition of the huge benefits of 145 psi 'strong steam' was a major turning point for engine technology.

A DIFFERENT KIND OF PUFFING CAN BE FOUND AT **56**

LEGISLATION FROM A TRAGEDY

The shirtwaist – a woman's blouse styled like a man's tailored shirt – was all the rage in the early twentieth century. On 25 March 1911, a fire broke out at the Triangle Shirtwaist Factory in Manhattan, New York. The fire started on the eighth floor (possibly from a cigarette butt or from a spark: no one is sure), and the fire brigade arrived quickly. However, their ladders did not reach that high, and their hoses were not powerful enough to douse the flames. As the fire raged, many of those trapped inside died from the smoke and heat. Some tried to run down the fire escape, but it collapsed, killing 24. And about 60 others, some of them holding hands, jumped to their inevitable deaths. The factory's workforce consisted largely of young women and girls, and 146 of them – most aged between 13 and 23 – died that day.

The Triangle Shirtwaist Factory fire marked a turning point in US legislation. The International Ladies' Garment Workers' Union led a 100,000-strong march through New York to campaign for better conditions, and elsewhere workers increasingly organised themselves into unions in order to voice concerns over questions of safety and working conditions. New York soon introduced new safety laws, and other states followed suit. In fact, numerous state and federal laws were enacted because of those 146 deaths.

THERE'S ANOTHER NEW YORK FACTORY AT **231**

147

Tabula rasa

Laurence Sterne's *Tristram Shandy* was published in nine volumes between 1759 and 1767. It's an oddity of a book: an anti-novel that appeared almost before the novel itself had been invented; a book that broke the rules before the rules had been devised; an autobiography that is so full of digressions that it barely reaches the beginning, never mind the end; a tale told by a narrator who constantly interrupts himself to discuss the writing of his book; a learned text full of allusions; frustrating, infuriating, sometimes difficult, and often very funny.

In *Tristram Shandy*, the reader is frequently invited to engage with the physical reality of the book as printed object. Sterne makes copious use of graphical devices, and we are treated to an intricate system of asterisks, crosses, dashes of varying (and significant) length, squiggly lines representing the narrative course of the book, and marbled pages – not to mention short chapters, missing chapters, chapters out of sequence…

…and a totally black page (see 73). But the black page is balanced later in the book by its exact opposite. In volume 6, lost for words adequate to describe the beauty of Widow Wadman, Sterne leaves a page completely blank, and invites the reader to 'call for pen and ink – here's paper ready to your hand. – Sit down, Sir, paint her to your own mind – as like your mistress as you can – as unlike your wife as your conscience will let you…'

It hardly seems necessary to mention that the blank page is numbered 147.

TO SPECIFY STERNE'S BLANK PAGE FOR THE INTERNET, TURN TO **255**

148

Lost in translation

Blood Reserve 148 is the 'home' of the Kainai (Blood) tribe in what is now southern Alberta. On 22 September 1877, members of the Kainai tribe – as part of the Blackfoot Confederacy – met with representatives of the British Crown and the Dominion of Canada at Blackfoot Crossing on the Bow River about 100 kilometres east of what is now the city of Calgary. The place was a traditional spot for hunting bison, which were numerous, but on that day in 1877 it took on a new significance.

The Confederacy members assumed that they were about to discuss a peace treaty that would involve sharing their traditional lands with European settlers. The representatives of the British Crown, on the other hand, sought nothing less than the complete surrender of First Nations land. The idea of land ownership was totally foreign to the Confederacy members, and they had virtually no idea what they were signing (even the translation of the treaty was woefully inadequate). But sign they did, and what they signed became known as Treaty Seven (between 1871 and 1921, there were eleven such treaties).

Treaty Seven resulted in the formation of restricted land (reserves) in which First Nations peoples, including the Kainai and the other members of the Blackfoot Confederacy, were forced to live. By 1877, numerous reserves, each one numbered, had been established. Blood Reserve 148 is the largest. Over the decades, its inhabitants have had to adapt to a new way of life, leaving behind their nomadic tradition. And most of the bison have gone.

FIND A EUROPEAN SETTLER AT **340**

149

Flying into trouble

British Airways flight BA149 left London's Heathrow Airport on the evening of 1 August 1990 on its way to Kuala Lumpur via Kuwait City and Madras. It made its scheduled stopover in Kuwait on 2 August, despite the fact that for several weeks beforehand Iraq had been staging a military build-up on the border, and Saddam Hussein had been issuing demands for Kuwait's surrender.

The plane landed at a deserted airport, and a few hours later the passengers and crew found themselves being transferred by the Iraqi military to various hotels in Kuwait where they were held hostage. Clearly, the invasion of Kuwait had already begun. Women and children were allowed to return home at the end of August, but some of the remaining hostages were used as human shields at key military locations. One passenger was killed, and one died in captivity, before the others were eventually released.

Conspiracy theorists speculate about why BA149 was allowed to touch down in the first place. Did the US and UK governments know that the Iraqi invasion of Kuwait had already started by the time BA149 had landed? Was the plane in fact carrying several SAS and/or MI6 personnel, who were using the flight in order to infiltrate the region? These questions remain unanswered.

Some of the survivors successfully sued BA for negligence in landing in Kuwait after the invasion had started, and for the loss of property. The plane itself was eventually blown up at the end of the Gulf War as the Iraqi forces retreated early in 1991.

FLY ON TO **172** FOR ANOTHER AEROPLANE

150

HARD-WIRED IN THE CORTEX

How many friends do you have on Facebook? How many useful contacts do you maintain on LinkedIn? How many people do you converse with on Twitter? Is it dozens, or hundreds, or thousands? In fact, the answer in each case is likely to be no bigger than the size of a Neolithic tribe, a Roman army unit, or a medieval village, and it may correspond very closely to the total population of the households on your Christmas-card list (if you still send Christmas cards). The maximum number of social contacts that each of us can handle is about 150.

This is Dunbar's number. It was proposed in the early 1990s by an evolutionary psychologist named Robin Dunbar, whose research on social bonding in several primate species showed that the size of the group in which the animals lived correlated well with relative brain size. Extrapolating to our own species predicted a group of 150 – and, sure enough, this matches the size of all sorts of social groups through human history.

Dunbar's number, it is argued, is hard-wired into the human brain, set by the size of the neocortex. Our biology places a limit on the number of people with whom we are able to maintain a relationship, regardless of the sphere in which those relationships exist. There is even one social networking service (called Path) that recognises this and makes explicit use of Dunbar's number, restricting each user to just 150 contacts.

HOW MANY FRIENDS FOR THE PRIMATE AT **288** ?

151

THE LONDON CHARIVARI

The first edition of *Punch* magazine was published on 17 July 1841. Its founders, engraver Ebenezer Landells and writer Henry Mayhew, got the idea for the magazine from a satirical French paper, *Le Charivari* (*charivari* means 'rough music'), and in fact the first issue of *Punch* was subtitled 'The London Charivari'. At an early meeting, the remark was made that the magazine should be like a good punch mixture – in need of lemon (a reference to the magazine's first editor, Mark Lemon) – whereupon Mayhew shouted: 'A capital idea! Let us call the paper *Punch*!'

Over the years, *Punch* developed a reputation as a defender of the oppressed. Early editions targeted leading politicians, including Prime Minister Sir Robert Peel, who was often referred to as Sir Rhubarb Pill. The magazine also drew attention to the high cost of the monarchy, pointing out for example that Prince Albert's annual allowance of £30,000 was three times more than the total amount spent on educating the country's poor. *Punch* was particularly admired for its cartoons, drawn by the likes of H. M. Bateman and John Tenniel, and, later on, Quentin Blake and Ronald Searle.

Sales figures remained impressive throughout the first half of the twentieth century, but a terminal decline set in during the 1970s and 1980s, and publication eventually ceased on 8 April 1992. Yet the magazine was in no sense a failure, for it had been published without a break for 151 years.

THE SATIRICAL MAGAZINE AT **94** IS STILL GOING STRONG

152

Between the devil and…?

The Walt Disney Company was founded in October 1923, and its film studio has produced an impressive number of feature films, starting with *Snow White and the Seven Dwarfs* in December 1937.

Disney's 152nd feature film – titled *Amy* – was released on 20 March 1981. It was preceded just a couple of weeks earlier by *The Devil and Max Devlin*, which was notable for two things: its (shocking at the time) use of profanities ('damn' and 'son of a bitch'), and its casting of much-loved 'good guy' Bill Cosby as the Devil. And then three months after *Amy* came the fantasy adventure film *Dragonslayer*, which was critically slated, although it has subsequently gained a bit of a cult following.

None of the three films made much money at the box office, but *Amy* – sandwiched between the Devil and the dragonslayer – was acclaimed because many of its characters were played by people with hearing difficulties who were not trained actors. Set in the early 1900s, the film tells the story of how Amy Medford, played by the British actress Jenny Agutter (b.1952, arguably best known for her appearance in *The Railway Children* in 1970), devotes her life to teaching sight-and-hearing-impaired students.

In 1982, Disney Educational Services used part of the film in its outreach programme, entitled *Amy-on-the-Lips* – although be warned that googling this is likely to lead to something altogether different. As for counting up the total number of films since Snow White and her dwarfs first appeared on celluloid…well, it's a lot.

153

Old magic and new science

One Hundred Fifty Three Chymical Aphorisms is the title of a little book printed in London in 1688, translated from the Latin original that had been published in Amsterdam a few months earlier. The author was Franciscus Mercurius van Helmont (1614–1698).

'Chymical' refers to alchemy, not chemistry as we know it today, and the 153 aphorisms belong to a world in which learned men sought the elixir of life and the philosopher's stone and puzzled over how to transmute base metals into gold. Alchemy was concerned with perfecting not only metals but also bodies and souls. In his aphorisms van Helmont sums it up as a search for 'a Catholick Medicine, most potent in perfecting the imperfect Metals, and in restoring of all diseasy bodies whatsoever'.

In the seventeenth century this was by no means the obvious nonsense that we so easily dismiss today. Van Helmont was a mystic but also a promoter of scientific progress. Now he is almost unknown, but in his day his work was taken seriously by the likes of Leibniz, Locke, Boyle, and Newton. It was a time when scientists were 'natural philosophers', and when old magic and new science rubbed along together quite happily – and in van Helmont's 153 aphorisms we get just a glimpse of an endeavour that looks very strange to us, but which is in fact intimately connected to the origins of modern chemistry and medicine.

FIND SOME RATHER MORE MODERN MEDICAL MAGIC AT **242**

154

What is your substance, whereof are you made?

Remarkably little is known about the life of William Shakespeare, and those who are eager to know more are often drawn to the sonnets. This sequence of 154 fourteen-line poems has been endlessly scrutinised for clues, and speculation about the identity of Mr W. H., the Fair Youth, and the Dark Lady has resulted in numerous interpretations, as commentators have puzzled over the details of the author's life, his sexuality, the meaning of each poem, and the structure of the sequence as a whole.

But how much of a window into the writer's soul do the sonnets really offer us? In Shakespeare's day the sonnet was in vogue as the ultimate poetic style in which to express the theme of love. So when Romeo and Juliet first meet and fall instantly in love, the first fourteen lines of their dialogue form a perfect Shakespearean sonnet, the highly stylised art form indicating the heightened passion of the scene.

Among the many interpretations of the sonnets, one of the wilder suggestions is that the length of the sequence is a conscious echo of the maximum length of an English sonnet, which (allowing for feminine endings, in which each line has eleven syllables) is 154 syllables. This is almost certainly nonsense, but in one respect at least it may be closer to the mark than the auto-biographical approach, in directing our attention to the artifice rather than the apparent emotion. At least some of the substance of Shakespeare's sonnets is in their style.

FOR THE PETRARCHAN SONNET, GO TO **317**

155

A PRIZE-WINNING LEAP

A dog flea can jump, on average, to a height of 155 millimetres – a much more impressive leap than that of the cat flea, which manages only 132 millimetres. The research that led to this discovery was carried out by Marie-Christine Cadiergues, Christel Joubert, and Michel Franc of the École nationale vétérinaire de Toulouse, and it was published in the journal *Veterinary Parasitology* in 2000.

Their work did not earn Cadiergues and her colleagues a Nobel Prize, but in 2008 it did bring them the IgNobel Prize for Biology – and they thereby joined an august group of scientists who have been recognised 'for achievements that first make people laugh, then make them think'.

The IgNobel Prizes have been awarded annually since 1991 by the journal *Annals of Improbable Research*. Recent winning projects have included a study on why onions make your eyes water (Chemistry, 2013), one on how the bones of a dead shrew dissolve inside the human digestive system (Archaeology, 2013), and the discovery that leaning to the left makes the Eiffel Tower seem smaller (Psychology, 2012).

Andre Geim has won both an IgNobel Prize (for levitating a frog) and a Nobel Prize (for discovering graphene). But fleas have only once jumped into the IgNobel list.

156

A Corsican export

In 1794, when the warships HMS *Fortitude* and HMS *Juno* failed
to take the sixteenth-century tower at Punta Mortella in Corsica,
the British attackers were impressed by the tower's design. In fact,
they were so impressed by its thick stone walls, its circular outline,
and its roof-mounted cannon that Punta Mortella became the
model for a series of small defensive forts built around the coasts of
Britain and Ireland.

Somewhere along the line the name got slightly scrambled,
and the British versions came to be known as Martello towers.
The first of them was built in 1803, and up until the end of the
Napoleonic Wars in 1815, 156 of these round, squat, bomb-proof
towers were built to defend the newly formed United Kingdom:
103 around the south and east coasts of England, 50 in Ireland,
and three in Scotland.

The design was also used elsewhere across the British Empire,
and there was another spate of building similar towers later in
the nineteenth century, but in Britain and Ireland only these
156 are the true Martello towers of the Napoleonic era. About
half of them survive to this day, with notable examples including
those at Aldeburgh in Suffolk, Jaywick near Clacton in Essex,
and Dymchurch in Kent. There are also several around Dublin
Bay, and the one at Sandycove on the southern shore of the bay
doubles as a James Joyce museum.

FOR SOMETHING ELSE ROUND, SQUAT, AND BOMB-PROOF, SEE **136**

157

KRAKATOA'S EYEWITNESS

In 2010, Indonesian census workers came across a woman who asserted that she was 157 years old. The South Sumatran villager, known as Turinah, claimed to have been born in 1853, the year in which the Crimean War started. She had an excellent memory, clear sight, no hearing problems, and had smoked clove cigarettes all her life. She also spoke Dutch quite fluently (Indonesia was a Dutch colony for centuries until 1945).

Unfortunately, there are no authentic data to prove Turinah's age; she claimed to have burned her identification papers to avoid being linked to an attempted communist coup in 1965. She was, however, able to give a very persuasive eyewitness account of the colossal 1883 eruption of Krakatoa.

Turinah's alleged age of 157 is so far above any other known figure that doubts have of course been expressed about the truth of her claim. To date, the only person verified to have lived beyond 121 years of age is Frenchwoman Jeanne Calment, who was born in Arles on 21 February 1875 and died on 4 August 1997. Men, of course, generally live shorter lives. As for Turinah, the jury is still out.

A REAL OR IMAGINARY MANHATTAN APARTMENT?

On 158th Street in New York's Manhattan stands a row of town houses which, at a certain angle, and in a fading evening light, could perhaps – with a large pinch of salt – be said to resemble a 'long white cake of apartment-houses'. Any high-school student of English literature should recognise this as F. Scott Fitzgerald's description of the apartment in *The Great Gatsby* (1925) where Tom Buchanan has an affair with Myrtle Wilson, and where he subsequently breaks her nose.

F. Scott Fitzgerald (1896–1940) was born in Minnesota but moved to New York as a child, and it was the buzz of that rapidly developing city that inspired him to write *The Great Gatsby*. The novel focuses on the spirit of the Jazz Age and on what it meant to be an American living in America during the 1920s. For this reason it is often regarded as one of the Great American Novels, along with Herman Melville's *Moby Dick*, John Steinbeck's *The Grapes of Wrath*, Toni Morrison's *Beloved*, Jonathan Franzen's *Freedom*, and a select few others.

158th Street does exist, but whether Fitzgerald relied more on real geography for that 'long white cake' idea or whether he drew solely on his imagination, we don't know and it doesn't matter.

VISIT SOME OTHER MANHATTAN RESIDENTS AT **100**

159

Neatly parcelled out

At the end of the eighteenth century the newly established US state of Georgia covered a vast stretch of land as far west as the Mississippi River, taking in most of present-day Alabama and Mississippi, but very little of it had been settled by the European Americans. A map from 1794 shows thirteen neatly delineated parcels of land along the Atlantic coastline and up the Savannah River bordering South Carolina, but the western lands are largely empty, bearing such labels as 'Country of the Cherokees', 'Country of the Creek Nation', and 'These parts are little known'.

The neat parcels of land are counties, the basic administrative units into which American states are divided. Having started with eight counties in 1777, Georgia had thirteen by 1794, and 24 by 1800 – but still the vast majority of the state belonged to the Cherokee and Creek nations.

In 1802 the state shrank to its present size and shape. At the same time thousands of settlers were moving in from elsewhere, increasing the population density (which led to the subdivision of existing counties) and extending the occupied territory (which created more counties to the west). By 1832, the entire state was parcelled out into 89 counties. By 1924 these had become 161, but three were merged into one in 1932, resulting in the 159 into which the state of Georgia is divided today. Georgia is second only to Texas in the number of its counties. 159 counties, no little-known parts, no Country of the Cherokees.

COUNT THE COUNTIES AGAIN AT **26**

BEATING RAPIDLY

Giving birth is stressful for the mother, and being born can be equally stressful for the baby. During labour and delivery, therefore, a careful watch is kept on the health of the baby, and the fetal heart rate is one of the key things that is monitored – with a simple ear-trumpet (Pinard horn), with Doppler ultrasound, or by means of more sophisticated electronic fetal monitoring (EFM).

Too slow or too fast is bad news, but what is the maximum normal rate? Above what rate should the midwife be worried for the health of the baby? There has been a certain amount of moving of the goalposts over the years, as committees and reviewers shuffle and sift their way through the evidence and the expert opinions – but a recent review carried out in Germany has concluded that the upper limit of normal is 160 beats per minute (bpm), and this matches the point at which 'reassuring' becomes 'non-reassuring' according to the latest NICE (National Institute for Health and Care Excellence) guidelines. The lower limit is generally set at either 115 or 120 bpm.

Compared with the heart rate of an adult, 160 beats per minute is fast. By the time the child has reached his or her mid-teens, the heart should have slowed down to the normal adult resting rate of 60–100 bpm.

FIND SOMETHING CONSIDERABLY FASTER AT **299**

161

The darker side of space

Bona fide astronomers might not know much about Fiorina 161, but the name is well known to aficionados of the *Alien* films, for it makes its appearance in *Alien 3* (1992, directed by David Fincher), and it is a planet. Orbiting around a binary star system in the equally fictitious Neroid Sector, Fiorina 161 is approximately 19.5 light years from earth, although its precise location is classified.

Fiorina 161 is home to not much more than a lead-smelting works and a small penal colony, and it is run by the unpleasant and unscrupulous Weyland-Yutani Corporation. The colony's inmates are all male, and they all have a history of physical and sexual violence on account of their 'double-Y' chromosome patterns. The unsavoury nature of the inmates is matched by that of Fiorina 161 itself. Although its atmosphere can support humans, it experiences ridiculous extremes of temperature, its surface water is acidic, and it is home to some particularly unpleasant creepy-crawlies.

Ripley, our hero (played by Sigourney Weaver), has to crash-land on Fiorina 161, killing her entire crew – but not, of course, the alien, which Ripley unwittingly seems to take with her wherever she goes in the universe.

FIND MORE INMATES AT **211**

A FITTING TRIBUTE TO BRUNEL

In 1831 a competition was held to design a suspension bridge that could cross the Avon Gorge in Bristol. The winner was a young engineer named Isambard Kingdom Brunel. Although work on the Clifton Suspension Bridge soon began, it rapidly ground to a halt – largely as a result of the Bristol Riots later that year, which severely dented the city's commercial confidence and led to a woeful lack of funds. Work started again five years later, but by the time of Brunel's death in 1859, lack of investment had once again brought the project to a virtual standstill.

The Institute of Civil Engineers decided to complete the bridge as a tribute to Brunel. They raised new funds, and the bridge was finally finished in 1864. The massive chains from which the bridge is suspended came from the recently demolished Hungerford Bridge (another of Brunel's designs) in London. These chains are anchored in tunnels in the rocks well below ground on each side of the gorge, with wrought-iron rods hanging from them to support the girders and decking. There are 162 of these rods, ranging in length from 0.9 metres in the middle to 20 metres at the ends. Go and count them as you walk across the bridge and back: there are 81 on each side.

BACKTRACK TO **47** FOR ANOTHER BRUNEL MASTERPIECE

163

Food for thought

Push your trolley around virtually any supermarket in the UK or the USA, and you can stock up on asparagus from Peru, grapes from Chile, potatoes from Israel, carrots from South Africa, and chicken from Thailand.

The Worldwatch Institute – whose aim is to accelerate the transition to a sustainable world – wants this to stop. In its 2002 'Worldwatch Paper No. 163: Home Grown: The Case for Local Food in a Global Market', the Institute asserts that the business of flying food around the world does considerable harm to exporters and importers alike. It consumes staggering amounts of fuel, generating greenhouse gases and contributing to global warming. It often forces producers to convert their land to monoculture, and to sell their produce to just one or two huge purchasers, forcing reliance on a potentially fickle market.

According to the Institute, this is not good for the consumer either. The further food has travelled, the more its vitamin and mineral content deteriorates. And long-distance food wipes out any possibility of face-to-face contact with local food producers.

So your weekly trolley might only trundle a couple of hundred metres, but much of the food it contains will probably have travelled many thousands of kilometres. In fact, the Worldwatch Institute calculates that the average plateful of food on the average American table has travelled about 2,400 kilometres, and in the UK food now travels 50 per cent further than it did two decades ago. That is certainly food for thought.

164

A persistent cartographic error

The name of James Cook is familiar to most people, largely on account of his expeditions to the southern hemisphere in the late eighteenth century, and for his arrival on the shores of what became known as Australia. That of Willem Janszoon is less familiar, yet 164 years before Cook set foot on Australia's eastern coast, Janszoon landed at Cape York in Queensland, and in so doing he was the first European known to have made landfall on this strange southern continent.

Janszoon (*c.*1570–1630), an employee of the Dutch East India Company, had been instructed to search for new trading opportunities beyond New Guinea. In December 1603, he set sail from the Netherlands in the *Duyfken*, and on 26 February 1606 he arrived at what is now the Pennefather River on the western shore of Cape York. He was not too impressed with what he found: the inhabitants were inhospitable (ten of his crew were killed when they went ashore), and the land was unpleasantly swampy.

Janszoon charted 320 kilometres of coastline, not realising that this was in fact a whole new continent, separated from New Guinea by the Torres Strait. His cartographic error persisted on Dutch maps for many years, until Captain Cook sorted it all out 164 years later, in 1770.

165

RIGHT BRAIN, LEFT BRAIN

Among the gruesome specimens in jars at the Hunterian Museum in London there is half a brain. It belonged to Charles Babbage (1791–1871), who is undoubtedly best known for his 'difference engines'. Although somewhat unwieldy, and never finished, these machines are regarded as the precursors of today's computers, and Babbage is often called 'the father of the computer'.

While Babbage may have used one half of his brain (perhaps the half in the Hunterian?) to create these machines, the other half (which currently resides in London's Science Museum) seems to have been preoccupied with something very different. Babbage was much vexed by public nuisances, and in 1864 he compiled a list of 165 of them. These included street music of all kinds, especially organ grinders, which inflicted untold misery 'upon multitudes of intellectual workers'. Also high on Babbage's list was almost anything involving children: he singles out the trundling of hoops (responsible for getting under horses' legs and throwing the rider) and the popular game of tip-cat (played with two irritatingly noisy sticks).

The organ grinders, hoop trundlers, and tip-cat players have pretty much all gone, but it would probably be easy enough to compile a new list of 165 nuisances in today's city streets, given half a brain.

THE GAME AT **16** MIGHT ALSO HAVE ANNOYED BABBAGE

166

Paddle and shovel come as standard

The Eastern Front saw some of the worst conditions of World War Two. Not only was the fighting ferocious, but starvation, exposure, and disease killed soldiers and civilians alike. The weather was often dreadful, and just getting around proved immensely difficult, for when the ground wasn't frozen solid it was wet, or muddy, or rocky, or all three.

The Germans had been using motorcycles with sidecars for reconnaissance purposes. These were reasonably good at crossing rough terrain, but they provided no protection from the atrocious Russian weather, and they could not cross any wide or deep body of water – and there was certainly plenty of that around.

Enter the Volkswagen 166 Schwimmwagen. This was an amphibious, four-wheel-drive, off-road vehicle, and it replaced the motorcycle–sidecar combination from 1941. The 166 Schwimm-wagen was small, lightweight, reliable, and simple to operate. It even came with a paddle in case of engine failure when afloat, and a shovel for digging it out of deep mud – although unfortunately reversing was virtually impossible.

Nearly 16,000 were produced between 1941 and 1944, but very few original ones survive, and they are now a collector's item, fetching a tidy sum at auction.

MORE MUDDY AND BLOODY WARFARE AT **300**

167

A ZIP-CODE LOTTERY?

In 2000 George Ryan, Governor of Illinois, commuted 167 death sentences to life imprisonment without parole. This came after revelations that twenty of the condemned were found not to be guilty of the crimes for which they had been sentenced. Eleven years later, the state's new governor, Pat Quinn, signed legislation which entirely abolished the death penalty in Illinois, and commuted the sentences of those still held on death row.

There were, of course, objections – not least from the Fraternal Order of Police. But many others, including the American Civil Liberties Union (ACLU), were quick to praise Quinn's decision, pointing out that judgements about who lives and who dies are all too often dependent upon people's socioeconomic status, their race, the skill of their lawyers, and where the crime took place.

This last point is certainly true. Over the last two decades, the death penalty has slowly declined in popularity in the USA, and several other states besides Illinois have also recently abolished it. Texas, however, has performed over 500 executions since 1976, and it is highly unlikely that it will relinquish capital punishment any time soon.

168

Taking a tumble

During the mid-twentieth century the USA came up with a theory as to why communism was spreading so rapidly throughout the countries of Southeast Asia, from China and Korea to Vietnam, Cambodia, and a whole host of others. They called this the domino theory, and it was used to draw attention to the communist threat and to justify American intervention around the world.

Domino theory takes its name from the domino effect, in which one small and often seemingly insignificant event can have a massive impact because it spreads – often very rapidly – from that first event to a whole series of others, one after another. And the domino effect gets its name from the domino show, in which dominoes (sometimes millions of them) are stood on end in long lines so that, when the first one is toppled, it topples the second one, which topples the third… and so on and so on. Although the domino show is a moderately recent phenomenon, it has become very popular. There is even an annual domino-toppling exhibition in the Netherlands.

A standard domino set has 28 tiles, with each half-tile displaying between zero and six spots, and the number of spots, or 'pips', totals 168. This is irrelevant for domino shows, or the domino effect, or domino theory. Those 168 pips are, however, crucial for the game of dominoes itself, which was invented sometime during the fourteenth century – in China. Which brings us back to communism.

169

FROM THE MOON TO OMAN

On 16 January 2002 a rather unusual-looking lump of rock was found in the Sayh al Uhaymir region of the Sultanate of Oman. Measuring 70 × 43 × 40 millimetres, it was light greyish brown and weighed a little over 200 grams. Further research revealed it to be no ordinary rock, but a lunar meteorite. It is now known as Sayh al Uhaymir (SaU) 169, and it is an impact-melt, KREEP-rich breccia – the acronym being formed from K (the chemical symbol for potassium), REE (rare earth elements), and P (phosphorus). Lunar meteorites such as SaU 169 are very rare. Most are discovered in deserts – particularly in Africa, Antarctica, and the Arabian Peninsula – where they have been left undisturbed for thousands, if not millions, of years.

Until the 1970s, there was no way of knowing where such meteorites had come from. But, having succeeded in landing a man on the moon and returning him safely to earth in the 1960s, the later Apollo missions were tasked with collecting samples of moon rock and bringing them home for analysis. These were shown to be quite different in composition from, and much older than, terrestrial rock. And comparisons with meteorites have revealed that some of these, including SaU 169, also originated from the moon. It is thought that SaU 169 comes from the moon's Lalande impact crater, which, after repeated asteroid bombardment over millions of years, launched some of its rock and dust into space. And then, around 10,000 years ago, it was captured by the gravitational pull of the earth and fell onto what is now Oman.

170

The ducks can look after themselves

Noah's Ark housed just 170 species of animal. If you find that hard to believe, you should consult the first edition of the *Encyclopædia Britannica*, which was published in Edinburgh in three volumes between 1768 and 1771. The first volume contains an article about the ark, accompanied by an engraving of what looks like a large floating garden shed, and the text is concerned almost entirely with the construction and capacity of the vessel.

Among the 'several points of curious inquiry' is the issue of the ark's dimensions. How can it have been big enough for all the animals that required accommodation? The answer is provided by a mixture of calculation and appeal to authority, with the writer concluding that 'the number of species of animals will be found much less than is generally imagined, not amounting to an hundred species of quadrupeds, nor to two hundred of birds; out of which, in this case, are excepted such animals as can live in the water. Zoologists usually reckon but an hundred and seventy species in all.' Frustratingly, the writer says nothing about the identity of those 170 species, other than that there were probably 'only seventy-two of the quadruped kind'.

The text then moves on to consider how many stalls the animals required (and therefore how many stalls each of the eight people had to clean daily), how much food was needed, and where it would have been stored. In fact, with just 170 species to accommodate, there was most likely 'a deal of room to spare'.

A QUICK SKETCH OF THE SECRET OF LIFE

Volume 171 of the leading scientific journal *Nature* was published in 26 weekly parts from January to June 1953. Altogether, it contains 1,168 pages, but a single article, barely a page in length, has attracted more attention than all the rest put together – more, perhaps, than anything else published by *Nature* in its entire 145-year history.

On pages 737–738, in the issue for 25 April, is an article by James Watson and Francis Crick entitled 'Molecular structure of nucleic acids: a structure for deoxyribose nucleic acid'. By today's standards, Watson and Crick's paper is unusually brief. It is also unusual for the fact that they were right. Unlike most first announcements of new ideas in science, their quick sketch of the structure of DNA (produced quickly because they were in direct competition with other scientists – such as Maurice Wilkins and Rosalind Franklin – to get there first) has needed almost no modification over the ensuing decades.

And if you are looking for the scientific understatement of the twentieth century, look no further: 'It has not escaped our notice that the specific pairing we have postulated immediately suggests a possible copying mechanism for the genetic material.' Although Watson and Crick were concerned only with the structure of a molecule, their discovery opened the door for answers to much bigger questions.

HELPING THE IRON CURTAIN TO RUST AWAY

On 28 May 1987, eighteen-year-old Mathias Rust took off from Helsinki in a Cessna 172 aeroplane and flew, alone, through the Iron Curtain to land in Moscow's Red Square.

Later, he said he had been doing his bit to ease Cold War tensions, hoping to build an 'imaginary bridge' between East and West. And maybe he succeeded – because several hundred Soviet military heads rolled as a direct consequence of the failure to stop the little plane. Maybe the flight of that Cessna 172 helped Mikhail Gorbachev purge the armed forces of those who did not support his reforms. Was Rust even partly responsible for the collapse of the Soviet Union?

Rust's escapade may have caused a stir, but his choice of aircraft was not so surprising. The four-seater Cessna 172 (the Skyhawk) was – and still is – the archetypal single-engined aircraft. It first flew in 1955, and has since been through count-less upgrades and variants. It is still in production, and has the distinction of being the world's most numerous aircraft type. For every Boeing 747 that ever flew, there have been about forty Cessna 172s.

ENJOY A LITTLE MORE COMFORT, BUT NOT MUCH, ON THE FLIGHT AT **272**

173

Where east is west and west is east

In the northern Pacific, the volcanic island chain of the Aleutians stretches a long way west from the mainland of Alaska. From Anchorage, it is over 1,000 kilometres to the tip of the Alaska Peninsula, and from there a further 800 kilometres brings us to Amlia Island, at 173 degrees west. But we still have 1,000 kilometres to go before we reach Attu Island, the westernmost of the Aleutians.

Although it is so much further west, Attu is actually Amlia's eastern twin, for the line of longitude at 173 degrees east runs straight across the middle of the island. Attu Island is the westernmost point of the United States, but its longitude places it well to the east of the vast bulk of the country. In other words, it is the furthest west, but the only American territory to the east of it consists of a dozen or so Aleutian islands.

To clarify matters, note that the easternmost point of the USA is much further west than almost anywhere else in the country. This is Semisopochnoi Island, at 179 degrees east, and there is nothing American to the west of it other than that handful of Aleutian islands, ending at 173 degrees east. Thus, the USA's westernmost point is a mere 500 kilometres west of its easternmost point. Glad that's all cleared up, then.

174

BURIED IN BUGS

The human genome project was completed in 2003, but *Homo sapiens* was by no means the first species to have its complete DNA sequence mapped out. That distinction belongs to a bacteriophage called phi-X-174 (ϕX174), whose genome was sequenced by Fred Sanger and colleagues in 1977.

A bacteriophage (phage for short) is a virus that attacks bacteria. Phi-X-174 specialises in *Escherichia coli*, but there are many other phages, targeting other bacterial species. Phages almost certainly outnumber all other organisms on earth combined, with a total world population estimated at 10^{31}. A random millilitre of water, or a pinch of soil, is likely to contain millions. If each phage were as big as a grain of sand, the surface of our planet would be covered in them to a depth of 80 kilometres. If they were the size of ladybirds, we'd all be buried in a layer of bugs over 50,000 kilometres deep.

Bacteriophages were discovered by the English microbiologist Frederick Twort in 1915, and they had a brief period in the lime-light as a treatment for bacterial diseases before being eclipsed by the development of antibiotics. Interest in them lingered on in the Soviet Union, however, and today, faced with the rise of antibiotic-resistant bacteria, researchers in the West are once again investigating the possibility of using them to fight infection. Based on ever more detailed knowledge of the inner workings of these viruses, genetically engineered phage therapy may not be so far away.

CHECK OUT **121** FOR ANOTHER WAY TO KILL BACTERIA

175

THERE WAS A YOUNG PAINTER CALLED ...

Edward Lear (1812–1888) is best known today for nonsense verse and nonsense drawings, but as far as Lear was concerned the silliness was only a sideline. His real career was as a serious artist. In his later years he was a landscape painter, but he first found fame as a meticulous recorder of natural history.

He 'began to draw for bread and cheese' when he was fifteen years old, and then in 1830 he started drawing parrots from life in the newly opened London Zoological Gardens, using the new technique of lithography to produce stunningly beautiful and detailed portraits of the birds. He tried to sell his work, but failed to attract many subscribers. In 1832, aged just nineteen, Lear gathered his prints together in a privately published single volume entitled *Illustrations of the Family of Psittacidae*, but only 175 copies were printed, and fewer were sold. Lear was no businessman.

Lear's talent, meanwhile, had been spotted by John Gould (1804–1881), who was just embarking on his own career as ornithologist, publisher, entrepreneur, and self-publicist. Gould employed Lear as an illustrator for a series of books on birds published through the 1830s, but he took most of the credit himself, even putting his own name at the bottom of some of Lear's lithographs. These books sold in their thousands and made Gould's fortune. In time, therefore, Edward Lear's work came to the notice of many more than 175 people – even if some of it was inscribed with the name 'Gould'.

TURN TO **42** FOR ANOTHER BEAUTIFUL BOOK

176

Transparent beauty

Built on the foundations of an earlier religious building, Chartres Cathedral in north-western France was consecrated in 1260. In 1979 it became a UNESCO World Heritage Site, for it is an exceptionally fine example of Gothic architecture.

The cathedral's huge flying buttresses enabled an unusually large number of windows to be incorporated into the overall design. In total, there are 176 stained-glass windows – the largest collection of medieval glass in the world – and nearly all of them are original. One of the rose windows was damaged by artillery fire during the French Wars of Religion in 1591, and more recently the corrosive effects of an increasingly polluted atmosphere have caused some problems, but by and large the windows have escaped harm. During World War Two, much of the stained glass was removed and put into storage until the war was over. Subsequently reinstalled, the glass is now protected by external secondary glazing.

Particularly dense glass was used in the windows, making the interior quite dark. In the fourteenth century, a few windows were replaced with lighter grisaille glass to improve illumination. But the light of the sun continues to shine through the remaining 176 stained-glass windows, just as it has for nearly eight centuries.

EVEN MORE WINDOWS AT **365**

177

A GOAL WORTH ACHIEVING

In 1990, as many as 177 out of every 1,000 children born alive in sub-Saharan Africa were expected to die before reaching the age of five.

The significance of the 1990 figure is that it is the official baseline against which progress towards the United Nations Millennium Development Goals (MDGs) is measured. In 2000 the UN set itself eight MDGs, mostly concerned with improving conditions in the developing world, and specifying targets to be achieved by the year 2015. Goal number 4 addresses child mortality, with the specific aim of reducing the global under-five mortality rate by two-thirds from what it was in 1990.

In many countries, progress has been impressive, though it is patchy, and a two-thirds reduction may yet be hard to achieve. Between 1990 and 2012 the rate for sub-Saharan Africa as a whole fell from 177 to 98. But it is notable that all 16 countries with rates still over 100 are in sub-Saharan Africa. In 2012, across the world, 6.6 million children died before their fifth birthday, mostly from preventable causes and treatable diseases such as diarrhoea, measles, malaria, and malnutrition.

For comparison, under-five mortality in the developed world was fifteen per thousand in 1990 and six in 2012. In the UK it now stands at five; in Iceland it is two.

THESE DAYS, **153** WOULDN'T BE CONSIDERED MUCH HELP

178

IT'S A WRAP

The artists Christo (b.1935 in Bulgaria) and Jeanne-Claude
(1935–2009, born in Morocco) were good at wrapping things.
Over the years they used various fabrics to wrap Berlin's
Reichstag, the Pont Neuf in Paris, parts of the rocky shoreline at
Little Bay near Sydney, a tower and a fountain in Spoleto in Italy,
and the Museum of Contemporary Art in Chicago. They also
wrapped a few trees – in Missouri in 1966, in New York in 1968,
and in Sydney in 1969.

On 13 November 1998 they began a new project – *Wrapped
Trees* – in the Fondation Beyeler and at the nearby Berower Park,
in Riehen, near Basel, Switzerland. Nine days and an awful lot
of man- and crane-hours later, no fewer than 178 trees had been
shrouded in 55,000 square metres of woven polyester fabric, held
in place by over 23 kilometres of rope.

The trees shimmered inside their translucent shrouds. As
visitors walked among them, colour and shape shifted as the light
changed, or the wind blew, creating a magical effect. And just 23
days later, the wrapping was removed, and the 178 trees returned
to their winter slumber. Christo commented: 'I think it takes
much greater courage to create things to be gone than to create
things that will remain.'

HOW MUCH WRAPPING WOULD THE TREE AT **111** HAVE REQUIRED?

IT MUST BE FEBRUARY'S FAULT

In any well-organised count from 1 to 365, there are 183 odd numbers and 182 even ones, and if the count is extended to 366 you end up with 183 of each. That's the way it is in this book: a neat alternation of odds and evens, all the way to the end. But not in the calendar. Six times, on the journey from 1 January to 31 December, an odd number (31 July, for instance) is followed by another odd one (such as 1 August) – with the result that there are only 179 even-numbered days in the year. And a leap year does nothing to even things up. In fact, it makes it more uneven, by adding yet another odd day.

Granted, dividing a 365-day year into 12 months is bound to lead to some unevenness, but you'd expect something a bit more even-handed. We can hardly blame the Roman emperor Augustus, even if he did steal a day from February to ensure that his month was no shorter than the one named after Julius Caesar, because that merely substituted one odd-numbered day for another.

So let's blame February – the month that nobody much cares for, the weakling month. If February had had the courage to claim a day from, say, March and take back the one that had been reassigned to August, we'd have something a bit more even than a mere 179 even days.

TOO CLEVER BY HALF?

How to measure intelligence? The IQ (intelligence quotient) test is one popular method. So if you really want to know how smart you are, you can take a test online or at one of the many sessions arranged by organisations such as Mensa in the UK. Depending on your result, you will probably either boast ad nauseam to your friends and relations, or keep schtum about the whole sorry business.

This kind of testing was based on research undertaken in the early twentieth century, notably by the American psychologist Lewis M. Terman, and subsequently by fellow American Leta Hollingworth, who was the first to conduct a longitudinal study of children with an IQ of 180 or above.

On a standard IQ test, most people will score 100. Score very much lower than this, around the 60 mark, and you might run the risk of being labelled 'a carrot'. This was the phrase used by one IQ test administrator during a recent interview on the *BBC Breakfast* TV show. Following numerous complaints, an apology was duly issued.

According to Hollingworth, a score of 140 or above is verging into egghead territory, while the dizzy heights of 180 mean you're a genius. Only about one person in every 2 million will be this much of a clever clogs.

Is it all nonsense? IQ tests may be great at demonstrating how good or bad you are at doing IQ tests, but perhaps that's all.

THE BRAIN AT **165** WAS CLEVER IN BOTH ITS HALVES

DOUBLE GOLD

Long before Dick Fosbury jumped 224 centimetres and into the Olympic record books with his eponymous high-jump flop at the 1968 Summer Olympics, fellow American Ellery Harding Clark made his own particular leap into the annals of athletics.

Clark, a 22-year-old Harvard student, competed at the very first Olympic Games of the modern era, hosted by Athens in April 1896. He won the gold medal for the high jump with an impressive leap of 181 centimetres. This was a major achievement, well ahead of his closest rivals, James Connolly and Robert Garrett. And of course Clark jumped forwards, rather than using the yet-to-be-invented Fosbury flop – a technique which, as Fosbury himself proved in 1968, enabled athletes to reach much greater heights.

But in terms of medals, Clark far out-jumped Fosbury, for in 1896 he also won the Olympic gold medal for the long jump, achieving a distance of 637 centimetres and demonstrating the kind of athletic versatility that would be near impossible today.

The current high-jump world record is a full 64 centimetres above Clark's 181. It was set by Cuban athlete Javier Sotomayor in 1993 in Salamanca, Spain. Sotomayor's record may have stood for more than two decades, but can he do better than Ellery Harding Clark at the long jump?

HOP BACK TO **155** FOR MORE JUMPERS

HOW MANY BLINKING TIMES?

It seems entirely plausible that a punk-inspired rock band whose albums include *Enema of the State* and *Take Off Your Pants and Jacket* would take its name from the number of occurrences of everyone's favourite four-letter F-word in an X-rated film – but is it true?

The band Blink-182 was formed in California in 1992. The original members were Mark Hoppus, Tom DeLonge, and Scott Raynor (who was later replaced by Travis Barker), and the name was originally just Blink. But an Irish band of that name threatened legal action, so 182 was added. Why 182? It is apparently the number of times that Al Pacino says 'fuck' or a derivative thereof in the film *Scarface* (1983).

At least, that's an explanation that surfaces from time to time on the Internet forums. Another theory is some sort of nonsense based on the letters RB (don't ask).

In any case (according to one earnest contributor to a music trivia website), if the *Scarface* theory is correct the band should be called Blink-226. Maybe someone should do a recount.

183

A second life for cigar boxes

On 17 August 1889, an art exhibition opened its doors in Melbourne, Australia, showing the paintings of a handful of artists – among them Tom Roberts, Charles Conder, and Arthur Streeton – who had begun to establish a name for themselves down under. The exhibition was unusual, because the vast majority of the works – there were 183 of them in total – were painted not onto traditional canvas but onto the lids of cigar boxes. Indeed, the '9 by 5 Impression Exhibition' took its name from the size of the cigar-box lids, which measured just 9 inches by 5 inches – but what became of the cigars is anyone's guess.

The exhibition was inspired by recent developments in impressionism in Europe. More importantly, however, the paintings on those cigar-box lids marked a significant turning point in the art of Australia, for the subjects chosen were mostly of Australian rather than European scenes, and the artists involved were turning increasingly to the landscapes, city scenes, and sunsets of Australia, rather than looking back to Europe.

Since then, the richness of Australia's artistic heritage has been celebrated with the inclusion of work by Aboriginal peoples (this would have been inconceivable in 1889), and many such works were exhibited at a recent (2013) show of Australian art at the Royal Academy in London. A handful of the 183 paintings from the Melbourne exhibition were also on view.

ANOTHER PAINTED SUNSET AT **206**

184

THE BOTTOM OF THE LAKE

BETTER DROWNED THAN DUFFERS IF NOT DUFFERS
WONT DROWN. The telegram from Mr Walker to his four
children, John, Susan, Titty, and Roger, marks the start of their
adventures in Arthur Ransome's *Swallows and Amazons*. Much
of the setting for the story was inspired by Coniston Water in
the English Lake District. In particular, Coniston's Peel Island
became Wild Cat Island, and played a central role in the story.

Swallows and Amazons was first published in 1930, when messing
about in sailing boats all day long, without any irritating adult
interference, was the perfect way to learn not to be a duffer, and
no Swallow or Amazon ended up at the bottom of the lake, for
they all soon learned how to tie a bowline and a clove hitch, and
tack against the wind, and sail at night without drowning.

Someone who did end up at the bottom of the lake was Donald
Campbell, who on 4 January 1967 launched his jet-propelled
boat – *Bluebird K7* – on Coniston Water in the hope of beating his
own world water-speed record, only to lose control of the boat
and crash. The remains of *Bluebird K7* and Campbell were finally
recovered in 2001. Campbell broke eight world speed records on
land and water. He was surely no duffer.

In Ransome's day, and in Campbell's, Coniston had a
maximum depth of 184 feet. Barring minor seasonal fluctuation,
the depth hasn't changed since then, even though the Ordnance
Survey maps now show it as 56 metres. Still more than enough to
drown a duffer, whatever the unit of measurement.

IMPERIAL MAPPING GIVES WAY TO METRIC ONCE MORE AT **190**

185

CHINESE ASTRONOMERS SAW IT FIRST

Dating from the fifth century, *The Book of the Later Han* records the history of the Chinese Han Dynasty from 6 to 189 CE. Among the events it records was the observation by Chinese astronomers, in the year 185, of a 'mysterious star'. It was visible between the constellations of Circinus and Centaurus, in roughly the same direction as Alpha Centauri, and it remained in clear view for eight months.

It is now thought that what the astronomers had seen was a supernova, and it has been labelled SN 185 (Supernova 185: the number comes from the year of its discovery). A supernova occurs when a large star runs out of fuel, collapses, and creates a dramatic burst of bright radiation that sends a shockwave into the interstellar medium, before fading away. SN 185 is believed to be the first recorded sighting of this rare but spectacular phenomenon.

The remnants of some supernovae have been detected using a combination of optical, X-ray, infrared, and other high-tech methods that include neutrino detectors operated by the Supernova Early Warning System. And recent research has raised hopes that the remnant of SN 185 has been discovered. Labelled RCW 86 (RCW refers to the cataloguing system devised by astronomers Rodgers, Campbell, and Whiteoak), the remnant is about 8,200 light years away, it has a radius of between 50 and 85 light years, and it would have been visible on earth about 2,000 years ago – an age that links it nicely with SN 185.

THE FIRST SMALL STEP INTO SPACE IS RECORDED AT **315**

186

SHADES OF RED

There are several systems for specifying colours, of which the best known are probably RGB (used on computer screens) and CMYK (used in printing). Another widely used one is the Pantone Matching System (PMS), a proprietary system that has become quite a commercial success. Part of the daily lives of designers and printers for many years, Pantone has more recently made it onto the high street in the form of a range of consumer products, from mugs to storage boxes, from chairs to bicycles, each boldly coloured and proudly displaying the relevant Pantone code. In this range, the red ones are code 186, often referred to as ketchup red.

Pantone 186 is also the shade of red that appears in the crosses of St George and St Patrick on the Union Jack. Or at least it is the colour recommended for that purpose by the Flag Institute. It is just a suggestion, not an official standard – and indeed the flag itself has no official status as a national symbol, either.

In many other contexts, people are fussier about the precise Pantone shade. Don't try painting a Royal Mail pillar box or a London bus with Pantone 186 – because that's a completely different (though at a casual glance virtually indistinguishable) red, officially specified in both cases as Pantone 485. The red on the American flag, on the other hand, is Pantone 193 ('old glory red'), while the Canadian one uses Pantone 032.

FIND AN ICONIC RED OBJECT AT **278**

187

A NUMBER FOR MURDER

Gangsters spend much of their time trying to avoid police officers. And police officers spend at least some of theirs chasing gangsters. But in California, gangsters and police officers have at least one thing in common, for they all know exactly what 187 refers to.

187 can be found in the California Penal Code, which dates from 1872. Although the code has seen many amendments and revisions since then, it still underpins the application of criminal law in the state. The code is divided into six parts, which are further subdivided into titles, chapters, and, finally, sections. Section 211, for example, refers to robbery, 285 to incest, 314 to indecent exposure, and 451 to arson. But probably the best-known section number in the Penal Code is 187 (one-eight-seven), which denotes murder: 'the unlawful killing of a human being, or a fetus, with malice aforethought'.

On the street, 187 has become a simple and instantly recognisable shorthand for the crime of murder, and it is used by those running from the law as well as those trying to enforce it. In California the punishment for 187 ranges from a lengthy prison sentence to the death penalty.

IN THIS BOOK, ARSON IS AT **233**

MEMENTO MORI

A search for a picture of a human skull on the Internet may take you to Holbein's *The Ambassadors* (1533), with that strange elongated shape in the foreground, or to the diamond-encrusted platinum skull that is Damien Hirst's *For the Love of God* (2007) – but sooner or later you are likely to come across the twentieth American edition of *Gray's Anatomy*, published in 1918 and now long out of copyright. In that edition of the world's most famous anatomy textbook, Figure 188 is a fine engraving of a human skull in profile, with the constituent bones labelled and coloured in various pastel shades.

The first edition of *Anatomy Descriptive and Surgical*, with words by Henry Gray and illustrations by Henry Vandyke Carter, was published in London in 1858. It was an instant success, and a second edition appeared in 1860. Gray died (aged only 34) in 1861, but the book lived on under a succession of editors and artists on both sides of the Atlantic.

Over the years, different editions, British and American, have included different images of the skull, sometimes relying on drawings, sometimes using photographs. In its most recent incarnation (the fortieth edition, published in 2008 to mark the book's 150th anniversary) *Gray's Anatomy* has a profile of a skull that bears a striking resemblance to Figure 188 in the twentieth American edition. The immortal anatomy book still contains this striking memento mori.

FOR ANOTHER ANATOMY LESSON, TURN TO **33**

189

First, catch your turtle

'Ingredients – a turtle, 6 slices of ham, 2 knuckles of veal, 1 large bunch of sweet herbs, 3 bay-leaves...' It's not quite as arresting an opening line for a recipe as 'First, catch your hare', but to modern sensibilities it is nonetheless a bit startling. This is the recipe for turtle soup in the first edition of Mrs Beeton's *Book of Household Management*, where it appears as entry number 189. (Just make sure not to confuse it with number 172, which is mock turtle soup.)

Isabella Beeton, the original domestic goddess, compiled her advice on running a household (mostly, but not entirely, concerning cookery) in the late 1850s. It was published in instalments, and then came out in book form in 1861. It was a massive best-seller, every bit as successful as today's equivalents, and spawned a whole series of later editions and imitations. Isabella died in childbirth at the age of 28 in 1865, but her name lives on.

Most of Mrs Beeton's recipes are for everyday fare, but turtle soup at number 189 is certainly an exception to the rule – for it is 'the most expensive soup brought to table' and 'an article of luxury', with 'some hundreds of tureens...served annually at the lord mayor's dinner in Guildhall'.

For the record, the phrase 'First, catch your hare', popularly thought to have been coined by Mrs Beeton, appears nowhere in her work.

THERE'S A LESS LUXURIOUS INGREDIENT AT **48**

190

Overlapping mapping

Although the Ordnance Survey had been doing its detailed mapping of Great Britain at a scale of 1:2,500 since the middle of the nineteenth century, it continued to publish maps in untidy imperial scales such as 1 inch to the mile (1:63,360) until the early 1970s.

The seventh and last series of these 1-inch maps was published between 1952 and 1972, and some readers may well remember them with a certain fondness. They were the maps with red covers that preceded the magenta (pink? purple?) 1:50,000 series, and the whole of Scotland, England, Wales, and the Isle of Man was covered in 190 sheets.

At least, the numbering went from Sheet 1 (Shetland Islands, Yell & Unst) to Sheet 190 (Truro & Falmouth) – but in later printings there were only 189 maps in the series. Sheets 138 (Fishguard) and 151 (Pembroke) overlapped by 35 kilometres, so in 1965 they were combined into a single larger-than-normal sheet, numbered 138/151.

The current 1:50,000 series (first published in 1974 and named *Landranger* since 1980) covers the whole country in 204 sheets, with most of Pembrokeshire squeezed into Sheet 157.

SURVEY SOME EARLIER CARTOGRAPHIC CONFUSION AT **164**

PARTIES AND NON-PARTIES

The Kyoto Protocol, which was adopted in December 1997 and
entered into force in February 2005, was intended to give the
United Nations Framework Convention on Climate Change
(UNFCCC) some teeth by setting legally binding targets for
reducing emissions of the main greenhouse gases that contribute
to global warming.

Currently (mid-2014), 191 states are parties to the protocol.
That's all but four of the UN's 193 members, plus a couple of
small non-UN states, which on the face of it is pretty impressive.
But look at the states that are missing: Andorra, South Sudan,
Canada, and the USA. Yes, the whole of North America plays no
part. The USA signed the protocol in 1998 but has no intention of
ratifying it. Canada withdrew from Kyoto in December 2012.

The Kyoto Protocol sets compulsory targets only for
'developed' countries, allowing developing nations to adopt a
less rigorous approach, and in addition a number of industri-
alised countries that were party to the first commitment period
(2008–2012) have taken on no targets for the second (2013–2020).
The net result is that (among others) China, India, Russia, and
Japan can be added to the USA and Canada as, in effect, non-
participants. Between them, these six countries are responsible for
over 58 per cent of the world's carbon dioxide emissions. Formal
participation by 191 nations begins to look less impressive.

FOR MORE ON UNITED NATIONS MEMBERSHIP, SEE **51**

KEEPING SECRETS FROM BIG BROTHER

'If you want to keep a secret, you must also hide it from yourself.'
In an Orwellian future, Big Brother is most definitely watching
you, and keeping secrets is impossible, as Winston Smith found
out to his cost. At the time of publication, in 1949, George
Orwell's 1984 seemed a long way into an unlikely future. But now
we have 192.com.

192.com was set up in 1997 as an alternative to British
Telecom's directory enquiries. It contains details of numerous
residential and business records across the UK, yet there are
concerns over whether the information it provides not only
constitutes an invasion of privacy, but could also make identity
fraud easy. A government-backed organisation called Get Safe
Online warns of the perils of revealing too much personal
information on social media sites. And yet virtually all such
information is available for a small fee at 192.com, together
with details concerning how long you have lived at your present
address, the estimated value of your property, and who lives
next door.

As Winston commented in *Nineteen Eighty-Four*, perhaps nothing
is your own except the few cubic centimetres inside your skull.

CREEP BACK TO **134** FOR MORE SECRETS

193

Lost in the Great Storm

The Great Storm of 1703 caused widespread damage across southern England and the English Channel. In just a few days, in late November, whole towns were flattened, thousands of trees were uprooted, and hundreds of windmills were destroyed. Conditions at sea were even more atrocious, and numerous ships, and lives, were lost.

Among the Royal Navy's losses was HMS *Newcastle*, a fourth-rate ship of the line. She had been built at the 'sailor town' of Ratcliffe on the north bank of the River Thames in 1653, and had seen her first action two years later, when she sailed into Porto Farina, Algiers, with fourteen other warships and destroyed a Barbary pirate fleet. She was later involved in skirmishes with the French, the Dutch, and the Spanish. But the Great Storm of 1703 put an end to the *Newcastle*'s career. She foundered at Spithead in the mouth of the Solent, and, although some of her crew were saved, 193 perished.

In total, the Royal Navy lost thirteen ships, the merchant navy lost 40, and as many as 10,000 people are believed to have died at sea and on land. Daniel Defoe was not alone in thinking that the storm had been an act of divine wrath. 'No pen could describe it, nor tongue express it, nor thought conceive it unless by one in the extremity of it.' The Great Storm remains one of the worst storms ever recorded in Britain.

FIND A LESSER STORM AT **293**

FROM NON-STATE OBSERVER TO NON-MEMBER STATE

Palestine is not among the 193 members of the United Nations. It wants to become UN member state number 194.

The Palestine Liberation Organization (PLO) was granted non-state observer status in 1974, and since then the path towards the goal of full membership has not been easy. In 2011 a campaign under the banner of 'Palestine 194' culminated in the submission of an application to become the 194th UN member. This application remains stalled, but in November 2012 the UN General Assembly upgraded Palestine to the status of a non-member observer state.

By coincidence, 194 is also the number of a UN Resolution that is often cited in support of the Palestinian cause. UN General Assembly Resolution 194 was adopted in December 1948, towards the end of the Arab–Israeli War when several hundred thousand Palestinians had fled or been expelled from their homes, and its Article 11 addresses the issue of refugees. From one perspective, it clearly establishes that the Palestinian refugees have an inalienable right of return, but those on the other side of the argument stress that the resolution grants that right only to those 'wishing to . . . live at peace with their neighbours'.

Assuming that this is eventually sorted out and Palestine is finally admitted to the UN as a full member state, will it become the 194th, or will Kosovo get there first? But that's another story.

THE UN'S MILLENNIUM DEVELOPMENT GOALS ARE DISCUSSED AT **177**

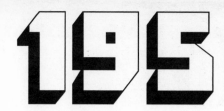

FREE FALL

On 14 October 2012 Felix Baumgartner stepped out of a pod attached to a helium balloon 39 kilometres above the earth, setting a new world record for the highest parachute jump. On his free-fall descent he also became the first skydiver to break the sound barrier, reaching a speed of 1,342 kilometres per hour.

How could this be? The terminal velocity of a human body falling through the air is 195 kilometres per hour, so how could Baumgartner exceed this by a factor of almost seven? The answer is right there in the question. The key words are 'through the air'. In a vacuum, a falling object accelerates under the influence of gravity at a rate of about 10 metres per second per second, and it carries on accelerating until something stops it. But an object falling through the air is subject to drag (air resistance), and the terminal velocity is the speed at which the drag balances the pull of gravity such that the object stops accelerating. For a human body in normal atmosphere, in a face-down free-fall position, terminal velocity is about 195 kilometres per hour – though adopting a different posture, such as feet first, can make a considerable difference.

Felix started his jump so high up that he was in effect jumping in a vacuum, and therefore there was no terminal velocity. As he descended and the air became denser, the situation progressively changed. Just before he opened his parachute, at about 1,500 metres, he would have been falling at a much more respectable 195 kilometres per hour. Approximately.

FIND ANOTHER ACCELERATING OBJECT AT **97**

196

A key to the hieroglyphs

The Rosetta Stone was carved during Egypt's Ptolemaic period, in 196 BCE, and its importance for Egyptology lies in the fact that it is inscribed with the same message in three scripts (hieroglyphic, demotic, and Greek), which in 1822 enabled Frenchman Jean-François Champollion to decipher hieroglyphs. This was the first time in well over a thousand years that their meanings were understood.

Under the terms of the 1801 Treaty of Alexandria, the Rosetta Stone became British property, and one year later it took up residence in the British Museum in London, where it still has pride of place in the museum's Egyptology section, although controversy over its rightful home remains to this day.

The Rosetta Stone was originally unearthed near the Egyptian port of Rosetta (now Rashid) in 1799, during Napoleon's Egyptian campaign. In 1917, amid concerns about heavy wartime bombing of London, it went underground again, this time to a station on the Postal Tube Railway beneath Holborn, where it spent the remainder of the war.

The date of the Rosetta Stone's original discovery was 15 July, which by neat coincidence is the 196th day of the year – and St Swithun's Day.

A MORE ANCIENT WRITING SYSTEM APPEARS AT **322**

HOW LONG IS TOO LONG?

At 197 minutes, David Lean's *Doctor Zhivago* (1965) is a long film. Perhaps this was necessary. After all, Boris Pasternak's novel (from which Robert Bolt's screenplay was adapted) is well over 500 pages long, and most of the story is set against the complex historical backdrop of World War One and the Russian Revolution. Pasternak's book was banned in the Soviet Union, so filming took place in Spain, with most of the snowy bits filmed in Finland and Canada.

The film was not shown in Russia until 1994. But elsewhere, despite mixed reviews at the time (it was too long; it was too romantic), it proved a perennial favourite. It won five Academy Awards, and it remains one of the most popular and commercially successful films of all time.

David Lean had a penchant for making long films, among them *The Bridge on the River Kwai* (1957) at 161 minutes, *Lawrence of Arabia* (1962) at 216 minutes, and *Ryan's Daughter* (1970) at 195 minutes. But these pale into insignificance compared with a number of other mainstream, but probably less well-known, films. Claude Lanzmann's *Shoah* (1985) is 566 minutes long in its UK version, while Joris Ivens's *Comment Yukong déplaça les montagnes* (*How Yukong Moved the Mountains*, 1976) runs for 763 minutes. That's a lot of popcorn to get through.

ENJOY SOME MORE POPCORN WITH *DR ZHIVAGO* AT **284**

198

THE LULLABY OF LONG WAVE

Insomniacs from Jersey to Lerwick will be familiar with the soothing strains of 'Sailing By', an extract of which is broadcast on BBC Radio 4 FM and on 198 kHz long wave at around 0045 hours every night. The length of the extract played varies, depending on how much time needs to be filled – for this piece of light orchestral music, composed by Ronald Binge in 1963, is a signal for sailors, alerting them to prepare for the Shipping Forecast, which follows at precisely 0048 hours.

The Shipping Forecast is broadcast three more times during the day: at 0520, 1201, and 1754 GMT. The BBC still uses the now outmoded long-wave frequency of 198 kHz, because – unlike shorter-wavelength signals – this can be received clearly in any of the 31 Sea Areas around the British Isles. So whether you're sailing the icy waters of South East Iceland, or approaching port in Plymouth, or dodging the waves in Dogger, the forecast can be relied upon to provide up-to-the-minute details of wind speed and direction, precipitation and visibility, as well as warnings of what to expect as conditions change.

The forecast always starts with: 'And now the Shipping Forecast, issued by the Met Office on behalf of the Maritime and Coastguard Agency.' And the details that follow adhere to a precise format, always in the same order, and always limited to 370 words. Too many for this book, but perhaps the long-wave lullaby is just long enough to lull landlubbers to sleep.

199

One step at a time

The fishing port of Whitby on the coast of North Yorkshire is famous for many things. It was the home of the eighteenth-century explorer Captain James Cook; it is a fossil hunter's paradise, featuring three ammonites on its coat of arms and offering countless articles fashioned from Whitby jet in its many gift shops; it is the setting for some key scenes in Bram Stoker's *Dracula*, and today plays on its gothic connections with a twice-yearly Whitby Goth Weekend. And there are the ruins of Whitby Abbey, overlooking the town from the East Cliff.

The abbey lies just beyond St Mary's Church, which is reached by means of another famous landmark, the 199 steps, also known as the Church Stairs. There have been steps here for many centuries, and the present stone structure dates from about 200 years ago. The steps are worn by the passage of thousands of feet – including, apparently, those of Count Dracula in the guise of an immense dog, for it was here, where 'the churchyard hangs over the laneway to the East Pier', that he first made landfall in England and disappeared into the darkness.

A restoration project undertaken in 2005 is marked by a plaque set into the wall recording the names of sponsors, each of whom adopted a step. Step 14, for example, celebrates Nell the sheepdog, and step 146 is 'Nick and Louise's Wedding Step'. There is no step commemorating Dracula, but step 13 is named in honour of the Whitby Goth Weekend.

200

DO NOT PASS GO

Whether you're the Scottie dog, the wheelbarrow, the battleship, the top hat – or, up until 2013, the iron – each time you pass Go you can enjoy collecting £200 (or $200, or 200 euros, or 200 drachmas, depending on which country and decade you're in). But beware the card that reads: 'Go to jail. Go directly to jail. Do not pass Go. Do not collect £200.' Once behind bars, you will have to use the 'Get Out of Jail Free' card, or roll a double on the dice, or pay a fine, in order to smell the sweet fresh air of liberty once more.

The board game of Monopoly first appeared in the 1930s in America, and soon spread around the world, encouraging its players to drive all their opponents into bankruptcy through the collecting of rent and the trading of houses and hotels. It's a ruthless game. There's no room for altruism, or philanthropy, or overly sentimental random acts of kindness to neighbours or strangers.

But if your heart is not really focused on property development, just think what else you could do with £200, awarded for doing nothing more complicated than passing a square on a board during a three- to four-hour game in which there's plenty of time to indulge in flights of imagination beyond the city streets, while you await your next turn.

TOSS A COIN, INSTEAD OF ROLLING THE DICE, AT **92**

201

LAST ONE STANDING

Egypt's Cheops Pyramid (aka the Great Pyramid of Giza) originally consisted of 210 stone layers, but only 201 now remain, for the pyramid's topmost layers have been weathered away by time and the desert wind. Yet its visual impact is still astounding, as are its statistics, even where they can only be estimated: 2.3 million limestone blocks; a mass of 5.9 million tonnes; a volume of 2.5 million cubic metres; 146.5 metres tall – the world's tallest man-made structure for more than 3,800 years, until surpassed by the 160-metre spire of England's Lincoln Cathedral in the 1300s.

Constructed between 2584 and 2561 BCE, the Cheops Pyramid is by far the oldest of the Seven Wonders of the Ancient World. It is also, sadly, the only one still in existence. Much as one would have liked to pay one's respects at the Temple of Artemis at Ephesus or at the Statue of Zeus in Olympia, or go for a wander through the Hanging Gardens of Babylon, these are all long gone. But at least the Great Pyramid remains, nine courses short of its former glory but nevertheless providing more than just a hint of the magnificence of those six other lost wonders.

SAIL ACROSS THE MED TO **274** FOR MORE ANCIENT STONE MONUMENTS

202

Galloping into history

The Bayeux Tapestry records the events which led up to the Norman invasion of England and the Battle of Hastings in 1066, including the moment when King Harold was apparently mortally wounded by an arrow in the eye. It consists of eight strips of unbleached linen which have been sewn together to form a continuous panel 50 centimetres high and an impressive 70 metres long.

The tapestry lends itself admirably to the counting of things: 626 human beings (only 3 of whom are women), 41 ships, 49 trees, 55 dogs, 37 buildings, 57 Latin inscriptions, 8 colours, and well over 500 assorted lions, dragons, and other beasties.

Especially prominent are the horses. There are 202 of them (outnumbering women by 67 to 1), and they appear across the entire length of the tapestry: lined up ready for action, galloping en masse, tumbling head over heels as they unseat their riders, and dying in ditches.

Despite all this counting, some things remain a bit of a puzzle. Why is the Bayeux Tapestry so called, when actually it is a work of embroidery (it is stitched, rather than woven)? Who made it? Where and why was it made? And how sure can we be that the figure with the arrow in his eye really is Harold?

THE BEAST AT **1** IS SOMEWHAT HORSE-LIKE

203

THE MOSQUE WITH A CATHEDRAL AT ITS HEART

Two hundred and three years. That's how long it took to build what is now known as the mosque–cathedral (*mesquita–catedral*) of Córdoba, in Andalucía, Spain. Work began in 784, and was completed in 987. The building started life as a mosque, shortly after the Islamic conquest of the Iberian Peninsula – but during the thirteenth century Christian rule was re-established, and the building was converted into a Catholic church. Various architectural additions were made to it over the following centuries, yet none has matched the original Islamic architecture. The building is especially admired for its hypostyle (a hall with its roof supported by columns), whose forest of 856 pillars makes a great place for games of hide-and-seek.

The centre of Córdoba, with the mosque–cathedral at its heart, is now a World Heritage Site. Yet for all its Islamic splendour, Muslims are not allowed to use the building for prayer; in April 2010, when two Muslim tourists knelt to pray, they were escorted outside.

THERE'S ANOTHER WORLD HERITAGE SITE AT **338**

204

THINKING INSIDE THE BOX

How many squares on a chessboard? The obvious answer is 64. But award yourself a bonus point if you said 204. In addition to the sixty-four 1 × 1 squares, the chessboard also contains the following: one 8 × 8 square, four 7 × 7 squares, nine 6 × 6 squares, sixteen 5 × 5 squares, twenty-five 4 × 4 squares, thirty-six 3 × 3 squares, and forty-nine 2 × 2 squares. As any calculator or schoolchild will inform you, that adds up to 204.

This is the kind of puzzle that does the rounds of social media sites. To deploy a well-known phrase, it necessitates thinking outside the box – or perhaps, in this case, inside the box, for all the squares are definitely in there somewhere.

For even more bonus points, try calculating the number of rectangles on a chessboard. The answer is 1,296.

205

FILLED TO THE BRIM

A standard oil drum, the steel drum that has been ubiquitous
since World War Two, the kind you might make into a garden
incinerator or a barbecue, the one that can be turned into a drum
for a steel band, the kind you see piled high in scrapyards, is a
44-gallon drum. Sorry, a 55-gallon drum. No, it's a 200-litre
drum. It's actually all of these. Forty-four imperial gallons is very
close to 200 litres, and although 55 US gallons is more like 208
litres it is still near enough for all these terms to be used inter-
changeably. Internationally, it is generally known as the 200-litre
drum.

So why, you may ask...? Because the standard capacity of the
drum, regardless of what it is called, is in fact 205 litres. More or
less, at any rate (you can squeeze in a few more drops if you insist).
And the term '205-litre drum' seems to be catching on.

Just make sure not to confuse an oil drum with an oil barrel.
Oil outputs and oil prices are quoted in units of barrels – and the
standard barrel for such purposes is 42 US gallons, or 159 litres.

WOULD **304** PROVIDE THE RAW MATERIAL FOR AN OIL DRUM?

206

Orange and blue harmony

Herblay, Opus 206? This sounds like a musical composition, but actually it's a painting by the French neo-impressionist Paul Signac (1863–1935), who was clearly stirred by something in the nature of music, and who often named his artworks using terminology more commonly associated with music. Indeed, the parallel developments of music and the visual arts are exciting and complex, and there can be no doubt that a resonance between the two art forms has inspired the work not just of Signac but also of many others, among them Kandinsky, Schönberg, Cage, Klee, Mondrian, Paolozzi, J. A. M. Whistler, and Modest Mussorgsky. Mussorgsky's composition *Pictures at an Exhibition* (1874) was inspired by his visit to an art exhibition; each of its ten movements represents one of the artworks on display. In a similar vein, John McCabe wrote *The Chagall Windows for Orchestra* (1974) after seeing Marc Chagall's stained-glass windows in the synagogue of the Hadassah Hospital in Jerusalem.

Paul Signac, like fellow Parisian artist Georges Seurat (1859–1891), worked in the pointillist style; this developed the short brush strokes of impressionism into dots of pure colour which, when juxtaposed, can create a shimmering effect. His *Opus 206* (1889) – which currently hangs in the Kelvingrove Art Gallery and Museum in Glasgow – depicts a view across a still lake to distant trees and a darkening sky. Signac uses dots of the complementary colours orange and blue to create a calming visual harmony.

MORE PICTURES AT AN EXHIBITION ARE ON DISPLAY AT **117**

207

HYPERINFLATION

Germany, 1923. Having suffered an expensive defeat in World War One, the government adopts a policy of printing whatever money it needs to cover its costs. The value of the currency falls dramatically. A loaf of bread that sold for 250 marks in January costs 200 billion marks by November. Prices double every four days. The daily inflation rate hits 21 per cent.

Zimbabwe, 2008. Land reforms and mass emigration have led to a decade-long decline in economic output, while costly involvement in a war in the Congo and further unpaid debts have prompted a policy of simply printing money. As the currency declines in value, banknotes with a face value of 100 trillion Zimbabwean dollars are printed. By mid-November, prices double in just over a day, equating to a daily inflation rate of 98 per cent.

Hungary, 1946. World War Two has devastated the country, and debt-fuelled support of the German war effort has left a large hole in the national finances, on top of which massive war reparations are due to the USSR. In spite of bankers' warnings, printing of money goes into overdrive. As a result, inflation takes off, and by July prices are doubling every fifteen hours. This is the highest rate of hyperinflation ever recorded, measured at 207 per cent per day.

COULD YOU HOPE TO RECOUP YOUR LOSSES AT **49** ?

208

Keeping the beat

In 1814, in Amsterdam, Dietrich Nikolaus Winkel created the world's first mechanical musical chronometer. The German inventor Johann Maelzel then took (some might say stole) Winkel's idea, added a scale, called it a metronome, patented it, and marketed it under his own name.

Traditional mechanical metronomes such as those made by Maelzel almost invariably go up to a top speed of 208 beats per minute (bpm). However, it was not until 1817 – and Beethoven – that any composer had stipulated a specific tempo on a score, preferring to use the traditional Italian terminology: *andante*, *allegro con brio*, *largamente*, and so on.

Almost all music is played well below that metronomic maximum of 208, and although it is not clear why this particular maximum was chosen, it could well be because virtually no music is played faster than that. But there are, of course, exceptions, especially in some of the bebop jazz of the 1940s and '50s; for instance, Charlie Parker's 'Shaw Nuff' gallops away at a *prestissimo* 380 bpm.

But whether the metronome charges along at 208 beats per minute, or at a much more sedate pace, musicians rarely play precisely in time with it. The mechanical metronomic beat cannot convey a *rallentando* or an *accelerando* or a *sostenuto* – the rhythmical ebb and flow that is at the heart of the music.

FOR A NOTABLY METRONOMIC TEMPO, BEAT YOUR WAY BACK TO **144**

209

Dangerous debromination

BDE-209, otherwise known as deca-BDE, otherwise known as decabromodiphenyl ether, is one of a family of flame-retardant chemicals called polybrominated diphenyl ethers (PBDEs) that have been widely used since the 1970s in all sorts of plastics and textiles. There are 209 different kinds (congeners) of PBDEs, containing between one and ten bromine atoms in different arrangements. The name deca-BDE (from the Greek *deka*, ten) tells us that this is the one with the full complement of ten bromine atoms, while the name BDE-209 reflects the fact that it is the last in the sequence.

The fire-resistant properties of PBDEs have saved many lives, but at a cost. They are persistent organic pollutants, found in house dust, soil, and drinking water – not to mention in the tissues of polar bears and in human breast milk throughout the world. The related polychlorinated biphenyls (PCBs) have been banned for decades, but the case against the PBDEs is less clear-cut. Those with lower numbers of bromine atoms are highly toxic and have been withdrawn from use, but governments and international organisations have been slower to act on BDE-209, on the assumption that it is inert and therefore safe. The problem, however, is that over time it may lose bromine atoms (a process called debromination) and degrade into the more dangerous forms.

In Europe, BDE-209 has been banned from electronic equipment since 2008, but it continues to be used in other applications. The search for suitable alternatives goes on.

A FLAME RETARDANT WILL PROBABLY BE UNNECESSARY AT **77**

A PERFECT POISON FROM POLAND?

In 1898, Marie Skłodowska-Curie and Pierre Curie stumbled upon the chemical element polonium, and named it after Marie's native land, Poland. Polonium (atomic number 84) is a naturally occurring but rare element, and all of its 33 isotopes, of which the best known is polonium-210, are radioactive.

On 1 November 2006, Alexander Litvinenko (1963–2006) fell seriously ill shortly after drinking tea with two companions in a London hotel. He was admitted to hospital, but died just three weeks later. An autopsy revealed that his body contained significant quantities of polonium-210. Litvinenko – a former FSB (Federal Security Service) officer in his home country of Russia – had been a vocal opponent of Putin's regime, and had fled to the UK in 2000, where he and his family had been granted asylum.

Two years earlier, on 11 November 2004, former Palestinian leader Yasser Arafat (1929–2004) had died unexpectedly and suddenly, after a short illness. The cause of his death was unclear. Seven years after the Litvinenko case, on 6 November 2013, Arafat's body was exhumed at the request of his widow, whereupon a Swiss medical team discovered that it too contained exceptionally high quantities of polonium-210.

Perhaps it will never be entirely clear how either of the two men died. But there is no doubt that polonium-210 was capable of killing them, for it is not only extremely toxic – just 1 microgram is enough to kill an adult – but is also colourless, odourless, and hard to detect in the human body.

FOR A LIFESPAN NOT CUT SHORT, GO TO **70**

TATTOOS, TESTOSTERONE...
AND A CHICK FLICK

Throughout movie history, the prison film has been an enduring genre. From *Penitentiary* (1938) to *The Shawshank Redemption* (1994), from *Men of San Quentin* (1942) to *A Prophet* (2009), they certainly cover a lot of ground – much (but not all) of it packed with tattoos and testosterone.

Some, like John Sturges's *The Great Escape* (1963) and Oliver Stone's *Midnight Express* (1978), are loosely based on real-life events. There is death-row drama in Frank Darabont's *The Green Mile* (1999) and Tim Robbins's *Dead Man Walking* (1995), and sadistic drill routines in Sidney Lumet's *The Hill* (1965). Alternatively, there's Stuart Rosenberg's *Cool Hand Luke* (1967), showcasing anti-hero Paul Newman's blue-eyed charm; or, if you prefer, the sexploitation sub-genre of Gerardo de León's *Women in Cages* (1971). In David Fincher's *Alien 3* (1992) the action takes place in the suffocating setting of a prison colony on an isolated planet. Or you might well be glad of *Chicken Run* (2000), an action-packed 'chick flick' directed by Peter Lord and Nick Park.

A 2009 addition to the testosterone-fuelled end of the spectrum is the Spanish film *Celda 211* (Cell 211), directed by Daniel Monzón. The plot centres on a new and inexperienced prison officer, a pregnant wife waiting anxiously at home, a riot, fleeing prison officers, betrayal, a mass escape, some Basque ETA freedom fighters thrown in for good measure – oh, and lots of violence. It doesn't end well.

IT ENDS RELATIVELY WELL FOR SOME OF THE PRISONERS AT **167**

A BY-PRODUCT

When Daniel Gabriel Fahrenheit (1686–1736) invented the mercury thermometer and wrote some numbers alongside the column of mercury, why on earth did he set the freezing point of water at 32 degrees and the boiling point at 212 degrees? Why did he not do it the 'sensible' way, like Anders Celsius, and make the scale run from 0 to 100?

Fahrenheit claimed he set zero at the freezing point of brine, but others have suggested that in fact he used the coldest temperature he recorded in his home town of Danzig one winter, or that he borrowed it from a Dane called Ole Rømer who had simply made it up, and invented the story about brine later to make it look respectable. Having established his zero, he then appears to have defined 100 degrees as (approximately) the temperature of the human body, or 'blood-heat'. Or maybe he set blood temperature at 96, which was arrived at by multiplying Rømer's scale by 4 and adding a bit…

However he did it, one thing is clear: Fahrenheit never set the boiling point of water at 212 degrees – that's just the way it turned out when the scale was extended upwards, a by-product of the juggling with the numbers assigned to ice and blood.

Pedants and purists may wish to note that the normal boiling point of water at sea level, at a pressure of 1 atmosphere (101.325 kPa), is in fact 211.9 °F (99.97 °C, 373.12 K), which is of course different from the boiling point at a standard pressure of 100 kPa, which is 211.3 °F (99.61 °C, 372.76 K). Approximately.

BILINGUAL MAPPING/MAPIO DWYIEITHOG

Aberystwyth, on the west coast of Wales in the county of Ceredigion, is a lively seaside resort and market town. It is also home to the National Library of Wales. Established in 1907, the library is a legal deposit library, meaning that it is entitled to receive a copy of everything published in the UK and Ireland. Among its holdings of maps are the Ordnance Survey Explorer maps, which, at a scale of 1:25,000 (4 centimetres to 1 kilometre) are beloved of walkers, for they show the details not just of rights of way, but also of cliffs, marshes, MOD firing ranges, and other areas best avoided – as well as the location of pubs for that thirst-quenching pint or three at the end of a hard day's slog. Aberystwyth and its surroundings appear on Explorer Map 213, and, this being Wales, the information on the map is in Welsh as well as English. Indeed, Aberystwyth is at the heart of a strongly Welsh-speaking area, with over half the population of Ceredigion being able to speak and/or read and write Welsh.

In 2000, fifty rather older maps were stolen from the library, and the thief sold them on to private collectors for about £70,000. He was duly arrested and received a four-and-a-half-year prison sentence. Even OS Explorer Map 213 wouldn't have helped him navigate his way out of that predicament. But if, unlike him, you're walking the coastal path, or inland along the rivers or over the hills, perhaps take the laminated version of Map 213, for, this being Wales, the weather can be exhilarating in a damp kind of way (and they can't show that on the map, can they?).

YOU MIGHT GET EVEN WETTER AT **184**

214

A RADICAL SOLUTION

How are the entries in a Chinese dictionary arranged? To Western eyes, it looks an impossible task. There are thousands of characters (as many as 50,000 in a comprehensive dictionary), and there is no obvious way of putting them in order. With nothing resembling ABC, how is it done?

The answer lies in the concept of the radical. Radicals (*bùshǒu*) are the graphical components or building blocks from which the characters are constructed, and according to the standard *Kangxi* list of radicals (first compiled in the year 1615) there are 214 of them. A typical written character is a combination of a radical and another element, and one common pattern is that one of these elements suggests the meaning while the other provides the pronunciation. For example, the character for oxygen (*yǎng*) is built from the radical for air (*qì*) and a second part (*yáng* – which on its own would mean sheep) to show the pronunciation.

Each character is derived from one of the 214 radicals. In the dictionary, the radicals are ordered according to the number of strokes of the pen (or brush) required to write them, from the simplest (one stroke) to the most complex (seventeen strokes), and under each of them the characters that belong to it are also arranged from simplest to most complex.

Not quite as easy as ABC, but perfectly manageable once you get used to it.

FOR SOMETHING THAT REALLY IS AS EASY AS ABC, SEE **123**

215

Memorable meals?

To stand out on the high street, a restaurant needs not only a reputation for serving good food but also a catchy name. So what is the restaurateur to do?

You could simply indicate the type of food you serve – whether it's the Steak House or the Vegan Gourmet. You could hint at the ethnicity of the food (or make it blindingly obvious) with a name like Giuseppe's or Jade Palace. Maybe you should name your establishment after yourself or a relative. Momma's Pasta might be nice, and Bob's Bistro is reassuringly down to earth – but you should probably think twice if your name is McDonald. There's always the well-worn pun: how about Lettuce Eat, or Lord of the Fries? Alternatively, what was the building before you turned it into a restaurant? Perhaps the Old Post Office would deliver the right sort of marketing message, and serve as a name for an establishment that serves a memorable meal.

If all else fails, just give up trying and name it after its address. It's commonly done. Among many real-life examples: the Two Fifteen Bistro at 215 Dominion Rd, Auckland, New Zealand; Mulhollows Bistro 215 at 215 Miracle Strip Parkway, Fort Walton Beach, Florida; Caffè Nazionale 215, Via Nazionale 215, Rome; Le 215 Restaurant Lounge, Saint-Priest, France...

216

LICENSED TO SELL

The name's Martin, Aston Martin. Specifically, an Aston Martin DB5, registration number BMT 216A. It was James Bond's car. Not his only car, not his first car, but certainly his best-known car. It featured in the film *Goldfinger* (1964), equipped with all the gadgets, and then the same vehicle, bearing the same number plate, was used in *Thunderball* (1965).

In later Bond films there are a couple of DB5s with different registrations, other Aston Martins, and other makes of car. And then in *Skyfall* (2012) we see it again – a silver Aston Martin DB5 (though this time it was in fact a model), registration BMT 216A.

Strangely, the first screen appearance of BMT 216A was not in a Bond film, but in an early 1964 episode of the TV series *The Saint*, starring Roger Moore – several months before the release of *Goldfinger*, and nine years before Moore took on the role of James Bond. It was not only the same registration number, but the very same car. It was the first DB5 to be built, and it had simply been assigned BMT 216A when registered.

The DB5 was also big news for Corgi Toys, who launched their own version to coincide with *Goldfinger* in 1964, and over the years Corgi and other toy manufacturers have produced numerous models, some with number plates such as JB 007, but most displaying the authentic BMT 216A. James Bond's Aston Martin, in its various guises, is the biggest-selling toy car of all time.

217

THE GLASWEGIAN TEA CEREMONY

Drink tea, not alcohol! This might well have been the battle cry of Miss Kate Cranston in 1903, when she commissioned fellow Glaswegian Charles Rennie Mackintosh to design a new tea room at 217 Sauchiehall Street in her home city.

Cranston, who was a staunch supporter of temperance, and who just so happened to be the daughter of a tea merchant, already had three successful tea rooms to her name – all alcohol-free, of course. The Willow Tea Rooms was her fourth, and she gave Mackintosh free rein to do pretty much what he liked. He certainly embraced this freedom, for he designed virtually everything – windows, doors, mirrors, chairs, cutlery, and even the waitresses' uniforms.

Like many Western artists and architects at the time, Mackintosh was inspired by all things Japanese, especially its art and design. This new craze even led to the creation of a new word: *Japonisme*. Renowned for its economy of style, its restraint in terms of colour and decoration, and its use of natural materials, *Japonisme* complemented the art movement known as modernism, which similarly rejected ornament and artifice.

After various refurbishments and expansions over the years, the Willow Tea Rooms still thrives at 217 Sauchiehall Street. And it is still an alcohol-free zone.

BREW UP SOMETHING UNDRINKABLE AT **285**

218

AN ICON FOR A NATION

In 1956, Melbourne hosted the southern hemisphere's first Olympic Games. Was Sydney perhaps looking for a grand project of its own, wishing to steal some of the limelight from its rival? Or was the timing pure coincidence? In any event, a high-profile international architectural competition to design the new Sydney Opera House was launched early in the year, with the closing date set for December when the Olympics would be in full swing.

Scheme number 218 was one of the last designs to be submitted. In January 1957 it was declared the winner, and Danish architect Jørn Utzon was appointed to design what was destined to become one of the twentieth century's most iconic and instantly recognisable buildings.

Construction started in 1959 but was not completed until 1973 – by which time disagreements between architect and city authorities had led to Utzon walking out on the project, never to return to Australia.

In many details, the finished construction differs from the original that was sketched out in submission 218. It was completed ten years late and cost fourteen times as much as was originally budgeted – but it has certainly done the job as envisaged by the competition organisers. In 2007, Sydney Opera House was added to the UNESCO World Heritage List, the youngest cultural site ever to be so listed.

TO TEST THE ACOUSTICS OF THIS SHELL-LIKE BUILDING, TRY **125**

TABLOID JOURNALISM

'To bring out a New Paper at the present day; when so many others are already established and confirmed in the public opinion, is certainly an arduous undertaking.' When he wrote the editorial for the first issue of the *Daily Universal Register*, published on 1 January 1785, the editor–proprietor John Walter was clearly concerned about the competition, and he told his readers he had 'resolved to sell the REGISTER *One halfpenny* UNDER the price paid for seven out of eight of the morning papers'.

In its early years, the newspaper – which was relaunched as *The Times* in 1788 – was full of scandal and gossip, and partly supported by backhanders intended to keep particular scandals out of its pages. In 1789 its editor was jailed for libel. It was not until several decades later that it acquired its reputation as the fearless 'Thunderer', and subsequently became the newspaper of the establishment, a 'newspaper of record', the very essence of what we now call a broadsheet.

Competition was still an issue 219 eventful years after its first publication. In 2004, therefore, under the ownership of News International and the editorship of Robert Thomson, and in line with a trend established by some of its rivals, the format of the paper was changed from broadsheet to tabloid (although the word used by *The Times* itself is 'compact'). Some might suggest that it was an appropriate change, given the origins of the newspaper as a scandal-sheet 219 years earlier.

220

I have measured out my life...

The Domesday Book records the results of a survey of England carried out in 1086. Its purpose was to record the state of the land, who occupied it, who owned what, how much it was all worth, and how much tax was due – so it is not surprising that Domesday is full of terms describing the measurement of land holdings. Along with the more familiar yards, miles, and acres, the text is littered with rods, perches, leagues, bovates, virgates, yokes, carucates, hides, sulungs – and furlongs.

A furlong (furrow-long) was the length of the furrow ploughed by a team of oxen before the plough was turned, but it also referred to the area that the team could plough in a day (also known as an acre – a strip 1 furlong long and 1 chain wide). The precise length or area of a furlong varied from place to place, but it was the very basis of medieval open-field agriculture. The daily life of the peasant was measured out in furlongs.

Since the thirteenth century, a furlong as a measurement of length has been set at 220 yards. Like those other Domesday units, it is no longer in everyday use – except, curiously, in horse racing.

PLOD BACK TO **124** FOR SOMETHING RELEVANT TO MODERN PLOUGHING

221

CONDUCT UNBECOMING IN THE LIBRARY

On 5 October 1789, George Washington borrowed a book from the New York Society Library, which at that time was located in the same building as the president's office. The book in question was *The Law of Nations* by the Swiss legal expert Emer de Vattel. Subtitled *The Principles of Natural Law Applied to the Conduct and to the Affairs of Nations and of Sovereigns*, it was a suitably worthy topic for the first president of a new country. However, Washington's own conduct left something to be desired, for he never returned the book.

In 2010, when the library staff were undertaking an inventory of books in the library's ledger for 1789–1792, they discovered that *The Law of Nations* was still missing – 221 years after Washington had borrowed it.

The original copy has not been unearthed. However, a replacement was bought online for $12,000 by Washington's Mount Vernon estate, and this was duly presented to the library on 20 May 2010 amid a degree of embarrassment – and indeed relief, for the head librarian, Mark Bartlett, commented: 'We're not actively pursuing the overdue fines.' Taking inflation into account, these would have been about $300,000.

CATCHING SHADOWS

At the start of the twentieth century, the ethnologist Edward
Curtis set out to compile a comprehensive photographic record
of Native American culture. Curtis asserted that he wanted to
document 'the old time Indian, his dress, his ceremonies, his life
and manners'. Published in 20 volumes between 1907 and 1930,
Curtis's project was titled *The North American Indian*. It contained
more than 2,000 photogravure images, covering more than 80
tribal groups.

The North American Indian was published in a limited edition.
Curtis had planned to produce 500 sets, but only 222 were ever
printed, partly because costs had escalated, but also because the
work's reception was decidedly mixed. Although there was no
doubting the ambitious scale of the project, or Curtis's skill with
a camera, he was accused of staging many of his scenes. Native
Americans themselves didn't much care for his work either: they
called Curtis the 'Shadow Catcher', alluding to the idea that he
had perhaps taken more than just photographs.

Although Curtis died in virtual anonymity, in recent years
there has been renewed interest in his work, not least because it
provides a visual record of how non-native people tended to view
– and treat – Native Americans.

223

A date to remember

The 223rd day of the year (excluding leap years) is 11 August. This date has witnessed many events – the first ascent of the Eiger (1858), the birth of children's author Enid Blyton (1897), the death of abstract expressionist Jackson Pollock (1956), and the accidental collision between Zola Budd and Mary Decker in the 3,000-metre Olympic final (1984), to name just a small handful. These are all certainly worth at least a line or two in the papers. And what happened on day 223 in 1999 was most definitely newsworthy and memorable.

It was a Wednesday, and millions of people around large chunks of the world took time off to spend much of the day looking skywards, for this was the date of a total solar eclipse. It was reckoned to be the most viewed eclipse in human history because it passed over areas of high population density in Europe, continuing its journey across Egypt, Turkey, Iran, and the Indian subcontinent, and ending in the Bay of Bengal.

In mainland Britain the path of totality crossed the far south-west (in Cornwall and south Devon), the crowds were out in force, and for up to 2 minutes and 2 seconds their world was plunged into darkness. Afterwards, the traffic jams leaving Cornwall were also newsworthy and memorable.

The next total solar eclipse over mainland Britain is not due until 23 September 2090 – the 266th day of the year – but what else will happen on that date is anyone's guess.

THERE'S A LOT MORE LOOKING SKYWARDS AT **266**

TONS OF GALLONS, MILES OF MINUTES

How many gallons are there in a ton? How many minutes make up a mile? Both those questions look a bit cock-eyed, because surely a gallon is a measurement of volume while a ton is a unit of weight, and minutes measure time whereas miles delineate distance.

Both gallon and ton are complex and shifting concepts. A gallon at least has the decency always to refer to volume, even if it's a different volume in different parts of the world (American readers look away now...), but a ton may be a unit of either weight or volume. The tonnage of a ship is a measurement of volume (in origin, the word refers to the capacity of a *tun*, a large barrel), but it is as well to be aware that there are displacement tons, freight tons, and register tons, and they are all different.

Lurking under the surface of the confusion, however, is a good old-fashioned ton, sometimes called a water ton. And for those of us old enough to remember that 'a pint of water weighs a pound and a quarter', that 8 pints make up a gallon, and that a ton is 2,240 pounds, it is easy enough to work out that a ton of water occupies a volume of 224 gallons. So, as a unit of volume, a ton is exactly that: 224 gallons.

And the minutes and miles? A minute is a measurement of angle as well as time (it's a 60th of a degree), and a nautical mile (now defined as 1,852 metres) was originally a minute arc of latitude. So, at least at sea, there is one minute in a mile.

THE VARIOUS TONNAGES OF SHIPS RESURFACE AT **320**

225

Flying south-west

Looking at the map, it is clear that travelling from Norwich to Southampton, or from Las Vegas to Los Angeles, will take you in a south-westerly direction. In fact, in both cases, the direction is exactly south-west – in other words, a bearing of 225 degrees. To follow a straight line like that you really need an aeroplane, and assuming you do not have your own you'll want a commercial flight. In which case, forget trying to get from Norwich to Southampton – but you can indeed fly from Las Vegas to Los Angeles.

Southwest Airlines might be able to help. Based in Dallas, Texas, Southwest was the world's first low-cost, no-frills, budget airline when it was established in 1971, and today it is the world's largest, with a fleet of almost 600 aircraft serving 89 destinations around the USA. Its two-letter code is WN. And sure enough, one of its routes is from McCarran International Airport, Las Vegas, Nevada, to Bob Hope Airport, Burbank, California, just outside Los Angeles. One of the flights on that route is WN225. And on that flight, passengers and crew must surely take satisfaction from the fact that the airline name, the flight number, and the direction of travel can all be expressed by the number 225.

LEAD POISONING?

The Franklin Expedition set off on 19 May 1845 in the ships *Erebus* and *Terror* in search of the Northwest Passage from the Atlantic to the Pacific. It ended in tragedy, for none of the crew, or Captain Sir John Franklin himself, ever returned.

In 1850 three makeshift graves were discovered on Beechey Island in the Canadian Archipelago of Nunavut, but what had happened to the ships or to the rest of the men was unclear. In the 1980s the three bodies were exhumed and the bones and hair of one of them (that of stoker John Shaw Torrington) were found to contain 226 parts per million of lead – a toxic amount that would have resulted in both physical and mental deterioration, and ultimately death.

Perhaps the lead came from the solder that had been used to seal the cans of food on board the ships. Perhaps it came from the ship's lead water pipes, or from pewter tableware (which used to contain lead), or from lead-wicked candles. However, recent research suggests that the wide distribution and high overall concentration of lead in Torrington's body is more likely to be the result of chronic exposure, which would have begun well before the expedition set out. Furthermore, it is of course entirely possible that Torrington and the others died of starvation, hypothermia, pneumonia, tuberculosis, scurvy, sheer exhaustion, or any combination thereof, although all these would have been exacerbated by lead poisoning. Today, exactly what happened to Franklin and his men, and why, remains a mystery.

MORE CANS (AND BOTTLES) AT **330**

227

On being eaten at sea (or not)

A few days out from Manila, with 'a sound like a monstrous metallic burp', the ship sank, and Richard Parker found himself adrift in a lifeboat for 227 days. We have omitted a few details, but that in essence is the plot of Yann Martel's *Life of Pi*, published in 2001 and turned into a Hollywood film, directed by Ang Lee, in 2012.

Richard Parker is a Bengal tiger, and the name is significant, as is the fact that his companion Pi survives for 227 days without being eaten – for there are least two other cases, one fiction and one fact, in which the name Richard Parker is associated with being eaten at sea.

In Edgar Allan Poe's *Narrative of Arthur Gordon Pym of Nantucket* (1838), four shipwrecked sailors draw lots to see who will be eaten, and the loser is Richard Parker. And then in 1884 the yacht *Mignonette* sank in the south Atlantic, and a real-life Richard Parker was eaten by his three companions in the lifeboat, leading to a famous court case, providing rich pickings for anyone keen on coincidences, and no doubt contributing to Yann Martel's choice of name for the tiger in *Life of Pi*.

FOR MORE ON SURVIVAL AT SEA WITHOUT BEING EATEN, SEE **28**

228

BLACK DAYS

The 1929 Wall Street Crash was marked by many Black days. Black Thursday (24 October 1929) was swiftly followed by Black Monday (the 28th), and Black Tuesday (the 29th) came hot on its heels. With each passing day, the Dow Jones Industrial Average took hit after hit from panic selling, until by 11 November it stood at 228 – a drop of 40 per cent since September.

Although there were some small recoveries over the next couple of years, by July 1932 the USA was in the depths of the Great Depression. Many thousands lost their jobs as shops and factories closed, and more than 20,000 companies went bankrupt, including over 1,000 banks. There was no benefit system for those who had lost their jobs, and the suicide rate soared. President Hoover's ideal of rugged individualism rang hollow for those who were forced to live in squalid conditions in campsites constructed out of flimsy cardboard – ironically called Hoovervilles. Not surprisingly, Hoover was heavily defeated in the November 1932 presidential election, and the new president, F. D. Roosevelt, introduced the New Deal, whose three Rs – relief, recovery, and reform – helped to get the country slowly back on its feet.

On 19 October 1987, the market crashed all over again – and again in 2008. But, so far at least, nothing has quite matched the crash of 1929.

EXPANDING WAISTLINES, SHRINKING CONFECTIONERY

There are 229 calories in a Mars Bar. Oh, if only it were that simple...

In the old days, when a Mars a day helped you work, rest, and play, before the advent of the obesity crisis, and before confectionery manufacturers developed a social conscience, you knew where you were with a Mars Bar (as long as you weren't in the USA, where an altogether inferior product was sold under that name). A Mars Bar completely filled its packaging, it weighed 65 grams, and it had about 290 calories.

Since then, the packaging has got roomier and the bar inside has got smaller. A cut to 58 grams and 260 calories came in 2009. The manufacturers claimed it was a public health initiative, but later admitted it was actually a cost-cutting exercise. And then in 2013 another cut was announced, this time proudly trumpeted as part of a pledge to help reduce the nation's waistlines. The Mars Bar now weighs a mere 51 grams and contains just 229 calories.

For those who hanker after the calories of yesteryear, there's always the deep-fried Mars Bar.

HARMONISATION THE EASY WAY

Until the mid-1990s, the domestic electricity supply in the United Kingdom was delivered at 240 volts, while in most of the rest of Europe it was 220 volts. This disparity was perceived as a barrier to trade, so the European Commission agreed to harmonise the voltages and impose a standard 230-volt supply across the whole of Europe.

Even those whose grasp of Ohm's law is a little hazy will appreciate that changing the voltage might make a difference. It would indeed. The power delivered to an appliance, measured in watts, is directly proportional to the voltage. So did light bulbs start to glow a little more dimly in Britain? Did electric kettles suddenly come to the boil more quickly in Greece?

Oh no. European bureaucracy is cleverer than that. Rather than insisting on any actual change in the voltage delivered – which would have involved new supply equipment and considerable expense – the Commission simply amended the legal voltage limits. The Electricity Quality and Supply Regulations (EQS) were tweaked to specify that a nominal 230 volts would encompass a range from 10 per cent below to 10 per cent above that value (anywhere between 207 and 253 volts). So British light bulbs continue to spark into life at 240 volts, and Greek kettles bubble along nicely at 220 volts – but both of them are now officially receiving 230 volts.

THE ELECTRICIAN AT **271** MIGHT HAVE OTHER THINGS ON HIS MIND

231

A FAME FACTORY

Given the existence of 50 Marilyn Monroes in the *Marilyn Diptych*, *Eight Elvises*, *200 One Dollar Bills*, and any number of Campbell's soup cans, Andy Warhol could have found a place almost anywhere in this book. But 231 is surely his rightful home, for 231 East 47th Street, New York, was the original address of his Factory.

When Andy Warhol set up the Factory in early 1964 he had already been famous for rather more than 15 minutes. He was a notorious and often controversial figure in pop art, and had already produced those screen-print Marilyns and soup cans. The Factory had once been a simple factory – a cold-storage warehouse that had also at various times housed a brewery, an electrical work-station, a cigar manufacturer, and several wood-working operations. With its walls painted silver and lined with foil, it became an art studio, a film studio, and a gathering place for artists, performers, drug users, drag queens, the Warhol Super-stars, and assorted underground figures (including Velvet ones).

The Factory moved on from 231 East 47th Street to another location in 1968, and then on again a few years later. A long list of famous names is associated with it. Warhol himself, famous at least partly for being famous, died in 1987 at the age of 58.

YOU'LL FIND JUST ONE DOLLAR BILL AT **292**

232

SERIALLY CONNECTED

In the distant past (as far back as the 1990s) you connected peripheral devices such as printers, mice, and modems to a computer via serial ports and parallel ports, which you found by fumbling around at the back of the big grey box under the desk amid the dust bunnies and the discarded sandwich wrappers. The serial port was the little one with nine pins, and no matter how hard you tried (it was dark back there, and the cable was never quite long enough to reach comfortably), it took at least three attempts to get the plug into the socket the right way round.

This is not the place to explain the technical differences between parallel and serial communication. Suffice to say that the serial port was the older and slower technology, and it used a standard known an RS-232. This defined the physical wiring, the voltage and other electrical settings, and the communications protocol. The original RS-232 standard was for a 25-pin connection (like a parallel port), and it was later adapted for the smaller 9-pin version.

The RS-232 port was once an essential part of every computer, until some of its functions were taken over by the PS/2 port. But that too has now been swept aside by USB connectors (universal serial bus – still serial, but faster) and increasingly by Bluetooth, Wi-Fi, and other wireless wizardry.

HOT, BUT WHO'S BOTHERED?

In a book about numbers it seems only right to devote a little space to another well-known book with a number in its title – but the only way of fitting Malcolm Bradbury in is to convert him to degrees Celsius, so his novel appears here as *Celsius 233*.

Fahrenheit 451, published in 1953, is a novel set in a future in which books are banned and burned. The title refers to the temperature at which paper bursts into flame. And ever since, Bradbury has been accused of getting it wrong. Some commentators have suggested that he got Celsius and Fahrenheit confused (so perhaps his book is set in a future in which books are gently warmed), while others have argued over flash points versus auto-ignition, spontaneous combustion versus kindling temperatures.

The physics texts themselves are somewhat contradictory, but it seems pretty clear that the temperature at which paper will spontaneously ignite in the absence of a flame or spark (its auto-ignition point) is generally in the range 210–250 °C, depending on the type of paper, how tightly packed it is, and many other factors. In essence, then, Bradbury was right.

But at the end of the day the temperature itself has no bearing on the plot, so the whole thing is a non-issue. Piggy's spectacles in *Lord of the Flies* are, however, another matter ∴

234

A DAY OF SILENCE

When Lisa Clayton sailed into port at Dartmouth, South Devon, in *Spirit*, on 29 June 1995, she entered the record books as the first woman to circumnavigate the world, single-handed, non-stop, and unassisted. Clayton kept a log (subsequently published as *At the Mercy of the Sea*), in which she recounted her adventures. Her epic voyage lasted 285 days, but it's not that number that is scrutinised here. Rather, it's what happened on day 234 of her journey that merits inspection: namely 8 May 1995, when she was becalmed in the Atlantic just north of the Equator.

The day before (day 233) was spent 'waiting, waiting, waiting' for wind, and feeling in very low spirits indeed. The day after (day 235) was almost equally miserable, with nothing much to report except a rapidly diminishing supply of matches, and a silly mistake sailing over a submerged rock (fortunately no harm done). But what about day 234? Well, here's the strange thing: it seems that absolutely nothing at all happened that day, for there is no log entry. Nothing to write? Perhaps only a fellow circumnavigator would fully understand the sheer loneliness, boredom, and frustration of the voyage, but we can all surely forgive Clayton her silence on that one May day.

CHANGING THE FACE OF THE WORLD

Uranium 235 is fissile, meaning that it can readily be split, releasing a huge amount of energy. It makes up just 0.7 per cent of naturally occurring uranium, but in the early 1940s a great deal of it was dug up at the Shinkolobwe mine in the Congo (now the DRC) and sold to the USA. Upon arrival in the States, it went through a process of isotope enrichment at Oak Ridge in Tennessee. It was then transported to an isolated laboratory at Los Alamos, New Mexico, where, as part of the USA's Manhattan Project, it was used to build Little Boy – the nuclear bomb that destroyed the Japanese city of Hiroshima on 6 August 1945, and helped to bring World War Two to a close.

It is impossible to know for sure how many hundreds of thousands of civilians and others were killed by Little Boy (and by Fat Man, the plutonium bomb that was dropped on Nagasaki just three days later). Suffice to say that the discovery of nuclear fission in 1938, and the uses to which that scientific discovery was put, changed the face of the world for ever.

THERE'S MORE RADIOACTIVITY AT **210**

236

INVASION OF THE CLOTHES EATERS

There are about 60 species of butterfly and 2,500 species of moth in the UK, but on the whole the moths are ignored, if not actively disliked. And there is one species that gets more than its fair share of the bad press and gives moths in general a quite undeserved bad name. Based on the checklist of British Lepidoptera published in 1979, this species has a Bradley & Fletcher number of 236; it is *Tineola bisselliella*, otherwise known as the common clothes moth.

The common clothes moth originated in Europe but now has a worldwide distribution, having taken to a jet-set lifestyle in suitcases full of clothes. The adults are small and grey-brown, and they live a secretive life in dark places and hidden corners, mostly indoors. Their larvae feed on woollen clothing, upholstery, carpets, and other fibres.

The scientific literature tells us that *Tineola bisselliella* is in decline owing to the increasing use of man-made fibres – but the popular media would suggest otherwise. For a measure of humanity's obsession with the clothes moth, and the level of panic it induces, note the frequency of newspaper headlines such as 'Invasion of the clothes eaters', or try a Google search for 'moth' and see how many of the top hits refer to this species and ways to kill it.

THE ANIMAL AT **5** IS MORE CLOSELY RELATED TO US THAN TO ANY INSECT

237

One way to get rid of a headache

It just happened. The person had beautiful eyes. I wanted to get a job. Someone dared me. It's fun. I was pressured into doing it. I wanted to get rid of a headache. These are just a few of the 237 reasons why people have sex, according to a paper published in 2007 in the journal *Archives of Sexual Behavior*. A book by the same authors (Cindy Meston and David Buss, *Why Women Have Sex*) was published in 2009, using the list of 237 reasons generated by the earlier research as the basis for an exploration of the female experience.

In the academic paper the 237 reasons were organised statistically into four major groupings (physical, goal attainment, emotional, insecurity). There is plenty of evolutionary psychology in here, linked to the Darwinian concept of sexual selection – but there is also sociology, economics, game theory, religion, even criminology.

The top reason, for both men and women, was simply 'I was attracted to the person', while at the bottom of the list was 'I wanted to give someone else a sexually transmitted disease.' Perhaps it's just as well – for the sake of one's faith in human nature – that that one came last.

FIND ANOTHER WAY TO RID YOURSELF OF THAT HEADACHE AT **81**

238

FISHING FOR PENGUINS

Penguin (order Sphenisciformes, family Spheniscidae). Loves fishing and all kinds of sushi. Enjoys the outdoor life. Not bothered by biting-cold winds and blizzards for months at a time. Not keen on flying (can't get airborne at all, actually), but great at waddling and tobogganing, and is a superb swimmer. Natty dresser; especially smart in black and white. Good with eggs. Fidelity no problem. Usually found in the southern hemisphere, but available for guest appearances in films and cartoons.

Penguin Books. Founded in 1935 by Allen Lane, after he had suffered the frustration of having nothing to read at Exeter railway station. Inexpensive paperbacks for the mass market. Sold in station bookstalls and popular high-street stores. All subjects: fiction, politics, science, the arts. Distinctive smart cover design, using bands of colour according to series. Hugely successful. Each title numbered according to date of publication. Found on bookshelves all around the world. Companions: Pelicans and Puffins.

Penguin Book No. 238. Title: *The Compleat Angler, or the contemplative man's recreation*. Author: Izaak Walton. Originally published 1653, reissued by Penguin November 1939. Price: 6d. Yellow and white. Prose and poetry. Songs and anecdotes. Wood engravings by Gertrude Hermes. A reminder of a long-lost rural life in seventeenth-century England. A celebration of the spirit and art of fishing. Good sense of humour. No strings attached.

PLENTY MORE FISH IN THE SEA FOR THE ANIMAL AT **350**

239

The mystery of the misplaced museum

'My dear fellow,' said Mr Sherlock Holmes, as we sat on either side of the hearth in what I was beginning to suspect was the wrong house, 'what is it that troubles you so?'

'I have for many years understood,' said I, 'that your lodgings were at 221B Baker Street. Why then, when we dined at my club last evening, did you inform that fellow that he could call on you at number 239?'

'I am afraid that your long-held impression is erroneous. You have been too easily misled by the plaque on the front of this establishment.'

'For heaven's sake tell me, then,' I ejaculated, 'how have you deduced the correct numerical identity of this "Sherlock Holmes Museum" in which we now find ourselves?'

'As to the address,' said Holmes, 'suppose for a moment that we visualise a street oriented approximately on a north–south axis, with the numbering arranged in such a way that the houses on the eastern side bear even numbers, while those opposite are numbered sequentially with odd numbers. Having established this much, it is so transparent that even a Scotland Yard official could see through it. It will not have escaped your notice, I trust, that the estate agent immediately to the south of where we are now seated is numbered 237, and the small restaurant to the north is 241. I hesitate to use the word elementary, my dear Watson, but...'

VISIT ANOTHER LONDON MUSEUM AT **138**

240

A pound per sheet...

The Penny Black was the world's first gummed postage stamp. It was introduced in May 1840 and revolutionised the postal service of the United Kingdom.

Penny Blacks were printed in sheets of 240 stamps (20 rows of 12), with the position of each individual stamp identified by a pair of letters in its bottom corners, from AA for the stamp at the top left-hand corner of the sheet to TL for the one at the bottom right. Furthermore, the sheets were printed from eleven different engraved plates, with myriad little differences from plate to plate, and some of the plates were reworked. So collectors today have at least 2,640 different individually recognisable Penny Blacks to look for. Hours of harmless fun.

With 20 rows of 12 penny stamps, a row could be bought for a shilling and a whole sheet for £1 (240 pence). If you were lucky enough to find a complete sheet today, it would be worth rather more than that. But don't worry, you won't. The only surviving complete sheets are in the British Postal Museum in London.

THERE'S ANOTHER POSTAGE STAMP AT **259**

...BUT HOW MANY SHEETS?

Amble down the supermarket aisle past the displays of what is rather coyly described as 'bathroom tissue', and you'll be confronted by a dazzling display of the art of marketing. There's the occasional package emblazoned with a cloud, a butterfly, or a feather, but it's mostly cuddly animals. Yes, cute and fluffy is what sells toilet paper: rabbits, bears, kittens, koalas, and of course puppies.

Underneath the packaging, they all look much the same. If they're not white, they may be pink, or peach, or the palest blue, but all are pastel. And the rolls are all about the same size, too – in every case, the diameter is between 11 and 12 centimetres and the height of the roll is 10–11 centimetres.

But the uniformity conceals an astonishing variety. Read the small print. What do you get for your money? The average number of sheets per roll is somewhere in the low 200s, but the range is from 160 to 360. Clearly, there are other factors to take into account – such as how thick, how absorbent, how quilted and cushioned and soft and luxurious the product is – but it's as well to keep an eye on the number of sheets per roll, and per pound.

As for those puppies on a well-known British brand – at the time of writing, they offer an oddly precise number: 'Average 241 sheets per roll.'

FOR PRECISION IN MEASURING PAPER PRODUCTS, SEE **297**

242

A DUTY TO INVOLVE AND CONSULT

Once upon a time – and it wasn't so long ago – Doctor knew best, and patients had to accept whatever was dished out in the way of health care. But patients have become 'consumers' and 'service users', and the role of the doctor is now to inspire, support, and help each of us as we take a more active role in managing our own health.

So hospitals are abuzz with patient participation, person-centred care, shared decision making, health consumerism, health advocacy, patient empowerment... The jargon piles up almost as fast as the initiatives themselves.

What applies on the clinical front line applies also at the policy level, and again there is a plethora of jargon – from public consultation to stakeholder engagement, from openness and accountability to patient and public involvement. In this context, health-care organisations often use another little piece of jargon: 'Section 242 duty'. This is a reference to Section 242 of the National Health Service Act 2006, which imposed a general obligation on all NHS bodies in England to consult and involve service users in the planning, provision, and delivery of services.

Although the 2006 Act has been partially superseded by later legislation, and the structure of the NHS has changed (even the organisations that replaced the organisations established by the 2006 Act have now been swept aside), the Section 242 duty remains in place – and it is still often referred to by that label.

MORE MEDICAL FADS AND FASHIONS AT **296**

243

SUPERSTITION, SCIENCE, AND SELLING INSURANCE

At last, in January 2011, anyone living at number 13 could breathe a sigh of relief. There was no longer any need to worry about having an unlucky address. Science came to the rescue, ousting mere superstition, and proved that in fact the unluckiest house number in Britain was 243.

This was the headline result of a survey carried out by price-comparison website confused.com, which specialises in insurance. The survey was based on insurance claims over a four-year period, and during those four years 45 per cent of people living at a house numbered 243 had claimed on their home policies, compared with only 18 per cent of those at number 13.

A year earlier, a similar survey – also carried out on behalf of an insurance company – had revealed that the unluckiest house number was 33. And in mid-2012 it had apparently become 166. It's not possible that all of this scientific endeavour is in fact part of a publicity stunt by the insurance industry, is it?

PAY DAY FOR A METAL DETECTOR

A recently ploughed field in Staffordshire, UK, might not sound like a promising location for a thrilling event, but on 5 July 2009, near the village of Hammerwich, Terry Herbert was out there with his metal detector when the machine gave a satisfying 'ping'. Digging began, and over the next five days enough gold, silver, and other precious objects – a veritable hoard – were unearthed to fill no fewer than 244 bags.

The excavation continued – with funding from English Heritage and Staffordshire County Council – and thousands more items were discovered. Many of them were decorated with garnet, and most were military: swords, helmets, pommel caps, hilt plates. There were also a few Christian crosses.

The Treasure Valuation Committee valued the hoard at £3.285 million. Under the provisions of the 1996 Treasure Act, this is the amount that must be paid to the finder and landowner (shared equally) by any museum that wishes to acquire the hoard. The Birmingham Museum & Art Gallery and the Potteries Museum & Art Gallery made a joint bid for it, and the sum was eventually raised.

The Staffordshire hoard has been dated to the seventh or eighth century. It is the largest collection of Anglo-Saxon gold and silver metalwork ever to have been unearthed, and it must renew the hopes of anyone who is thinking of consigning the metal detector to the garage or selling it on eBay.

THERE IS ANOTHER ANGLO-SAXON CREATION AT **12**

CATALOGUING IN CYBERSPACE

In libraries the electronic age dawned well over 50 years ago, and since then card catalogues have made way for online search systems, while author indexes and subject lists have metamorphosed into metadata. An essential step in making the transition was to devise a way of coding the elements represented on the old catalogue card so that they could be handled by computers. In the 1960s, therefore, an international standard called MARC (machine-readable cataloguing) was developed. In its latest manifestation (MARC 21) this is still the basis for the storage and exchange of bibliographic metadata.

In the MARC coding scheme, field 245 is the title statement. In most systems that use MARC, field 245 is a compulsory field, often the only compulsory field: every record must have at least a 245 tag, even if no other information is entered.

With a good old-fashioned book you know where you are. The title appears on the cover, and on the title page, and with luck it's the same in both places. But as the material to be catalogued increasingly encompasses electronic resources, it gets harder. Web pages often have multiple titles, or no obvious title of any sort. What is a cataloguer to do? How can a 50-year-old cataloguing standard be stretched to accommodate modern electronic formats? At the interface between cyberspace and everyday reality, the best brains among the metadata managers puzzle over how to find something sensible to put in the 245 field.

THERE'S MORE LIBRARY CODING AT **294**

THERE AND BACK AGAIN

The Andover and Redbridge Canal, in Hampshire, was completed in 1794 during the heyday of canal-building. It carried coal and slate along its 34 kilometres from Redbridge to Andover, and it transported agricultural produce in the other direction. The canal was not a great commercial success, but it managed to survive for over 60 years, finally closing in 1859.

A long stretch of the canal was quickly filled in and converted into a railway line – railways, like canals, prefer flat routes. This opened in 1865, and it was called the Sprat and Winkle Line – probably because it carried seafood from Southampton to Andover. And in the other direction it took passengers to the seaside. During both world wars, it transported troops from Salisbury Plain to Southampton, and thence to France, although for many this was a one-way journey.

Like so many railway lines, the Sprat and Winkle Line closed in the 1960s. But this was still not the end of the line, for parts of its route were incorporated into the Test Way, a 79-kilometre footpath between Walbury Hill in West Berkshire and Eling in Hampshire. And in June 2011 sections of the old canal and railway line became Route 246 of Sustrans' National Cycle Network. Sustrans works to develop sustainable methods of transport, and its cycle network uses traffic-free and quiet routes to enable cyclists to travel safely and scenically. But one wonders whether their saddlebags are loaded with either sprats or winkles, whichever direction they're travelling.

ROUND THE CLOCK

Not so long ago (in 1946, to be precise), when the Texas-based Tote'm convenience stores changed their name to 7-Eleven to reflect their extended opening hours, the idea of being able to buy groceries any time from 7 a.m. to 11 p.m. was unheard of. But when a convenience store with a logo clearly based on that of 7-Eleven was created in the *Grand Theft Auto* series of video games a few decades later (in 2002), it was somehow inevitable that it would be called 24/7. For in the meantime the 24/7 culture had sprung up and spread across the world, to the point that opening around the clock had become almost the norm. Today, whether an enterprise offers groceries or plumbing, IT support or recruitment services, insurance or car hire, it had better be able to offer it 24 hours a day, seven days a week – and of course the development of e-commerce has made it so much easier.

Reflecting the growth of the always-open approach to business, the phrase '24/7' originated in America sometime around the early 1980s. Today it has achieved commonplace – not to say clichéd – status, appearing daily not only in discussions of business objectives but also in the names and logos of countless companies and organisations. 24/7 is actually quite an unusual coinage, a member of the exclusive club of everyday expressions (9/11 is another) that consist solely of numbers.

CATCH UP WITH SOME MORE CATCHY CLICHÉS AT **110**

248

LAWS FOR LIVING

Jewish law has a plethora of *mitzvot* (commandments). These are given in the Torah, and they cover all manner of topics: worship, business practice, war, food, clothing, sex, leprosy, love. Some of the *mitzvot* are based on what must surely be universally accepted rules about how to live a decent life (do not kill other people; do not steal; do not commit incest; return lost property; give charity according to one's means). Others are particular to the Jewish faith (do not boil meat with milk; do not wear garments made of wool and linen mixed together; affix the *mezuzah* to the doorpost of your house). And some are, well, just plain common sense (do not eat a worm found in fruit).

There are 248 positive *mitzvot* (a figure which, in some traditional Jewish texts, matches the number of bones in the human body). There are also 365 negative *mitzvot* (for the number of days in the year). That makes a total of 613, although not surprisingly many of them can no longer be followed: sacrifices and slavery, stoning and decapitation, for example, are no longer acceptable, even though they were included in the original 248 positive *mitzvot*.

Nonetheless, the *mitzvot* remain at the heart of what it means to be not just Jewish but human. Treat others with kindness; help a neighbour with his or her burden; love the stranger.

FIND FURTHER RELIGIOUS GUIDANCE AT **114**

249

THE MUMMY'S CURSE

A craze for all things Egyptian swept across Europe and America during the nineteenth century, stemming from Napoleon's Egyptian campaign (1798–1801) and the subsequent scientific studies of the artefacts of ancient Egypt. Meanwhile, horror fiction was equally popular, from *Frankenstein* (1818) through to *Dr Jekyll & Mr Hyde* (1886) and *Dracula* (1897). Strangely, however, it took a while for the two themes to come together. A few tales about mummies were published in the first half of the century, but even Edgar Allan Poe does not seem to have seen the horror potential of bringing a long-dead corpse back to life – his story 'Some Words with a Mummy' (1845) describes not a chilling encounter but a friendly chat.

The honour of launching the mummy's career as an icon of popular horror culture goes to Sir Arthur Conan Doyle, whose short story 'Lot No. 249' (1892) tells of an Oxford student who buys a shrivelled mummy at an auction (hence the title) and then works out how to restore its 'lurid spark of vitality', before sending it out across the town to wreak vengeance on his enemies. In the end, he is forced to hack the mummy to pieces and burn it, but the mummy – or at least the countless imitations that it spawned – lives on, lurking in the pages of horror comics and reanimated nightly in cinemas around the world.

SOME LARGER SCARY MONSTERS ARE FOUND AT **305**

250

A press that made an impression

When Charles, 3rd Earl Stanhope (1753–1816), invented his printing press in 1800, it represented a major advance over the old wooden presses. The cast-iron frame made the whole machine stronger and more rigid. The enlarged and reinforced platen (the metal plate that presses the paper down onto the type) could cope with sheets of paper twice as big. The series of compound levers made it easier to apply pressure, requiring less effort on the part of the pressman and resulting in a sharper impression. The value of the new press was quickly appreciated – not least by *The Times* newspaper, which employed a 'battalion' of them, and by the engraver Thomas Bewick, who looked forward to seeing his next book printed more cleanly and clearly.

But the Stanhope press was essentially the same piece of kit as printers had been using since the middle of the fifteenth century. For all its advantages, it was still a hand press, printing one sheet of paper at a time and requiring every operation to be performed by hand. Above all, it brought almost no improvement in the speed of printing. Just like Gutenberg's press, the Stanhope press worked at a maximum rate of about 250 sheets an hour.

The first real advance in printing speed came some years later with the steam-powered rotary press. By the end of the century that had been ushered in by the Stanhope press, the printing presses of *The Times* had an hourly output measured in the tens of thousands. A further century on, newspapers are now printed on presses that run at up to 100,000 sheets per hour.

FOR *THE TIMES*, TURN BACK TO **219**

251

A foggy set of rules?

It was certainly foggy in London Town when Fred Astaire sang, strolled, and danced his way through George and Ira Gershwin's 'A Foggy Day' and into the heart of *A Damsel in Distress* (1937) – all while wearing full evening dress, and casually drawing on a cigarette in that insouciant way of his.

And no doubt the last thing on Astaire's mind that night was where, how – and indeed whether – he could park his car in the fog-bound capital. But had he consulted the UK Ministry of Transport's *Highway Code*, which was first produced in 1931, he would have found hundreds of rules and guidelines that are designed to promote road safety, including some concerned with the tricky matter of parking.

These days, details of how to park when a pea-souper is swirling around the city streets are given in Rule 251 of the *Highway Code*, which reads: 'It is especially dangerous to park on the road in fog. If it is unavoidable, leave your parking lights or sidelights on.' Now that sounds sensible. But one can't help worrying over the question of unavoidability: could Fred Astaire have been destined to drive endlessly around the smarter districts of London until 'the sun was shining everywhere' – as the song goes – and parking was possible?

Both the *Highway Code* and 'A Foggy Day' have stood the test of time. The latter is now a standard in the canon known as the Great American Songbook, while the former – including Rule 251 – is required reading for any aspiring driver in the UK.

ENCOUNTER INCLEMENT WEATHER OF A DIFFERENT SORT AT **118**

THE GREAT DYING

About 252 million years ago there was a dramatic change in the earth's climate. Atmospheric carbon dioxide concentrations increased, oxygen levels fell, ice sheets disappeared, and polar regions were transformed into temperate zones, as hotter and drier conditions spread across the globe. Does any of this sound familiar?

Of course it did not happen in an instant, but in geological terms it was a rapid event, taking place over a mere million years or so. This was the end of the Permian period and the start of the Triassic, and it was the greatest natural disaster in the history of the planet. The Permian–Triassic Extinction Event, also known as 'The Great Dying', killed off 96 per cent of marine species and 70 per cent of terrestrial vertebrates. It was a far bigger catastrophe than the Cretaceous–Palaeogene mass extinction that wiped out the dinosaurs 187 million years later.

The cause of the Permian–Triassic extinction is unclear, but the most likely candidate is a massive volcanic eruption in what is now Siberia, where molten basalt spread over an estimated 7 million square kilometres, releasing a massive dose of greenhouse gases into the atmosphere and leading to global warming and ocean acidification. The volcanic activity may in turn have been set off by an asteroid impact. Will the impact of humans, 252 million years later, have similarly catastrophic consequences?

CARBON DIOXIDE CONCENTRATIONS ALSO FEATURE AT **280**

253

BAKERLOO SEATS

On the London Underground there are seven carriages on a Bakerloo Line train. If each carriage has 36 seats, and if every seat is occupied and there are no standing passengers, then the train is carrying 253 people (252 passengers + 1 driver). Such mundane details matter, because *253* is also the title of a story by Geoff Ryman which explores the histories, thoughts, and eccentricities of an imaginary 253 characters on that Bakerloo Line train in a seven-and-a-half-minute journey from Embankment to the Elephant & Castle – and Ryman devotes exactly 253 words to each character.

253 was initially produced as a website in 1996, and hypertext links connecting one character to another enabled the story to be read in a non-linear way that emphasised the similarities between people. Two years later a print version was published under the title of *253: The Print Remix*, which won the Philip K. Dick award. In this version, no such links are possible, so the story is read in the more conventional linear way – which, the author argues, draws out the differences between the characters portrayed, rather than focusing on what they have in common.

Curiously, however, it appears that Ryman got his sums wrong. The 1972 Mk 2 Tube Stock used on the Bakerloo Line in the mid-1990s (and still in use today) in fact has three carriages with 36 seats and four with 40, making a total of 269 seats per train (including the driver), not 253.

FOR A NON-LINEAR NARRATIVE IN FILM, SEE **71**

A BLUFFER'S TRUNCATED GUIDE TO
POKER PROBABILITIES

Whatever version of poker you are playing, whether it's straight,
stud, draw, flop, or Texas hold'em; whether it's online or on The
Strip, or if it involves a different kind of strip; whether you're
playing for money or for chocolate buttons – you are playing the
cards, the odds, and the people. But mainly the people. Poker,
famously, is not a card game but a people game that happens to be
played with cards. A poker player needs to be able to read minds,
and to bluff convincingly.

However, this is not a psychology textbook.

All forms of poker use a 52-card pack with four suits, and each
player bets on a hand of five cards. The hands are ranked in a set
order, reflecting the statistical likelihood of being dealt each hand.
So a royal flush beats a straight flush, which beats four of a kind,
which beats a full house, which beats a flush, and so on – but the
odds against any of those are too big for this book. The best poker
hand that we can accommodate is a straight (five consecutively
numbered cards of mixed suits). The odds against being dealt a
straight are 254 to 1.

That's all. This is not a maths textbook.

255

background-color:#FFFFFF

Lurking behind every beautifully designed webpage are hyper-text markup language (html) tags, which control the structure, and cascading style sheets (css), which determine the appearance, including the colours used.

The colours are specified by means of the RGB (red, green, blue) colour model, which has been the official web standard for almost as long as the World Wide Web has existed. Unlike the subtractive CMYK system used in printing (in which each colour absorbs light, and therefore the more colours, the darker), RGB is an additive system, based on projecting coloured light, and more of each colour means lighter. So mixing red and green (for example) results in yellow, setting all three colours to zero (no light) is black, and projecting them all together at maximum intensity produces white.

Each of the three base colours has 256 possible settings, from 0 (none) to 255 (maximum). So rgb(0,0,0) is black, rgb(255,0,0) is red, rgb(0,0,255) is blue, rgb(255,255,0) is yellow, rgb(122,122,122) is mid-grey, rgb(90,90,130) has a distinct blue tinge, and so on *ad infinitum* (or at least *ad* 16 million or so). Usually, however, colours are specified not in decimal but in hexa-decimal (base 16) notation, in which the digits are 0–9, A–F.

If this page were a webpage, its white background colour would be specified as background-color:rgb(255,255,255), or – in hexadecimal – as background-color:#FFFFFF.

FIND A WHOLE ROW OF WHITE THINGS AT **52**

256

Going up...

Just imagine if breaking the bounds of earth and travelling into space were as simple as going up in an elevator, with no need for expensive, dangerous rockets. In 1895, Russian rocket scientist Konstantin Tsiolkovsky (1857–1935) came up with just such an idea. His space elevator would be tethered to the earth at one end and attached to some kind of geostationary satellite at the other. Never mind the fact that man-made satellites of any sort (geo-stationary or otherwise) had yet to be invented – Tsiolkovsky was definitely on to something.

The cable between earth and satellite would clearly need to be not just very long but strong – and had Tsiolkovsky lived another 30 years he would have witnessed the invention of Kevlar, a synthetic fibre which has a breaking length of 256 kilometres. The breaking length means that a cable made of Kevlar can be 256 kilometres long and still support its own weight if it is anchored only at the top. So, in theory at least, Kevlar could be suspended 256 kilometres above the surface of the earth and not break.

But that is still nowhere near enough to reach any geo-stationary satellites, which orbit at around 35,000 kilometres above us. It looks as if the space elevator will have to wait a bit, and Kevlar will have to be content with terrestrial applications – body armour, racing sails, ropes, and frying pans.

FOR SOMETHING ELSE THAT IS FAMOUSLY LONG AND STRONG, SEE **241**

257

A wealth of bathrooms

The Istana Nurul Iman palace, completed in 1984, is the official residence of the Sultan of Brunei. It is reputed to be the biggest palace in the world. It has over 1,700 rooms, and 257 of them are bathrooms.

Brunei (or Brunei Darussalam) is an independent state on the island of Borneo. It has an area of 5,765 square kilometres (a little bigger than the English county of Norfolk) and a population of 415,000. Having decided not to join the Malaysian Federation after World War Two, it gained its independence from the UK in 1984. In terms of per-capita GDP it is the fifth-richest nation in the world, with its wealth based on oil. Its capital is Bandar Seri Begawan, and on the outskirts of the city is the sultan's palace, with 257 bathrooms.

The Sultan of Brunei is the absolute ruler of Brunei. The present sultan, Hassanal Bolkiah, has been on the throne since 1967. He is also prime minister, finance minister, minister of defence, and head of the Islamic faith in his country. A few years ago he was the richest person on the planet. He is the proud holder of countless honorary degrees, military honours, and other awards from around the world, and he lives in a palace with 257 bathrooms.

THAT MANY BATHROOMS COULD SPELL TROUBLE – SEE **312**

258

NUMBERS THAT DON'T TELL THE TRUTH

It is usually notoriously difficult to calculate the number of casualties in any individual battle, let alone a whole war. For example, the estimated number of British casualties at the Battle of the Somme in 1916 is an uncertain 420,000, while the French lost 'about' 200,000, and the Germans 'somewhere in the region of' 500,000. As for total casualties for the whole of World War One, 'over 37 million' is the most frequently quoted figure.

There are, however, accurate records for the 1982 Falklands War – a very much smaller war, fought over days (74 of them) rather than years, and focused on a comparatively tiny geographical area. By the time of the Argentine surrender, on 14 June, there were 258 British casualties (255 military personnel and three Falkland Islanders).

But these numbers only tell part of the story. In addition to those 258 fatalities, 777 British personnel were wounded, some of them very badly indeed. The Argentine figures are much higher: 649 killed, 1,068 wounded, and 11,313 captured. And the mental scars are borne by both sides.

A NUMBER THAT DOES TELL THE TRUTH IS **80**

A COLLABORATIVE STAMP

Norwegian postage stamps are all catalogued and assigned standard numbers (prefixed by NK) in a publication called *Norgeskatalogen*. Within that sequence, NK-259 is a striking and unusual stamp. It is printed in red and it shows a helmeted soldier in battle, with bayonet fixed, and behind him the Norwegian and Finnish flags. At the top are the words 'Den Norske Legion' (the Norwegian Legion).

NK-259 was issued in August 1941, with a face value of '20 + 80' – meaning that in addition to the 20 øre postal fee a surtax of 80 øre was levied, to support the volunteers fighting in the Norwegian Legion. This was a brigade formed by the pro-Nazi Quisling regime in collaboration with the Waffen-SS, to fight alongside the German army. It had been intended that the Norwegian volunteers would be sent to Finland (hence the Finnish flag on the stamp), but in the event they found themselves in Russia, taking part in the siege of Leningrad. The Legion was disbanded in 1943.

Today, NK-259 is one of the more valuable Norwegian stamps of the 1940s, because not many were printed and they did not remain in circulation for long. Norway was liberated by the Allies on 8 May 1945, and a week later all stamps issued during the Nazi occupation, including NK-259, were withdrawn from sale and banned from postal use.

260

Sitting comfortably

The British education system is often criticised for sending children to school too early, and for imposing too rigid a set of standards and targets even for three- and four-year-olds. But if a child is attending nursery school, no one is likely to argue against the school providing equipment that conforms to an official standard, to ensure that it is well designed, ergonomically suitable, comfortable, safe, and the right size.

There is of course an array of standards covering all of this. At the start of the school day, the child should hang his or her coat on a hook that is at an easily reachable height and securely fixed (that's covered by British Standard 5873). The playground equipment must be safe and appropriately sized (BS EN 1176), and surrounded by a fence that conforms to BS EN 10223. The toilets must also be designed to meet the particular requirements of the children (BS 6465).

Within the classroom, BS EN 1729 applies. It deals with *Chairs and Tables for Educational Institutions*, and specifies, among other things, the appropriate dimensions of furniture for children of different ages. For children aged three to four and just starting out on their formal education, chairs should have a seat height of 260 millimetres. There is even a colour-coding system indicating the size of the furniture. For sizemark 1 (260 millimetres), the feet of the chair should be orange.

COMPENSATIONS FOR BEING GROUNDED

Flying off to Finland? Soaring away to Slovenia? Hoping to get airborne to Austria? Anyone flying anywhere in or out of the European Union will be glad of the existence of EU Regulation 261. It came into effect on 18 February 2005, and it established the rules concerning compensation and assistance to passengers if their flight is delayed or cancelled, or if they are denied boarding for reasons such as overbooking or if half the cabin crew fall sick and there is no one to replace them.

If this happens to you, you could well be entitled to a re-routed flight (probably not via the Seychelles, though), or to overnight hotel accommodation (probably not the seven-star option, however), as well as meals and other refreshments (probably not the champagne, sadly), transport from airport to hotel and back again (not in the limousine, unfortunately), and the truly exciting opportunity to enjoy two telephone calls, fax or telex messages, or emails to tell your loved ones/boss/parole officer of your predicament. You may also be in line for cash compensation and a refund of the cost of your original ticket.

Not surprisingly, the airlines themselves are reluctant to advertise EU Regulation 261 any more widely than they absolutely have to, but it definitely helps to soften the blow for the passenger who's stranded in Spain or marooned in Malta or unexpectedly idle in Italy.

THE AIRCRAFT AT **129** WOULD NOT HAVE BEEN COVERED

262

The madness of William Shakespeare

The word 'mad' occurs 262 times in the complete works of Shakespeare. That fact alone is sufficient for a book like this, but it might also be a good starting point for someone engaged in a study of that little word as it has slipped and slithered its way through centuries of English-language usage, encompassing a range of shifting meanings from insane to infatuated, from uncontrolled to unwise, from frenzied to furious. Today, there is a clear difference between British and American usage, with the word primarily meaning insane on one side of the Atlantic and angry on the other.

For Shakespeare, 'mad' clearly had both these meanings, and the whole range in between. When Hamlet tells Rosencrantz and Guildenstern: 'I am but mad north-north-west...when the wind is southerly I know a hawk from a handsaw', it is pretty clear that he is referring to insanity, but what does King Lear mean by: 'I prithee, daughter, do not make me mad'?

As so often in Shakespeare, it's hard to pin down exact meanings. And there is further uncertainty in the figure 262 quoted above. This is based on the *Harvard Concordance*. Consulting the online Open Source Shakespeare *Concordance* would have resulted in this account appearing at 247. The number, of course, depends on which works are included in the canon, which text is followed, and how compound words and derivatives such as mad-brained, madly, and madness are treated. Anyone who needed to know the number for certain would be mad not to cross-check it all carefully.

THERE IS ANOTHER LIST OF WORDS AT **102**

A BOOKISH ENCOUNTER

Deep in the fiction section of the public library, Celia hesitated.
What should she choose? Which title would best console her
through the long lonely evenings that loomed? But as she reached
tentatively towards the shelf she felt a presence behind her. Could
it be? She hardly dared believe...Yes, in a moment, he was there.

'But I...' she attempted.

'Shhh,' he demanded, his deep tones barely rising above a
whisper. 'I know a series of books that has described 29,500 kisses
and 10,325 weddings in the last half-century.'

'But...' was the extent of any protest she had time to make –
then his arm brushed her elbow, as he deftly plucked a pink-bound
hardback from 'Authors H–L'.

'There you are,' he declared, and thrust the book into her
willing palms.

'But how do you know...?' she breathed.

Firmly he grasped the tome once more, and for a moment
their hands met, before she yielded the volume to his forceful grip.
He turned the publication over, and her eyes followed the urgent
jab of his finger as he indicated the publisher's name.

'Mills and Boon,' he asserted. 'You can also check out the
ISBN, or International Standard Book Number, which is printed
just above the barcode. You see the digits 263 in the middle there?
That's their publisher identifier. It identifies Mills and Boon.'

'Yes,' she sighed, gazing at the insistent vertical lines of the
barcode, as the librarian silently withdrew.

A VISIT TO **39** MIGHT HELP DECIPHER THAT BARCODE

264

A big hole in the ground

Strictly speaking, the Ngorongoro Crater in northern Tanzania is not a crater but a volcanic caldera, a feature formed when a volcano collapses in on itself. Had the massive volcano not collapsed 3 million years ago, there would be a mountain at Ngorongoro to rival Kilimanjaro.

But collapse it did, creating a landscape feature that now makes a major contribution to Tanzania's foreign earnings by luring visitors from far and wide to see the herds of elephants, wildebeest, and zebras, alongside one of the densest populations of lions on the planet. The crater is the centrepiece of the Ngorongoro Conservation Area, and also the focus of a difficult balancing act for the Tanzanian authorities as they try to maintain the area's stated aim of sustainable multiple land use, encompassing conservation, tourism, and the cattle-herding culture of the Maasai people.

With a floor area of 264 square kilometres, the Ngorongoro Crater is generally described as the world's largest intact caldera. But it is dwarfed by several flooded calderas, and by many others where the rim is no longer intact, such as the Aira Caldera in southern Japan, Toba in Indonesia, and La Pacana in the Andes, which is almost ten times as big as Ngorongoro. And when the supervolcano beneath Yellowstone National Park in the USA erupts – any day now – the result is likely to be a caldera big enough to swallow up several Ngorongoros.

SEE **252** FOR AN OLDER VOLCANIC EVENT

265

Monkeying around with birds

'Monkey basting the roast' is the intriguing title of a vignette that appears on page 265 of the first edition of Thomas Bewick's *A History of British Birds Volume Two*, published in 1804. Bewick (1753–1828) is best known for his detailed and exceptionally beautiful wood engravings of flora and fauna, based on his own keen observation of the natural world.

The second volume of the *History of British Birds* was published seven years after the first. It covered water birds, and it contained 101 figures illustrating coots and curlews, sandpipers and snipes, grebes and gallinules. So why on earth is there an engraving of a monkey in there too?

In addition to the main subject matter, Bewick's *British Birds* contained a number of vignettes when space allowed. Many are humorous, and they have become as highly regarded as the figures they accompany – if not more so. The monkey on page 265 is an especially fine example; it sits on a three-legged stool by a roaring fire, basting a chicken which is strung up in front of the flames, fat dripping onto a tray beneath, while a pot boils furiously.

The monkey is of course irrelevant to the book's subject matter, but this particular vignette is doubly curious. Not only does it depict a mammal, rather than a bird, but the bird roasting on the fire is the wrong kind of bird, since it is not a duck or a goose or a swan, but a chicken – and so, strictly speaking, it belongs in Bewick's first volume, which covers land birds.

FIND ANOTHER FINE ENGRAVING AT **188**

266

BLACK PERILS, SECRET ASSIGNMENTS, AND DESERT ADVENTURES

Captain James Bigglesworth (aka Biggles) served with 266 Squadron, flying Sopwith Camels, Hawker Hurricanes, Supermarine Spitfires, and Hawker Hunter jet fighters in a rather improbably lengthy career that spanned two world wars and earned him the Distinguished Service Order and the Military Cross and bar. His creator, Captain W. E. Johns, was himself a World War One pilot, and after the war he wrote no fewer than 96 Biggles titles, among them *Biggles and the Black Peril*, *Biggles' Secret Assignments*, *Biggles Defends the Desert*, and, of course, *Biggles of 266*.

W. E. Johns died in 1968, and these days Biggles himself is probably mostly of interest only to book collectors. But what of 266 Squadron? Formed in September 1918, the squadron – unlike Biggles – was no fiction, and indeed it saw plenty of action in World War One, carrying out anti-submarine patrols and other missions. In World War Two, now renamed 266 'Rhodesia' Squadron, it flew Spitfires at Dunkirk and in the Battle of Britain. After several reincarnations, the squadron was finally disbanded in 1964. Like Biggles himself, the squadron hails from an era now gone, but certainly not entirely forgotten.

WILLING VOLUNTEERS

Between July 2004 and May 2007, a brave band of 267 patients was recruited from a range of clinics, hospital wards, and out-patient departments across England to take part in the VenUS II clinical trial.

VenUS II was a study of maggot debridement therapy (MDT), in which live fly larvae are used to clean dead and infected tissue from a wound. The Mayans used maggots for this purpose many centuries ago, and during the American Civil War in the 1860s a Confederate army surgeon, J. F. Zacharias, found that it was an effective way of preventing gangrene. Since then it has become a surprisingly mainstream treatment, especially for leg ulcers.

In VenUS II, it was found that dead and dying tissue was cleared away more quickly by maggots than by standard treatment with a gel dressing designed to promote wound healing, but maggot therapy made no difference to overall healing. Other studies have produced similar results. A systematic review published in 2012 concluded that more investigations are required.

How easy was it to persuade the 267 volunteers to take part in VenUS II? How easy will it be to carry out further studies?

FOR MORE ON THE AMERICAN CIVIL WAR, GO BACK TO **34**

268

ET TU, JOHN WILKES BOOTH?

An actor playing the part of Mark Antony in Shakespeare's *Julius Caesar* has many lines to commit to memory, with the longest unbroken passage occurring in Act 3 Scene 2 – a speech of 268 words that begins 'Friends, Romans, countrymen'.

On 25 November 1864, towards the end of the American Civil War, the play was staged at New York's Winter Garden Theatre for one night only, and the man who had to memorise those lines was a 26-year-old actor by the name of John Wilkes Booth. He and his two brothers, sons of the well-known tragedian Junius Brutus Booth, were on stage together to raise money for a statue of Shakespeare that stands to this day in Central Park.

Five months later, on 14 April 1865, John Wilkes Booth visited another theatre – Ford's Theatre in Washington DC – where he shot and killed President Abraham Lincoln. The man whose father was named after one of the chief assassins of Caesar in Shakespeare's play, and who had himself acted in that play, became an assassin.

The 268-word speech provides another link to the assassinated president. Lincoln's most famous speech, the Gettysburg Address, is generally said to contain 271 or 272 words – but several versions of it exist, and one of them (the so-called Hay copy) runs, by neat coincidence, to exactly 268 words.

269

NUMBERS IS HARD, LET'S WRITE ABOUT TALKING DOLLS

As soon as Barbie opened her mouth, she was in trouble. All she'd said was 'Math class is tough', and before she knew it those pesky feminists were accusing her of reinforcing gender stereotypes and putting girls off studying mathematics and science. Never mind math class – life is tough for a talking doll.

The Teen Talk Barbie edition of the Barbie doll was released by manufacturers Mattel in July 1992. Each doll was programmed to say a randomly selected four phrases from a total of 270, including 'I love shopping', 'Wanna have a pizza party?', 'Party dresses are fun', and 'Do you have a crush on anyone?' Very soon, her words of wisdom had entered urban folklore in slightly modified form as 'Math is hard, let's go shopping.'

In response to criticism from the American Association of University Women, among others, Mattel pointed out that 'Math class is tough' was only one saying out of 270, and that the doll also said 'I'm studying to be a doctor.' But they soon backed down, and by October 1992 the offending phrase had been deleted. And so Teen Talk Barbie came to have a repertoire of just 269 sayings.

IS THE MATH AT **359** TOO HARD FOR BARBIE?

270

NOT JUST RABBITS AND LETTUCES

Beatrix Potter's 23 stories of foxy gentlemen and puddleducks, hedgehogs and lost handkerchiefs, rabbits and lettuces, are familiar to many of us, not just for the text but for their characterful watercolours.

Also moderately familiar is Potter's career as a Lake District farmer; in fact she bought her farm, Hill Top, with the proceeds from the books. But there is another, less well-known, side to Beatrix Potter. In 1888, at the age of 22, she started studying and painting fungi, and by 1901, one year before publication of her first children's story, *The Tale of Peter Rabbit*, she had already produced a set of 270 meticulously observed watercolours of fungus specimens. She also made microscopic studies of these, and her paper on spore germination was presented to the Linnean Society in 1897. However, because she was a woman – and therefore barred from attending the society's meetings – her paper was presented by her uncle.

Fifty-four years after her death, in 1997, the Linnean Society issued a posthumous apology to Beatrix Potter. Today her watercolours of fungi are now admired and appreciated for their artistic merit and beauty, and the important contribution that Potter made to the field of mycological research is now recognised.

GO TO **265** FOR ANOTHER ILLUSTRATOR OF NATURAL HISTORY

271

CHECK THE GARAGE, THE LOFT, THE GARDEN SHED...

Nature Morte Verre (Still Life Glass), *Papier Colle Pipe et Bouteille* (Copy Paste Pipe and Bottle), *Nu Assis* (Sitting Nude): these three artworks are among the 271 previously unknown drawings, prints, and collages by Pablo Picasso that recently came to light in a rather unexpected and somewhat controversial manner. A retired French electrician, Pierre Le Guennec, who had installed a security system in Picasso's villa near Cannes before the artist died in 1973, claimed that the artworks had been 'thank you' gifts from Picasso.

Le Guennec had stored the artworks in his garage for many years, before deciding to travel to Paris in 2010 to get the collection valued with a view to selling it. Picasso produced more than 20,000 works during his career, but hundreds are listed as missing, because they were either stolen or given away. Indeed, Picasso, like many artists, was known for his generosity, yet the sheer quantity of works in Le Guennec's possession raises doubts about how he acquired them – not least in the minds of the artist's descendants.

UNEARTH ANOTHER VALUABLE HAUL AT **244**

NO FRILLS

On Monday, 26 September 1977, a Douglas DC-10 took off from London's Gatwick Airport bound for New York. The plane bore the legend 'Skytrain' on its fuselage, and the tail fin was emblazoned with 'Laker'. On board were 272 passengers, who had paid £59 each for the privilege of crossing the Atlantic on the first Laker Airways Skytrain flight.

For over seven years, the brash and energetic Freddie Laker had been engaged in a legal battle to get Skytrain off the ground, fighting to cut through the arcane regulations that governed air travel and offer a simple walk-on transatlantic service. Ranged against him were the major international airlines. It was the defining David-and-Goliath story of the 1970s, a charismatic and likeable entrepreneur taking on faceless bureaucracy and big business.

When Skytrain was finally granted a licence, its fares were about one-third of what the major carriers were charging. But the other airlines lowered their fares in response, and in February 1982 Laker Airways collapsed into bankruptcy, a victim of the early-1980s recession and predatory pricing by the major airlines. But Skytrain had shown the way. Intercontinental air travel could indeed use the low-cost model that had been established by the likes of Southwest Airlines within the USA. The 272 passengers on the first Skytrain flight have been followed by countless others, flown around the world by many no-frills airlines.

FOR MORE NO-FRILLS FLYING, SEE **225**

273

The sound of silence

On 29 August 1952, at the Maverick Concert Hall in Woodstock, New York, the pianist David Tudor sat at a piano in front of an audience and lifted the piano lid in readiness to give the first public performance of a recently composed piece of music. He did not, however, play a single note. A few minutes later, he stood up, took a bow, and left the stage. The performance had lasted just 273 seconds. Its title: *4'33"*. Its composer: John Cage.

While David Tudor sat in silence at the piano, the concert hall was wide open to the woods at the back. Attentive listeners could hear the sound of wind in the trees, the patter of raindrops on the roof, and, more audibly, towards the end of the piece, perplexed mutterings. Most of the audience considered the piece either a joke or an affront: indeed, this has been the general reaction of most people who have either heard it, or heard of it, ever since. From its composer's point of view, however, the performance was spectacularly successful, for *4'33"* demonstrated that it was impractical, if not senseless, to attempt to retain the separation of conventional musical sounds and non-intentional sounds, or to make any claim for true silence. *4'33"* is not a work of silence at all, but a demonstration of its non-existence, of the permanent presence of sounds, and of the fact that they are worthy of our attention.

274

SUN, SEA...AND STONE

For sun-seekers, the Balearic island of Menorca is a great destination for sun, sea, sand, and sangria. For archaeologists, it is the place to go for *talayots*. At the last count there were no fewer than 274 of these stone constructions scattered about the island. *Talayots* were built sometime around 1300 BCE during the Talayotic period, when the island's society began to be organised into something resembling small towns.

Talayots are built with large stones, and some are up to 8 metres tall, with an average diameter of about 15 metres. Some are quite well preserved, while others are now little more than a pile of stones. They are usually found together with other remains of prehistoric stone structures, including circular houses and chamber tombs (*navetes*), as well as T-shaped monuments (*taulas*) that stand up to 4 metres tall.

Their purpose, however, is uncertain. Perhaps they were lookout towers; perhaps they were used as signal posts. Some were certainly defensive, for they usually occupy elevated sites, as can be seen at Torre d'en Galmés, which has good views over the surrounding countryside.

275

The art and science of smiling

In June 2008 the *New York Times Magazine* published a profile of Tyra Banks (ex-model, actor, talk-show host, and all-purpose celebrity) which began 'Tyra Banks has 275 smiles,' and went on to describe how she had 'studied, honed and mastered the smile'. Through her scientific study of smiling, Tyra had apparently engineered an arsenal of 275 secret weapons – including the surprise smile, the seductive smile, the commercial smile, and the 'angry but still smiling' smile.

Smiling is indeed the subject of scientific study. Humans appear to be the only animals that smile (though countless pet owners would insist otherwise). The nearest equivalent in our nearest relatives is a tooth-baring grin, but that generally expresses fear or threat rather than pleasure, and the evolution of the human smile remains something of a mystery. Smiling is more frequent in human females than in males, probably because testosterone inhibits smiling in favour of scowling at rivals, and using an arsenal of a different sort – so perhaps Tyra is on to something there.

'Smiles come naturally to me,' said Tyra, 'but I started thinking of them as an art form at my command.' The Mona Lisa has made do with just one enigmatic smile for the past 500 years. Does Tyra Banks really need 275?

276

SECOND-BEST

The achievements of Eratosthenes, born in 276 BCE, are rather overshadowed by those of other Greek scientists such as Euclid, Aristotle, and Archimedes, and many people today may not even have heard of him. That's because poor old Eratosthenes was always second-best. In his lifetime, indeed, he was derided with the nickname Beta – the second letter of the Greek alphabet.

As second-best mathematician, Eratosthenes made major contributions to geometry, and devised an algorithm for identifying prime numbers that is still in use today. As second-best geographer, he produced one of the most accurate ancient maps of the world, he calculated the circumference of the earth to within 1 per cent of the true value, he invented a system of latitude and longitude, and he even invented the discipline of geography itself. As second-best astronomer, he catalogued the stars, calculated the distance from the sun to the earth, and devised a calendar that incorporated leap years. Eratosthenes was also second-best in history, philosophy, poetry, and many other disciplines.

As director of the library at Alexandria, Eratosthenes was the leading librarian of his day – but he was, appropriately enough, the second person to hold that post.

Today, Eratosthenes has a prime-number sieve and a lunar crater named after him. His achievements form part of the foundations on which modern science is built. Being second-best isn't so bad, if you're second-best at *everything*.

FIND ANOTHER ANCIENT GREEK AT **347**

NOT JUST A NUMBER

Throughout the world, buses carry numbers to indicate the route they are following. And sometimes the routes are named as well as numbered. Usually the name is frankly rather dull – like the Orange Line in York, or the South Busway in Pittsburgh – but occasionally it seems that the bus company's marketing department gets involved, and a route ends up with a catchier name. So in Kent the 277 bus that runs from the suburb of Sherwood to the centre of Royal Tunbridge Wells is known as the Sherwood Shuttle – with the name proudly displayed in the livery of the buses and on the bus company's website.

But in this case it is not just the route that is named, for three of the buses on the route are themselves individually named, in honour of three local residents, Jenny Bays, Keith Marden, and Brian Senior. This sort of thing is not all that unusual: in Brighton and Hove, West Sussex, and around King's Lynn, Norfolk, buses bear the names of local celebrities (sometimes fictional, sometimes non-human), while across the Atlantic in Madison, Wisconsin, they are named after the children of bus company employees. The 277 is unusual, however, in combining named buses and a named route.

MOVE ALONG TO **291** FOR MORE ON PUBLIC TRANSPORT

278

HOLD TIGHT, PLEASE

Typical. You wait three-quarters of a book for a bus, then two come along together.

Unlike the 277 in Kent, London's bus route 278 no longer exists. Or at least it no longer runs on the streets of London. In cyberspace, the 278 is thriving, alongside countless other historic buses, trams, and trains. There is a dazzling array of websites dedicated to documenting the history of Britain's transport infrastructure, impressive for their quantity of information, level of detail, and authoritative accuracy. And from such sources we can gather the essential facts about a London bus route that has not operated for over twenty years.

In the early 1960s the 278 bus ran from the Victoria and Albert Docks northwards to Wanstead Flats, and except on Sundays continued further north to Chingford Mount. Its route roughly followed the Lea Valley, passing close to what is now the 2012 Olympic Park. The route was altered in 1962, extended in 1965, cut back in 1968, reduced further in 1973 (by which time the iconic Routemaster buses were no longer to be seen bearing the number 278), then extended again, and so on – and by the time the 278 was finally scrapped on 25 September 1993 it was serving different places in the East End altogether.

279

HOW FAR CAN YOU ROLL A CHURCH?

Bucharest, the capital of Romania, was badly damaged by the Allied bombings of World War Two. It also suffered considerable damage during an earthquake on 4 March 1977. However, neither of these events changed the face of the city as much as President Nicolae Ceauşescu's 'systematisation' scheme of the 1980s. Ceauşescu had visited North Korea in 1971, and, inspired by the grandiose avenues of Pyongyang, he set out to remodel Bucharest as 'the first socialist capital for the new socialist man'.

Several square kilometres of the historic city centre were demolished to accommodate apartment blocks and government buildings. Churches, synagogues, monasteries, a sports stadium, and a hospital were bulldozed, together with more than 9,000 houses, whose residents were obliged to accept flats in the ugly new apartment blocks.

Sitting incongruously next to one of these blocks is the Mihai Vodă Church. Built in 1591 by Mihai Viteazul (Michael the Brave) and originally part of an Orthodox monastery, the church survived the bulldozers – but in 1985 it was moved 279 metres east on rails to its present location in order to make way for the ostentatious new Centrul Civic (Civic Centre). However, its cloisters and ancillary buildings were destroyed, and it now rests on a concrete platform that is unlikely to withstand the next major earthquake. The remodelling of central Bucharest was completed in 1989, just in time for the dictator's overthrow.

FOR A CHURCH THAT STAYED PUT, SEE **203**

280

Exponential change

Until about 1800, the concentration of carbon dioxide (CO_2) in the earth's atmosphere was around 280 parts per million (ppm), and this value is universally recognised as the pre-industrial baseline. Analysis of air bubbles trapped in Antarctic ice, along with other data, shows that it had been stable at around that level since the end of the last ice age some 11,000 years ago. Furthermore, for as long as 800,000 years carbon dioxide levels had been remarkably stable, fluctuating between 180 and 300 ppm, with lower levels coinciding with colder periods.

Things changed with the Industrial Revolution. Burning of fossil fuels and felling of forests increased carbon dioxide output and reduced its absorption, and the level of the gas in the atmosphere began to rise. Slowly at first, but then increasingly rapidly, exponentially, topping 400 ppm in 2013. The last time the earth experienced CO_2 levels like this was over 15 million years ago, long before humans arrived on the scene.

In 2008 (when the CO_2 level stood at about 385 ppm), an environmental movement named 350.org was founded to promote 350 ppm as a safe upper limit, and to campaign for political and community action to reverse the increase. Their aim is to reduce atmospheric levels to 350 ppm – which is still a long way above 280.

THERE'S MORE ON THE INDUSTRIAL REVOLUTION (AND REVOLUTIONS) AT **8**

SINGING ALONG

Elvis is alive and well and performing nightly in music venues across the world. Alternatively, if you prefer your dancing queen to your blue suede shoes, you can take your pick: Abbaesque, Björn Again, Abbacadabra, and a hundred others all offer an opportunity to relive the authentic ABBA experience, typically (according to their websites) with 'plenty of audience participation and sing-along moments'. Some of them have even spawned their own imitations, so you can enjoy a night out singing along to a tribute to an ABBA tribute band.

Or how about the Mersey Beatles, or the Counterfeit Beatles, or the Counterfeit Stones, the Cloned Stones, or (with refreshing honesty) Not The Rolling Stones?

Which brings us to Blank 281. Yes, by means of a simple vowel change and some shuffling of the numbers, even the California rock band whose name may (or may not) be based on an F-word count has its own tribute band. Having written about the original at 182, it's only fair that we should now pay tribute to the band that pays tribute to them. We're not sure how many sing-along moments you get at a Blank 281 gig, however.

FOR SOMETHING ELSE THAT COMES BACK FROM THE DEAD, SEE **249**

ALL THE WAY ROUND

The M25 motorway, completed in 1986 and constantly widened, upgraded, coned off, and dug up ever since, is 188 kilometres from end to end. But hold on. How can a circle have two ends? After all, the M25 is London's orbital motorway. That means it's an endless loop, and it takes you all the way round London, right? Wrong.

Because the M25 does indeed have two ends. One end is at Thurrock, and the other is at Dartford, just across the River Thames, and the bit that crosses the river between them and completes the circle (the Dartford Crossing) is a lowly A road, the A282. And that's why the M25 makes its appearance here, and not at 25 or 188 (or 234, for the number of its bridges).

A booklet published by the Ministry of Transport in 1986 to celebrate the opening of the orbital motorway promised that the new road would mean an end to traffic jams and bottlenecks. And we all know how well it has lived up to that promise. So there you have it: the M25 as a work of fiction. Some of it isn't even the M25, it's the A282.

283

A planet-sized error

The distinguished astronomer Giovanni Domenico Cassini was the first to notice it. When he spotted it through his telescope in 1672 he wasn't quite sure, but when he saw it again in 1686 he was confident enough to announce his discovery to the world. The planet Venus had a moon.

Through the eighteenth century and into the nineteenth, many astronomers confirmed Cassini's observation, though others failed to find anything. Some even suggested that it was an optical illusion – and then finally, in 1884, a Belgian astronomer named Jean-Charles Houzeau figured it out. The object was not a moon of Venus but a planet in its own right, orbiting the sun once every 283 days. He named it Neith, after a secretive Egyptian goddess of that name.

He was just as wrong as Cassini had been, of course – and in 1887 the Belgian Academy of Sciences demonstrated that all the observations could be explained either as imperfections in telescope lenses or as stars that were in fact thousands of light years beyond Venus. Just three years after it was first added to the map of the solar system, Neith was consigned to oblivion.

FOR A DIFFERENT ASPECT OF VENUS, SEE **267**

PICK-AND-MIX CINEMA

In 1933, the Regal Cinema opened in the town of Kingsbridge in south Devon, England, with seating for 284 people. The cinema closed in 1973, and today the building houses a betting shop, a bar, and a bingo hall.

Kingsbridge tells the story of UK cinemas in miniature. The opening of the Regal coincided with the start of a massive box-office boom, and cinema attendances across the UK rose to a peak of 1.64 billion in 1946 before declining through the 1950s and falling steeply in the 1960s and 1970s, largely owing to the spread of television. By 1973, cinemas were shutting down all over the country – and a decade later national admission figures had fallen to a low of 54 million. Video rentals had almost killed off the cinema industry.

Since the mid-1980s there has been a turnaround. By 2012, box-office numbers were back up to nearly 180 million. And, sure enough, in 2000 a new cinema opened in Kingsbridge. But rather than catering for 284 people all watching a film together, the Reel Cinema, housed in the former town hall, has three screens each showing a different film and seating a smaller popcorn-munching audience. Going to the movies has become a pick-and-mix experience in more ways than one.

285

Gasping for a cuppa

As every mountaineer knows, you can't make a decent cup of tea on the summit of Mount Everest. Of course, as you approach the summit you are more likely to be gasping for oxygen than for a nice cuppa – but that is probably just as well, because the water to make the tea won't boil properly anyway. The higher you climb, the lower the air pressure, and that not only makes it harder to obtain enough oxygen from the air you breathe, but also lowers the boiling point of water – in effect because when the water molecules are subject to less atmospheric pressure they find it easier to escape as vapour.

For every 285 metres of ascent, the boiling point of water decreases by 1 degree Celsius, so even a climb up Ben Nevis will have a measurable effect, and by the time you reach the top of the world's highest mountain, at 8,848 metres, your kettle will boil at just 69 degrees, nowhere near hot enough for a brew.

But what happens to the freezing point of water? Does that also change with altitude? The short answer is no. The long answer involves phase diagrams and some complex physics, and this really isn't that kind of book. So relax – no matter how many times 285 metres you ascend you can still enjoy a decent Scotch on the rocks, even if the tea is undrinkable.

COME BACK DOWN TO SEA LEVEL AT **212**

THE COMPATIBILITY CURSE

The Intel 286 microprocessor chip (otherwise known as the 80286) was introduced in 1982, just a decade after the first microprocessors and seven years after the first (kit-form) microcomputer. The 286 was not the first 16-bit chip, but in many ways it represented a great advance over its predecessors, not least because it could run the software written for them – it was backward compatible.

The 286 was itself soon overtaken by the development of 32-bit processors such as the Intel 80386, not to mention the chips built by Motorola – but it was not pushed aside, because the rapidly growing personal computer market helped it to a position of dominance that it held into the early 1990s. The commercial breakthrough came in 1984, when IBM adopted the 286 for its second-generation Personal Computer, the AT. Sixteen million of them were sold within six years, and the IBM clones that began to emerge at about the same time also used the 286 (or copies of it).

Commercially, then, it became advantageous to keep building new systems on the existing chips, and to create new chips by extending the old architecture, rather than to take a radical step forward. Backward compatibility became something of a curse, and it can be argued that the very success of the 286 held the computer industry back for several years.

For the record, the processor in a laptop today is likely to have 10,000 times as many transistors as the 286, and to run at 500 times the speed.

MEANWHILE, IN A PARALLEL UNIVERSE . . . SEE **128**

CLASSIFIED, NAMED, AND NUMBERED

Beyond the planet Mars lies the main asteroid belt, and among the millions of objects in orbit around the sun in that zone, debris left over from the formation of the planets, is 287 Nephthys.

287 Nephthys is an irregularly shaped lump of rock, about 68 kilometres across, orbiting the sun at an average distance of about 350 million kilometres and taking slightly more than three and a half earth years for each orbit. It was discovered in 1889 (a few weeks after 286 Iclea), and is now one of hundreds of thousands of catalogued and numbered asteroids, many of which have also been given names.

In this case, the name is that of an ancient Egyptian goddess of darkness, sleep, and mourning. Nephthys is the Greek form of her name; the Egyptians knew her as Nebt-het, and she was almost always portrayed wearing a head-dress in the shape of a house topped by a basket – which are in fact the hieroglyphs that spell her name.

287 Nephthys is officially classified as a *small solar system body*, along with other asteroids, comets, near-earth objects (NEOs), and the rather scary-sounding potentially hazardous asteroids (PHAs). But 287 Nephthys is by no means hazardous, and is unlikely ever to come anywhere near us. It's just good to know it's out there, classified, named, and numbered.

FOR A CONSIDERABLY LARGER SOLAR SYSTEM BODY, GO TO **318**

288

WALKING, NOT TALKING

In November 1974 several hundred pieces of fossilised bone were found scattered on a hillside in the Afar Depression, at the northern end of the East African Rift Valley in Ethiopia. The bones came from a single animal, and the find was catalogued as Afar Locality 288-1. She is better known as Lucy.

Lucy (AL 288-1) lived about 3.2 million years ago, and belonged to a species called *Australopithecus afarensis*. Lucy is so well known that palaeontologists must be rather tired of having to tell us that this was not a one-off discovery. In fact, although AL 288-1 is one of the most complete skeletons, several other specimens of *A. afarensis* have been found, not only in Ethiopia but also in Kenya and Tanzania, and many related species are also known.

It is uncertain whether *A. afarensis* is a direct ancestor of modern *Homo sapiens*, or just a close relative. One issue that has been settled, however, is that our ancestors walked before they talked. It is clear from the details of these skeletons from the Pliocene that walking on two legs evolved before the large brain that led to language, tool-making, and all our other familiar traits. It was bipedal locomotion that first separated humans from other apes.

MOVE FROM LUCY TO LUCILLE AT **355**

289

From Charles to Caroline

Charles Darwin wrote a lot of letters, and – let's face it – this book could have picked any one of them. Among the numerous recipients were the naturalist Alfred Russel Wallace (whose own studies of how species evolve prompted Darwin to publish his theory of natural selection), the botanist Asa Gray, the zoologist Thomas Henry Huxley, Darwin's publisher John Murray, the writer George Eliot, the geologist Charles Lyell, John Stevens Henslow (the Cambridge professor of botany who first suggested to Darwin that he join the *Beagle* voyage), and Darwin's closest friend Joseph Dalton Hooker, with whom he exchanged thousands of letters over more than forty years.

Yet despite this plethora of correspondence with the prominent figures of the day, some of the most poignant letters are those that Darwin wrote to members of his own family. Letter 289 in the collection of the Darwin Correspondence Project was written at the Bay of Islands in New Zealand on 27 December 1835, shortly after Darwin had visited the Galapagos Islands, and it was addressed to his sister Caroline. In it he praises the missionaries in Tahiti, expresses his disappointment with New Zealand (both 'the country and its inhabitants'), complains of seasickness, and is glad to be 'on the right side of the world' and heading home.

Many of Darwin's letters certainly provide invaluable insight into his intellectual development, but letter 289 demonstrates his kindness. 'Give my most affectionate love to my Father, Erasmus, Marianne & all of you. Goodbye my dear Caroline.'

GO TO **25** FOR A MISSING LETTER

290

CONNECTING YOU NOW

The volcanic island of St Helena in the South Atlantic is one of the remotest places on earth. The nearest land, apart from a few small rocks, is Ascension Island, 1,300 kilometres to the north-west. Discovered by the Portuguese in 1502 and then briefly claimed by the Dutch, St Helena was more or less left to the English by the late sixteenth century. In 1657 Oliver Cromwell gave the East India Company a charter to the island, and it became a British colony in 1659. It is now part of the British Overseas Territory of St Helena, Ascension and Tristan da Cunha.

Because of its isolation, St Helena was chosen as a place of detention for Napoleon after his defeat at Waterloo. He was exiled to the island in October 1815, and died there in 1821.

But what has any of this to do with the number 290? Well, if you want to make a telephone call to one of the island's 4,000 inhabitants you will find yourself using the International Direct Dialling code 290. In the twenty-first century, St Helena is no longer quite so cut off from the outside world.

FIND ANOTHER LUMP OF ROCK WITH NAPOLEONIC CONNECTIONS AT **196**

291

FOOTBALL HIGHLIGHTS AND A WARM SEAT

At the time of writing, Moscow has 190, Paris has 245, London has 270, Seoul has 291, and New York tops the list at 421. Seoul may not have as many underground stations as New York, but it is far busier, with well over 3 million passenger trips per year, and it currently has the longest route length in the world. CNN rated it the best subway anywhere, and in 2013 the BBC nicknamed it the 'super highway'.

Such accolades are perhaps well deserved. According to its users, Seoul's metro is consistently clean, safe, and efficient. It has also embraced twenty-first-century technology, with mobile-phone connectivity on all carriages, as well as screens that provide not only announcements about the next station, but also international news, stock prices and, yes, football highlights. It even has heated seats to keep your own seat warm during those bitter Korean winters.

Seoul's metro opened on 15 August 1974 with just one line. It currently has 19. But what with the current rapid economic growth of South Korea, and, in particular, of its capital city, plenty more new ones are scheduled to open in the next few years. Before too long, that number of 291 will have to be revised upwards.

GO BACK A FEW STOPS TO THE LONDON UNDERGROUND AT **253**

292

COUNTING THE PENNIES

There are 292 ways of giving change for a dollar, and there must be well over 292 websites listing all the possible ways of doing it. There are also websites that pride themselves on *not* listing the possibilities. 'We are here to teach mathematics – that is, to help you learn ways to answer questions like this for yourself,' proclaims one such site. And since this is not a maths book, and we are not here to teach mathematics, we will neither list the possibilities nor explain the methods.

292 is only the correct answer if changing a dollar means using just the five smaller coins – half-dollars, quarters, dimes, nickels, and cents. If a straight swap of a dollar bill for a dollar coin is allowed, the answer becomes 293.

Asking a similar question in Europe generates an answer that is considerably larger. There are 4,562 ways of changing a pound or a euro into smaller-denomination coins. That is partly because there are five 20-pence or 20-cent coins to the pound or euro, compared with four quarters to the dollar, but mainly because the additional 2-pence or 2-cent coin means that there are six coins to work with instead of five.

293

A STORM IN A PETRI DISH

In early 2011 it came to light that a well-known American drinks company had contracted out the testing of artificial flavour enhancers to a biotechnology research firm. Nothing unusual in that, but what caused a bit of a stir in pro-life circles was that the research was being carried out in the laboratory using an immortalised cell line called HEK-293.

An immortalised cell line is a useful tool in biochemical and genetics research, used in the development of vaccines, for testing drugs, for research into gene therapy, and also for less life-critical applications such as bio-engineering flavour enhancers for fizzy drinks. It is a population of cells derived from an animal or human source that is kept alive in the laboratory, and that keeps dividing indefinitely because the normal cell-death mechanism has been switched off. The HEK-293 cell line was developed in the Netherlands in 1973 by inserting some viral DNA into cells from human embryonic kidney (hence HEK), an experiment that finally succeeded at the 293rd attempt. HEK-293 has become a standard cell line in many areas of research. It is stable, easy to work with, and provides reliable and repeatable results.

What caused the stir was the fact that the cells that started the HEK-293 line came from an aborted fetus. Forty years after HEK-293 was first developed, there were calls for a boycott of a certain brand of drink, on the grounds that the company was 'using the bodies of aborted children to make its products' and was feeding us 'cells from babies victimized by abortions'.

UNEQUAL TREATMENT

The Dewey Decimal Classification (DDC) is used by libraries throughout the world to organise their stock, and has achieved a very respectable new lease of life as the basis for a range of web-based metadata systems. DDC classifies human knowledge into ten main classes, each of which is in turn split into ten, and so on. So 200 is religion, 290 is non-Christian religions, and 294 is 'religions of Indic origin' – a neat hierarchical arrangement, with relationships between subjects expressed by a simple numerical notation. And class 294 can easily be further subdivided: 294.3 Buddhism, 294.4 Jainism, 294.5 Hinduism, and so on.

So far, so good. But the decimal notation that is DDC's strength and has taken it through 23 editions spanning 140 years is also a weakness, for it implies not only that there is something natural in the organisation but also that the shorter the number the bigger the subject. All the 'Indic' religions (which between them account for over 20 per cent of the world's population) are squeezed into 294, just one of 100 three-digit numbers available for religion. Christianity gets 70 times as much space. The whole of Sikhism (294.6) apparently ranks equally with Paul's Epistle to the Ephesians (227.5).

The explanation is twofold. First, DDC was designed not as an organisation of knowledge (let alone objective reality) but of books in libraries. Second, the books in question were those on the shelves of the library in Amherst College, Massachusetts, in the 1870s, when Melvil Dewey was librarian there.

ANOTHER SNIPPET OF LIBRARY HISTORY CAN BE FOUND AT **221**

295

Following the fruit flies

John Glenn was not the first earthly creature to go into space. That honour went to a cluster of fruit flies on 20 February 1947. Their flight lasted 190 seconds, but they had no control over the situation and just as little idea about what was going on.

John Glenn was not the first human being in space. That honour went to the Russian cosmonaut Yuri Gagarin on 12 April 1961. Gagarin's flight lasted 108 minutes, and, unlike the fruit flies, he certainly knew what was happening. However, he had no control over the flight, for that was handled by a combination of automatic systems and ground control.

John Glenn was not even the first American in space. That honour went to Alan Shepard on 5 May 1961. His flight took just 15 minutes 22 seconds. But unlike Gagarin, Shepard had a degree of manual control of the spacecraft and could make adjustments to its orientation.

So what *did* John Glenn do? He was the first American to orbit the earth, on 20 February 1962. In fact, he out-orbited Gagarin by doing it three times rather than just once. Along the way, he took control of the spacecraft and made significant adjustments to its position. He recorded numerous observations of the stars, the weather, and landmarks on the earth below. And he prepared his position ready for re-entry and splashdown. Glenn's flight lasted 295 minutes (and 23 seconds!). He paved the way for all future manned space exploration – but he couldn't have done it without the fruit flies showing him the way.

296

Blood and guts

Doctors seem to prefer journals with short and snappy titles. The journal of the American Society of Hematology has been called *Blood* since it began publication in 1946, and the British Society of Gastroenterology's journal has always been simply *Gut*. Following this fashion, *Diseases of the Chest* changed its name to *Chest* in 1970, and the *British Heart Journal* became *Heart* in 1996.

The trend towards the short and snappy is also shown in the use of abbreviations as journal titles. Over the years the *Journal of the American Medical Association* became *JAMA*, the *Quarterly Journal of Medicine* changed to *QJM*, and the *Canadian Medical Association Journal* adopted the bilingual title *CMAJ–JAMC*.

Nor is the *British Medical Journal* immune. This is one of the world's leading medical journals, with a history going back to 1840. And yet in June 1988 the *British Medical Journal* ceased to exist, when the final issue of Volume 296 was printed. A familiar pale blue journal appeared a week later, sure enough, but from that point on it has borne the title *BMJ*, and that is now the journal's official title, both in print and online.

The *British Medical Journal*, Volume 1 (1840) to Volume 296 (1988). Cut short in its prime, but not yet RIP.

297

IT'S ALL ABOUT THE ASPECT RATIO

297 millimetres. That's a funny measurement for a piece of paper. Why not something nice and round like 300? Why does the A4 paper that we use daily in our homes and offices measure 297 × 210 millimetres?

The 'A' series of paper sizes, from A0 (the largest) to A10 (the smallest), is based on two simple principles. First, an A0 sheet has an area of one square metre; second, the ratio of the long side to the short side (the aspect ratio) is the square root of 2 (which, as any fule kno, is 1.4142...). Each size in the series is half the area of the one above it, with the length of the smaller size equal to the width of the larger one. So A3 is 420 × 297, A4 is 297 × 210, and A5 is 210 × 148 (measurements are rounded to the nearest millimetre). And the magic of the square root of 2 is that when you do this, the aspect ratio is maintained across the whole size range.

The practical and aesthetic benefits of basing paper sizes on the square root of 2 were first appreciated by the eighteenth-century German physicist Georg Christoph Lichtenberg. The system is now more or less universal, having been adopted as an international standard (ISO 216) in 1975. Except in North America, that is, where paper with weird names such as letter and legal (and even weirder formats) is still in use.

298

For ever young

Even a cursory browse in the children's section of any good library or bookshop will unearth a good-sized flock of puffins. Puffin Books was launched as a children's imprint in 1940 by Allen Lane of Penguin Books. The first titles were non-fiction picture books, but fiction soon followed, and since then Puffin Books – like Penguin and Pelican – has become renowned for publishing high-quality yet reasonably priced paperbacks.

Each Puffin fiction title was given a number. The first in the series, no. 1, published in 1941, was Barbara Euphan Todd's *Worzel Gummidge* (with the author's name misspelt on the cover of the first printing). And Puffin no. 298 was J. M. Barrie's *Peter Pan*, in which Peter and Tinker Bell lead the three Darling children to Neverland. The Puffin edition was published in 1967, when Kaye Webb was at the editorial helm and the Puffin imprint was expanding rapidly, increasingly republishing classics of children's literature as well as new fiction. The Puffin *Peter Pan* was a reprint of the 1911 Hodder & Stoughton version, which was called *Peter and Wendy*. This was an adaptation of a stage play by Barrie entitled *Peter Pan* (1904). And the play, in its turn, was based on a character who had first appeared in one of Barrie's earlier adult novels, *The Little White Bird* (1902) – which had also generated another spin-off in the form of a children's book called *Peter Pan in Kensington Gardens* (1906). From the start, Barrie clearly knew that Peter Pan had commercial potential.

Very like Puffin Books, in fact.

FOR PUFFINS IN THEIR NATURAL HABITAT, SEE **36**

AMAZING GRACE

At the speed of light, it would take about 514 billionths of a second to travel from bow to stern of USS *Hopper*, a guided missile destroyer belonging to the United States Navy. And the woman after whom the warship is named would have been more aware of this than most of us.

For USS *Hopper* is named in honour of Rear Admiral Grace Hopper (1906–1992), computer pioneer, designer of the programming language COBOL, the person who is popularly (but probably erroneously) credited with discovering the original bug in the system (it was actually a dead moth) and coining the term 'debugging', and who was affectionately known as 'Amazing Grace'.

In her later years, Grace Hopper was a well-known and entertaining lecturer, and one of her tricks was to help her audience visualise the speed of light by handing out pieces of wire cut to the length that light travels in 1 billionth of a second (a nanosecond). These lengths of wire were about 299 millimetres long. To be precise, each piece should have been 299.792458 millimetres, but cutting pieces of wire to that level of accuracy isn't easy.

ANOTHER HOPPER CAN BE FOUND AT **181**

300

'MY SUBJECT IS WAR, AND THE PITY OF WAR'

The Battle of Verdun was the longest and most costly battle of World War One on the Western Front. The battlefield was less than 10 square kilometres in extent, but in France and Germany it has come to represent the horrors of war, similar to the Battle of the Somme for the British.

In the winter of 1915–1916, German General Erich von Falkenhayn decided on a massive attack on the town of Verdun, which, with its huge forts (created after the humiliation of the Franco-Prussian war), was a place of great symbolic significance for the French. Although French intelligence had warned of Falkenhayn's plans, these warnings were ignored by the French Command, and consequently Verdun was utterly unprepared for the initial bombardment on 21 February 1916, in which 1,400 German guns opened fire. German infantry met little resistance for the first four days, but French reinforcements soon arrived, and over the ensuing months the area around Verdun was subjected to repeated attacks and counter-attacks. The hills above the town were ground into a wilderness of mud and blood. On 15 December a final French counter-attack pushed the Germans back, and by the end of the battle all of Verdun's forts were back in French hands.

In total the battle lasted 300 days. Both sides suffered very heavy casualties, and, after all that time, and all those deaths, no tactical or strategic advantage had been gained by either side.

SEE **78** FOR A MORE HARMONIOUS MONOTONY

FREEDOM OF EXPRESSION DENIED

Article 301 of the Turkish Penal Code states that 'a person who, being a Turk, explicitly insults the Republic or Turkish Grand National Assembly, shall be punishable by imprisonment of between six months to three years.'

Despite international condemnation, there have been a number of prosecutions under Article 301, with activists, artists, and writers especially targeted. These include Orham Pamuk (a Turkish writer, academic, and Nobel Prize winner, who in 2005 had drawn attention to the mass killing of Kurds and Armenians in Turkey) and Perihan Mağden (a journalist and writer, who was prosecuted after writing an article titled 'Conscientious objection is a human right').

Since 2008, the number of prosecutions under Article 301 has begun to fall, and Turkey is aware that it damages its international reputation – especially in the light of the country's application to join the European Union.

Amnesty International asserts that Article 301 is at odds with Turkey's international legal obligations, and calls on the Turkish authorities to 'terminate without delay all prosecutions against individuals under it, and to abolish the article in its entirety'. However, at the time of writing (May 2014), Article 301 is still in place.

THOSE AT **316** ARE NOT AFRAID TO EXPRESS THEMSELVES

302

It's simpler for worms

Biology is often rather messy. With rare exceptions, it doesn't lend itself to the sort of numerical precision that this book demands. We can specify that most species of starfish have five arms, and that a human spine has 33 vertebrae, but we cannot say with any certainty that a human heart beats 60 times a minute, or that a fingernail grows 37 millimetres in a year. These are at best approximations or averages. And when it comes to a question like 'How many nerve cells are there in a human body?' the best we can do is shrug and say: 'Maybe about 86 billion.'

But there are simpler animals in which such a question can be answered. The nematode (round worm) *Caenorhabditis elegans*, about a millimetre long, transparent, and known to its friends as *C. elegans*, has precisely 302 nerve cells, or neurons. For several decades, *C. elegans* has been widely used as a model organism in laboratory studies of genetics and neural development, and the fact that it has such a small, and fixed, number of neurons is a great help in those studies.

Life is much simpler for worms.

IS THE PRECISION OF THE BIOLOGICAL NUMBER AT **160** JUSTIFIED?

303

RULES OF ENGAGEMENT

Harry 'Breaker' Morant (1864–1902) was an English-born Australian, a horse-breaker, bush balladeer, and likeable rogue, who volunteered to fight for the British in the Boer War – and who, in January 1902, faced a court-martial, accused of murdering a number of prisoners of war.

In his defence, Morant did not dispute the killings. He was a lieutenant in the Bushveldt Carbineers, a special unit tasked with countering the guerrilla tactics of the Boers, and he said he had been acting on Lord Kitchener's orders to 'take no prisoners'. When challenged by the president of the court to quote the section of the regulations, he defiantly replied: 'As to rules and sections, we had no Red Book, and knew nothing about them. We were out fighting the Boers...we got them and shot them under Rule 303.'

Morant was suggesting that the Lee-Enfield .303, the standard British army rifle of the time, provided him with all the authority he needed. But it did him no good. He was found guilty, and just hours later he and one other officer, Peter Handcock, were executed by firing squad. Four others received lesser sentences.

The story of Breaker Morant has attained mythic status in Australia, with the British authorities accused of using him as a scapegoat to cover up a controversial no-prisoners policy. The case has been the subject of several books, a stage play, a successful film, and a recent unsuccessful campaign to have Morant and his co-accused pardoned. Rule 303 has achieved minor currency as a term for summary execution.

GAUGE THE SIZE OF THE RIFLE AT **308**

THE NUTS AND BOLTS OF STAINLESS STEEL

Steel is an alloy of iron containing a variable (but small) quantity of carbon, along with a few other elements. The trouble with steel is that it rusts – the iron reacts with oxygen to form iron oxide. So steel typically needs to be given some form of protective coating. For many decades, therefore, starting in about 1820, metallurgists experimented with different alloys in an attempt to produce something that did not corrode, and these efforts finally bore fruit in Sheffield in 1913, when Harry Brearley produced the first stainless steel. In effect, this is a self-coating steel. Chromium added to the alloy reacts with oxygen to form chromium oxide, which acts as a microscopically thin protective surface film.

Stainless steel is by no means a single uniform product. According to its crystalline structure, it may be austenitic, ferritic, or martensitic, and it also differs in the proportions of its constituent elements, depending on the intended application. This results in an array of tailor-made alloys, subject to a multitude of specifications and grading systems. The most common type is grade 304, also known as 1.4301 or 18/8. This contains 18 per cent chromium and 8 per cent nickel, and it is used for a wide range of applications, from nuts, bolts, sinks, and saucepans to cutlery and architectural panelling.

Surgical instruments, boat fittings, and body-piercing jewellery, on the other hand, are more likely to be made from grade 316, which has more nickel than grade 304 and an additional element, molybdenum, to make it even more corrosion-resistant.

FOR STAINLESS STEEL IN ALL ITS ARCHITECTURAL GLORY, SEE **319**

305

A lost world of water

Mount Roraima, located on the border between Venezuela, Bolivia, and Guyana, is undoubtedly an impressive sight. At 2,810 metres, it is the highest mountain in the Pakaraima range and it is thought to be about 2 billion years old, making it one of the oldest geological formations in the world.

It rains almost every day on Mount Roraima, giving rise to some impressive waterfalls, including Roraima Falls. According to the World Waterfall Database, Roraima Falls consists of four drops in total, with a combined height of 610 metres. Its biggest single drop is 305 metres, and it has an average width of just 23 metres.

Roraima's vital statistics are easily outdone by numerous other waterfalls, in terms of height, width, and sheer volume of water. But the waterfall is certainly one of the most awe-inspiring, for it tumbles over the mountain's sheer sandstone edge like a horse's tail blowing in the breeze.

Mount Roraima was the inspiration for Arthur Conan Doyle's *The Lost World*, published in 1912, and even today it is perfectly easy to imagine an iguanodon or stegosaurus roaming around on its tabletop summit.

EXPLORE ANOTHER ARTHUR CONAN DOYLE MYSTERY AT **239**

306

Enriched with E numbers

When it comes to food, E numbers are bad, and 'enriched with vitamins' is good. That statement needs a little qualification these days, because – at least in the developed world – we are now inclined to be suspicious of any food that is 'enriched' with anything. We value food that is natural and pure and unadulterated. But still we know that vitamins are good for us. And E numbers are bad.

E numbers are European Union codes for substances that can be used as food additives. They were first applied to colouring agents, and the system was later extended to cover a wide range of other substances, from preservatives and antioxidants to flavour enhancers and antibiotics. And some of those things are not only clearly good for us (at the appropriate dose) but also natural.

E 306, for example, is vitamin E (tocopherol). It is an antioxidant, helping to protect cell membranes, playing a role in the immune system, and possibly slowing the progression of dementia. It is found naturally in several foods, sometimes added to fortified foods, and of course is also used in skin-care products, where its antioxidant properties are beneficial.

307

MOUNTAINS, HILLS, AND MOLEHILLS

Garth Hill, a few kilometres up the Taff valley from Cardiff in Wales, is not just a hill – it's a mountain. Yet apparently it was not always so. At the beginning of the twentieth century, English surveyors came to measure Garth Hill and decided it was indeed a mere hill. Determined not to have their local landmark belittled by the English, the locals set to work. The story of how extra rock and earth was piled on top of Garth Hill to raise it above the 1,000-foot mark is told in *The Englishman Who Went Up a Hill But Came Down a Mountain* (written by Christopher Monger and turned into a film of the same name in 1995). Whatever the truth of the story, Garth Hill now measures 307 metres (safely just over the 1,000-foot threshold).

But at what height does a hill become a mountain? In the early twentieth century, the British Ordnance Survey's definition of a mountain was land over 1,000 feet high (hence the need to pile a few more rocks onto Garth Hill). Since then, the figure has shifted around a great deal, but there is in fact no universal definition. The *Oxford English Dictionary* asserts that a mountain is 'impressive or notable' in relation to its surroundings. Perhaps this explains why the Welsh tourist industry emphasises Garth Hill's panoramic views, distinctive shape, steep slopes, and rocky outcrops. Or is it just a case of making a mountain out of a molehill?

DESCEND TO THE COAST IN ANOTHER PART OF WALES AT **213**

308

GAUGING THE CALIBRE

Since the 1950s, the ammunition of choice for deer hunters, competition shooters, and police marksmen has been the .308 Winchester rifle cartridge – so named because the bullet has a diameter of 0.308 inches. It is the same gauge as the 7.62 NATO, also known as the 7.62×51mm cartridge (standard ammunition for military small arms in NATO countries), and the two rounds are pretty much interchangeable.

But 0.308 inches is 7.82 millimetres, so surely the commercial bullets must be a bit bigger than the 7.62mm military ones. How come they are the same gauge? The answer to the puzzle is that it depends on whether you measure across the lands or the grooves. A rifle barrel has helical grooves along its length to impart spin to the bullet, and the bits between the grooves are called lands. Both the commercial .308 and the military 7.62 cartridges are designed for a barrel with a groove diameter of 7.82 millimetres and a land diameter of 7.62 millimetres. They merely follow different naming conventions.

Yes, the terminology of rifle calibres can be pretty confusing. It should come as no surprise, then, to discover that .303 British is a larger gauge than .308 Winchester. It's all a question of lands and grooves.

THE FINAL TRAIN JOURNEY

Perhaps because their country is so large, long-distance travel –
by planes, trains, automobiles, and motorbikes – is a perennial
theme for American singers, film-makers, artists, novelists, and
poets. It provides a fitting hook upon which to hang thoughts
of homecoming, or of escape, or of aimless drifting, or even of
one's own inevitable final journey into death.

Johnny Cash (1932–2003) wrote his fair share of such songs –
and 'Like the 309' was his very last. It appears on the posthumous
2006 album *American V: A Hundred Highways*, which was recorded
just months before he died. It seems likely that the song was
inspired by a derailment on the Cotton Belt line which occurred
not far from Cash's home when he was twelve years old.

Cash's voice has become a frail whisper. But 'Like the 309' is
not really a sad song, even though Cash must have known that his
own death was just a little further along the track.

TRAVEL TO THE END OF ANOTHER LINE AT **246**

310

SHINING A LIGHT FOR GREEK WARRIORS AND DEEP-SPACE PROBES

Greek mythology tells the story of how the navigator Canopus used the stars to steer his ship from Greece to Troy. On board was Menelaus, king of Mycenae, who was in pursuit of his estranged wife, Helen. But it seems Canopus was more interested in what shone in the heavens above him than in the beauty that had launched a thousand ships. One of the brightest stars by which he steered his course now bears his name.

Canopus is 310 light years away from the earth and it used to belong to the constellation Argo-Navis, named after the *Argo*, the ship used by Jason and the Argonauts. But in 1792 French astronomer Nicolas Louis de Lacaille subdivided Argo-Navis into three – Puppis (the poop deck or stern), Vela (the sails), and Carina (the keel) – and Canopus is in the last of these three.

Canopus is the second-brightest star in the sky. Sirius is the brightest, but is very much closer to us (a mere 8.6 light years away), so Canopus is intrinsically much brighter: although its apparent magnitude is less, it has a greater absolute magnitude. It is a giant star, and it seems likely – many billions of years into the future – to become a slowly cooling white dwarf rather than a supernova. In the meantime, Canopus still serves as a guide to navigation. Today, across the 310 light years of time and space, deep-space probes use star-tracking cameras to calculate their position relative to Canopus and other guide stars.

AT **31** THERE ARE SEVERAL FIGURES STARING UP INTO THE HEAVENS

HATEFUL NUMBERS

The Number of the Beast (666) will have to wait for the sequel, but here's a number with similar connotations that is within range. The eleventh letter of the alphabet is K, and three Ks indicate KKK, the Ku Klux Klan. So 311 = three elevens = white supremacy in the USA. Obvious, when you think about it.

There is respectable evidence that 311 is indeed used with that meaning, and it is listed as a hate symbol on the website of the Anti-Defamation League. No wonder the Internet advice columns are awash with concerned American moms asking whether they should worry that their teenage sons have '311' tattooed on their wrists. Maybe 'awash' is overstating it, but we did find one. Just how worried should she be?

It turns out that 311 is also the name of a rock band formed in Nebraska in 1982 and still going strong, who have made it very clear that the use of 311 to refer to the Klan is 'a most unfortunate coincidence and one that is extremely disturbing to us. We would like to state for the record that this is completely at odds with our personal beliefs. We believe the only people worth hating are organized haters like the KKK.' If Mom doesn't like their music, maybe that's just a little worrying for her, but that's all.

312

Utter nonsense, no argument

A few years ago a story appeared in the international press claiming that the average couple has 312 arguments a year. The story came from a so-called study carried out by a British bathroom retailer.

The press release upon which the story was based referred to 'a study of 3,000 adults' but gave no information on how the sample was selected, or the questions asked, or any details of analytical methods. This is not science, it is marketing.

Unsurprisingly, given the source, six out of the top ten argument triggers were related to bathrooms (stubble in the wash-basin, leaving the seat up, not flushing, and so on), and the press release went on to say that 'bathrooms should be a relaxing place where people can unwind after a hard day' before concluding by offering 'solutions to problems' – which were of course available for purchase.

313

Looking out to sea

In March 1774, Captain James Cook dropped anchor at the remote Pacific island of Rapa Nui (Easter Island) in search of water and fresh provisions. Among the small party that went ashore were the botanist Johann Reinhold Forster and the artist William Hodges. They crossed a hill to the far side of the island, where they came across some of the hauntingly beautiful stone figures (*moai*) for which the island has subsequently become famous.

Forster wrote in his journal: 'There we found 7 stone pillars, 4 of which were still standing...These pillars stood on a kind of pedestall or stone elevation: in some places these elevations are made of regularly hewn stones sitting as regularly and as finely as can be done by a Nation even with good tools.' The stone elevations that Forster described are known as *ahu*. 313 of them have been discovered on Easter Island, and they were constructed sometime between 1100 and 1680 CE, by islanders whose tools were probably far from 'good'.

William Hodges later produced an oil painting of the scene, *A View of the Monuments of Easter Island (Rapanui)*. Any twenty-first-century visitor would see much the same view today; some *moai* have fallen or have been deliberately toppled, but many still stand on their original *ahu*, looking out to sea as if they could somehow recall who made them, and why.

LOOK OUT TO SEA AGAIN AT **331**

314

Sophisticated engineering

When billiards was invented in the fifteenth century, any old stick or mallet would do for striking the ball, but not any more. A modern billiards, snooker, or pool cue is a sophisticated piece of equipment, not only beautifully engineered but also beautifully finished, using inlays of contrasting woods and decorative transfers. Some of this improves the player's performance, and some of it is apparently intended to scare off the opposition. The logos and brand names recall motorcycles or shoot-'em-up video games. Cues branded as Harley Davidson, Mayhem, Outlaw, Viper, or Predator are clearly not for wimps.

The Predator 314 cue shaft (manufactured by Predator Cues of Jacksonville, Florida) is now in its second generation, known as the 314^2. It has, they proudly announce, a re-engineered front end, a multi-layered tip, a scratch-resistant ferrule, and a joint insert that is mounted in a solid phenolic core. The ten-piece splicing technique promises 22 per cent extra consistency, with a pure transfer of energy, and it will give you a 35 per cent advantage over a conventional cue. Apparently. It will also set you back several hundred dollars. Why it's called 314 is a bit of a mystery – but nonetheless this is highly engineered sports equipment, backed up by highly engineered marketing.

FOR A LESS MACHO GAME, GO TO **168**

AROUND THE WORLD IN
CONSIDERABLY UNDER 80 DAYS

'You must realise that it is hard to express my feeling now that
the test for which we have been training long and passionately is
at hand...To be the first to enter the cosmos, to engage single-
handed in an unprecedented duel with nature – could anyone
dream of anything greater than that? But immediately after that
I thought of the tremendous responsibility I bore: to be the first to
do what generations of people had dreamed of; to be the first to
pave the way into space for mankind.'

These words (in Russian, of course) were spoken by Yuri
Gagarin, just before he became the first human being to orbit the
earth, on 12 April 1961. Travelling in *Vostok I*, Gagarin reached
a maximum altitude of 315 kilometres above the surface of the
earth. His voyage lasted under two hours, yet it was, as he clearly
realised, a ground-breaking moment for the human race.

Sadly, Gagarin died in March 1968, aged 34, while test-
piloting a MiG-15 fighter jet. And just a year later, the first men
landed on the moon, which would have been impossible without
Gagarin's exceptionally daring first flight beyond the gravitational
pull of the earth.

316

Ambushed by a gospel

Ambush marketing is big business at major sporting events, as brands that have not paid millions to become official sponsors invent new tricks (and employ plenty of old ones) to get their logos in front of the television cameras and bring their products to the attention of spectators. And the organisers of the Olympics, or the World Cup, or the Super Bowl are equally determined to keep those images from the public gaze.

One strange slogan that sometimes appears, especially in the USA, is 'John 3:16'. What sort of big business is this? What is the message? The business is Christianity, and it is a reference to the Bible, St John's Gospel, chapter 3 verse 16, which (in the King James version) reads: 'For God so loved the world, that he gave his only begotten Son, that whosoever believeth in him should not perish, but have everlasting life.' This summary of an entire religion, distilled further into a simple numerical form, has been held up on placards at sporting events since at least 1980 – not only in America but around the world.

The same message can be found outside the sporting arena. If you keep your eyes open in the southern United States, you will see 'John 3:16' printed on T-shirts, shopping bags, drinks cups, and packaging of all sorts.

317

a-b-b-a, a-b-b-a

The Italian poet Francesco Petrarca (1304–1374), known in English as Petrarch, did not invent the sonnet, but he certainly made it his own. He wrote mostly (and prolifically) in Latin, but he is best remembered today for his poems in Italian, in particular for a collection called *Il Canzoniere*. Of the 366 poems, 317 are sonnets. Most of them are addressed to Laura (who may or may not have been a real person), and all but a handful of the 317 are Petrarchan sonnets – not only in the sense that they were written by Petrarch, but also because they adhere to the pattern that has come to be known as the Petrarchan sonnet.

A Petrarchan sonnet is tightly structured, both thematically and formally. Its fourteen lines are divided into an octave or octet (eight lines) and a sestet (six lines), and there is almost always some sort of shift or turn (in Italian, *volta*) at the start of line nine, so that the sestet counters or answers the octave. The rhyme scheme of the octave is *a-b-b-a, a-b-b-a*, and the sestet is typically either *c-d-e-c-d-e* or *c-d-c-d-c-d*.

In the early sixteenth century the sonnet was introduced to England, and to the English language, by Sir Thomas Wyatt. The form was then enthusiastically taken up and adapted by others, including William Shakespeare, who wrote a few of his own (though he used a different rhyme scheme).

Mind you, Italian word endings make it easier to find a rhyme. Could that be why Shakespeare wrote far fewer than 317 sonnets?

FOR MORE ON A-B-B-A, SEE **281**

318

KING OF THE GODS AND THE NIGHT SKY

It is appropriate that the fifth planet from the sun is named after the king of the gods, for it is a giant. Jupiter has a mass of 1.9×10^{27} kg, which is 318 times that of the earth. In fact, its mass is 2.5 times that of all the other planets in our solar system put together.

Like the other outer planets in our solar system (Saturn, Uranus, and Neptune), Jupiter is a gas giant. It consists of about 90 per cent hydrogen and 10 per cent helium, plus traces of water, methane, ammonia, and rock. Astronomers theorise that, if it gained more mass – through the accretion of passing asteroids, for example – Jupiter would experience gravitational compression, resulting in a shrinking but increasingly dense planet. But there simply isn't enough material in the solar system for this tipping point to be reached, so Jupiter looks set to be with us for a few more aeons yet.

Viewed from the earth, Jupiter is not the brightest natural object in the sky: our moon, Venus, and of course the sun easily outshine it. And in terms of mass Jupiter is a pretty puny god compared to the sun – whose mass is a great deal more than 318 times that of the earth. Closer to 333,000 times, in fact.

FOR A MUSICAL JUPITER, COME BACK DOWN TO EARTH AT **41**

BIGGEST IS NOT ALWAYS BEST

Skyscrapers may have been born in Chicago with the Home Insurance Building in 1884, swiftly followed by the Rand McNally Building (which was the first entirely self-supporting steel frame structure), but New York has had more than its fair share of high-rises: the Flatiron (1903), the Singer Tower (1908–1968), the Woolworth Building (1913), 40 Wall Street (aka Trump Towers, 1930), the Empire State Building (1931), and the Twin Towers of the World Trade Center (1970/71–2001). One of the most iconic is the Chrysler Building (1930) at 405 Lexington Avenue. Financed by Walter P. Chrysler (of automobile fame) and designed by William van Alen, it is a superb example of art deco architecture, complete with protruding eagles' heads, massive gargoyles resembling Chrysler radiator caps, and stainless-steel sunburst crown.

At 319 metres tall, the Chrysler Building was, for a brief period, the tallest building in the world. It sneakily beat 40 Wall Street to the top slot by adding a 38-metre spire at the last minute. But just eleven months later, the Empire State Building overtook it, and since then numerous taller buildings have been built – not just in New York but around the world. The Kingdom Tower, in Jeddah, Saudi Arabia, is currently under construction (expected completion date 2019) and will beat the Chrysler Building's 319 metres by a factor of three. No matter. According to New York's Skyscraper Museum, the Chrysler Building is the best loved in that city, and looks likely to remain one of the most instantly recognisable skyscrapers of all time.

GO BACK TO **158** FOR A RATHER SHORTER NEW YORK BUILDING

320

HOW BIG IS THAT SHIP?

Cargo ships, oil tankers, container ships, bulk carriers, and the many other vessels that transport goods across the world can be measured in various ways, based on weight, volume, or length. In general, ships are getting bigger, but there are of course limits, imposed for example by the widths and depths of channels and the capacities of port facilities. The shipping industry keeps tabs on this by means of a classification of vessel sizes, using colourful names such as Handysize, Aframax, and Malaccamax, all the way up to ULCC (ultra-large crude carrier).

One important limitation is the size of the locks in the Panama Canal. Each of the six locks in the canal is 320 metres long. To fit through, the vessel itself needs to be a bit shorter than this, and there are also specifications for beam and draught. If it is just small enough to fit it is referred to as a Panamax ship. Vessels that are too big have to take the long way round via Cape Horn (Capesize), but they might still be able to fit through the Suez Canal (Suezmax).

The Panama Canal is being remodelled, with a series of new locks due to open in 2015. Ships built to fit the new locks are known as New Panamax. The vessels are up to 366 metres long, so they might just squeeze in, but the locks, at 427 metres, are too long to fit in this book.

A PHOENIX FROM THE SNOW

An exceptionally cold environment – the sort that can be found on the steppes of Siberia, or high on the slopes of an Alpine mountain, or at the South Pole – is great for preserving things: woolly mammoths, human bodies, old aeroplanes. But whereas mammoths and human beings cannot (yet) be brought back to life, some old aeroplanes can.

On 4 December 1971, a US Navy Hercules transport plane named *Juliet Delta 321* was delivering supplies for the international Antarctic Glaciological Project when it crashed about 1,360 kilometres from McMurdo Station. No one was injured, but the plane was badly damaged. A salvage operation was deemed to be too expensive, so *Juliet Delta 321* was abandoned to the elements.

The years passed, and in November 1986 a team set out to assess the condition of the wreck. The aeroplane was buried deep in the snow, with just a small section visible. Digging began and continued for a month until the plane was freed from a 10-metre excavation pit. Much to everyone's surprise, it had not deteriorated at all since the crash fifteen years earlier.

The following summer, in November 1987, major repairs were made at the crash site. Working conditions were hazardous: fierce winds, snowstorms, and temperatures of minus 30°C were the norm. But it was these very conditions that had helped to preserve the plane in its snowy grave, and on 10 January 1988 *Juliet Delta 321* took to the skies once again – a phoenix rising not from the ashes but from the snow.

FOR A PLANE THAT NEVER TOOK OFF AGAIN, FLY BACK TO **149**

322

CUNEIFORM TRIPLES

In New York, in the library of the University of Columbia, among the books and the manuscripts, the paper and the vellum, is a lump of clay. It has been there since it was donated by the publisher, collector, and philanthropist G. A. Plimpton in 1936, and it is known as Plimpton 322.

Plimpton 322 is a Babylonian clay tablet dating from about 1800 BCE. It is only a few centimetres across, but to mathematicians its fascination is infinite. Impressed into the clay are fifteen rows of numbers, in four columns. They are in cuneiform script, using the Babylonian base-60 system, and in the 1940s researchers realised that they listed a series of Pythagorean triples – clearly the work of a mathematical genius, well over a thousand years before Pythagoras.

More recent research has come to a rather different conclusion. Plimpton 322 is not the work of a lone and far-sighted genius, but a product of its time and place. The columns of numbers happen to coincide with some modern mathematics, but they were in fact written as a teaching aid for use in school arithmetic classes, designed to help the teacher set a series of assignments concerning the geometry of triangles. As a publisher of educational books, George Plimpton would no doubt have been pleased with this interpretation.

323

Too much sugar and spice?

Throughout much of its history, America's *Saturday Evening Post* has been greatly admired for its covers. No fewer than 323 of these were painted by Norman Rockwell, whose career with the *Post* lasted for 47 years. His first cover, on 20 May 1916, was a humorous picture called 'Mother's Day Off'. His last, on 14 December 1963, was a portrait of John F. Kennedy, who had been assassinated just three weeks earlier.

Rockwell's artwork for the magazine was loved and loathed in equal measure. Many could identify with his pictures of happy families, fun-loving kids, sports heroes, and working folk, seeing their own lives reflected back to them in a palatable and usually light-hearted way. The art world, however, was not so impressed, asserting that, even when Rockwell tackled more serious subjects – for example, civil rights, poverty, and space exploration – his style was too saccharine, too simplistic, to be taken seriously.

But no one can argue that Rockwell's career was not a successful one. He painted the portraits of US presidents Eisenhower, Kennedy, and Nixon, as well as other prominent world figures. And in 1977 he received the Presidential Medal of Freedom, the USA's highest civilian honour, for 'vivid and affectionate portraits of our country'. He died in 1978.

PLENTY MORE SUGAR, BUT NOT SO MUCH SPICE, AT **339**

RAILWAY NUMBERS

If this book had indeed started not with a one-horned beast but on
a train from platform zero at King's Cross station, many numbers
would have flashed past the traveller speeding up the East Coast
Main Line – numbers on trains; numbers on poles, masts, and
gantries; numbers on bridges.

From the very start, the British railway network has needed a
way of uniquely identifying each section of track and every one of
thousands of bridges, tunnels, level crossings, and other features.
Under the system known as Engineer's Line References (ELRs),
the section of the East Coast Main Line from King's Cross to
Shaftholme Junction, a little way north of Doncaster, is ECM1,
and just south of Doncaster station is a road bridge over the
railway bearing the identifying mark ECM1/324.

This is Balby Bridge. There has been a bridge here ever since
the Great Northern Railway was built in the 1850s, and it has seen
more than its share of misfortune. On 9 August 1947, two express
trains collided just south of Balby Bridge, and eighteen people lost
their lives. Then, on 16 March 1951, another fourteen fatalities
resulted from a derailment immediately to the north of the bridge.

Some of the original cast-iron oval plates bearing the number
324 can still be glimpsed from the train as it passes under Balby
Bridge, but those that were accessible from the road have gone
– perhaps taken to add to somebody's collection of railway
memorabilia – and have been replaced by modern plastic
versions, which of course still display the number 324.

VISIT ANOTHER BRIDGE AT **162**

325

PLAY WELL

For any child growing up in the 1960s, a set of Lego bricks was as essential as Meccano, Monopoly, Coppit, or Cribbage for whiling away the long years until computer games and YouTube were invented. In those early days of Lego, all one needed was a box of basic brick-shaped bricks and a bucket-load of imagination to create a pirate ship that sailed across the vast blue ocean of the bedroom carpet, or a turreted castle that towered above the surface of the kitchen table until – all too soon – it was besieged by teatime.

Lego is a contraction of *leg godt* (Danish for 'play well'), and it has been encouraging children and adults to do just that since its invention by toy maker Ole Kirk Christiansen in the 1940s. Lego went through a number of minor design alterations before the Lego brick that we know today was patented in 1958. Yet the interlocking brick has always been its most important feature: easily put together, and just as easily taken apart.

The variety of Lego bricks is now mind-boggling, and every year new sets are introduced: recent additions include 'Batman', 'Superheroes', and 'James Bond 007'. But you can still buy a simple Starter Set of Lego, such as Box 5529, which contains 325 standard bricks in six bright colours and in the simple brick shapes of the original sets. That should be enough for any aspiring pirate captain or king of the castle.

326

From a wedding to a weeping

'Sweete Themmes! runne softly, till I end my song.' The year is 1596. It is a calm, sun-filled day. The meadows are full of daisies and roses, violets and primroses. And nymphs are making bridal crowns from the flowers. Two swans come softly swimming, as white as snow. It is a time of peace and plenty; of a merry London and a glorious England. The day is one of celebration, for a wedding is taking place, and not one, but two, couples are tying the knot. 'Sweete Themmes! runne softly, till I end my song.'

'Sweet Thames, run softly, till I end my song.' The year is 1922. It is winter. The wind crosses the brown land, and the Thames, which on summer nights was clogged with cigarette ends and empty bottles, is now bleak and empty. The nymphs have gone, and there is no sign of the swans. This is not a place for a wedding, but for weeping and the rattling of bones. 'Sweet Thames, run softly, till I end my song.'

1596: the date of Edmund Spenser's 'Prothalamion'. 1922: the date of T. S. Eliot's 'The Waste Land'. Two poems joined by London's river. Separated by 326 years.

TRY CROSSING THE RIVER WITH THE VEHICLE AT **166**

CAMEO APPEARANCES

As Alfred Hitchcock is to *Psycho, Vertigo, Rear Window*, and 36 more of his movies, so the number 327 is to the *Star Wars* films (not to mention the television series, the books, the video games, and the comics). Like the great director in so much of his own work, the number makes a series of unexplained cameo appearances throughout the *Star Wars* franchise.

In the original *Star Wars* film, the *Millennium Falcon* docks in Bay 327 on the Death Star, and in *The Empire Strikes Back* she lands on Platform 327 in Cloud City. Meanwhile, among the assorted spaceships can be found the Rian-327 Airspeeder, the 327-B Assassin-class corvette, and the J-type 327 Nubian Royal Starship. In one of the TV spin-offs Boba Fett adopts the clone trooper serial number 327. Then there's a space colony called Outpost 327…an elite squad of clone troopers known as the 327th Star Corps…a droid called 327-T…

This could take a while. Frankly, you'd be better employed trying to spot the moment when Hitchcock walks across the set in *The 39 Steps*.

328

An iconic sports car

In June 1936 a new car appeared on the racing circuit. It was the 2-litre BMW 328 two-seater sports car, and at its very first race it knocked the socks off all the competition. The event was the International Eifel Race, held that year at the Nürburgring in Germany. At the car's helm was German motorcycle and racing car driver Ernst Henne, who led from the front and achieved an average speed of 101.5 kilometres per hour.

The 328 was manufactured between 1936 and 1939. Its chassis was designed by BMW's chief engineer Fritz Fiedler, and it was stiff yet light – ideal for racing (it had a top speed of 150 kilometres per hour), yet also good-looking and comfortable.

The car enjoyed an impressive racing career before World War Two, coming first in its class in the 1939 24-hour Le Mans race, and winning the RAC rally in the same year. It continued to race for many years after the war. Only 426 were produced, and fewer than 200 are believed still to exist. The 328 retains its appeal in car-collecting circles: in 2013 a heavily restored 1938 model sold at auction for £785,500.

329

AN UNSOLVED CRIME

At 07:13 GMT on Sunday, 23 June 1985, Air India flight 182, en route from Toronto to Delhi via London, exploded in mid-air and crashed into the Atlantic Ocean off the south-west coast of Ireland. All those on board were killed.

The bombing took place against a background of serious unrest and massive bloodshed in India. In June the previous year hundreds of Sikhs had been massacred at the Golden Temple in Amritsar, in October Prime Minister Indira Gandhi had been assassinated, and the rioting that followed resulted in thousands of deaths across the country.

It quickly became clear that the bomb had originated in Vancouver. Canadian investigators had a great deal of evidence pointing towards Sikh extremists based in British Columbia, and linking the bombing of Air India flight 182 to another bomb that had exploded at Tokyo airport just an hour earlier. And yet the case dragged on for decades and the crime remains unsolved. The alleged mastermind was killed in India in 1992. One Canadian resident pleaded guilty to a single count of manslaughter in 2003 and was later also convicted of perjury. And in March 2005, almost 20 years after the bombing, Canada's longest criminal trial ended with the acquittal of two men on 329 counts of murder.

FOR SOMETHING ON THE BACKGROUND TO THIS EVENT, SEE **352**

330

Mind your pints and quarts

In his *History of the Worthies of England* (published in 1662), Thomas Fuller tells the story of the Reverend Alexander Nowell, Dean of St Paul's in the reign of Elizabeth I, who went fishing one day and accidentally left a bottle of ale in the long grass on the riverbank. And then 'he found it some days after, no bottle, but a gun, such the sound at the opening thereof: and this is believed (casualty is mother of more inventions than industry) the original of bottled-ale in England.'

Or so the story goes. It seems more likely that brewers were already experimenting with secondary fermentation in the bottle before Dr Nowell was surprised by the pop of a cork. Bottled beer was certainly widely available – though still something of a novelty – by the time Samuel Pepys recorded drinking 'several bottles of Hull ale' in London one November evening in 1660.

Pepys was presumably drinking pints or quarts, since the millilitre had yet to be invented. But anyone drinking beer from a bottle or a can these days is more likely to encounter it in units of 330 millilitres. Across most of the world, carbonated soft drinks also come in cans of that size. Why 330 millilitres? Perhaps because it's close to a third of a litre. Perhaps because it's based on the size of can that was used for peas in 1930s America. Whatever the explanation, it is unlikely to involve an absent-minded dean and a fishing expedition.

331

Lighting the way

If you happened to be sailing along the Atlantic coast near Monte Hermosa, Argentina, as night fell on 1 January 1906, you would have seen something entirely new. On this day, the Recalada a Bahía Blanca Lighthouse was lit for the very first time. The lighthouse is constructed of cast iron, in the shape of an octagonal pyramidal tower, and it's painted in alternating bands of red and white.

These days, the light is produced by an Automatic Identification System (AIS) beacon which emits a flash of light every nine seconds, with a range of 28 nautical miles. No doubt Ferdinand Magellan, who sailed past the Bahía Blanca on the first-known circumnavigation of the earth some 300 years earlier, would have appreciated its reassuring light.

There are 331 steps to the top of the Recalada a Bahía Blanca Lighthouse. It is the tallest lighthouse in the southern hemisphere, at 67 metres. The tallest in the world is reputed to be the Jeddah Light in Jeddah, Saudi Arabia, which, at 133 metres, is almost exactly twice as tall.

SURPRISINGLY ENOUGH, THERE ARE THREE MORE STEPS AT **334**

A SMART PHONE

Most telephones in daily use today no longer have buttons, let alone dials. Smartphones have largely taken over from 'old-fashioned' mobile phones, and perhaps the even more old-fashioned immobile telephone may not be with us for much longer.

Telephone model no. 332 belongs to a different era. The 332 was introduced by the British Post Office in 1937. Like its predecessors the 162 and 232, it had a combined mouthpiece and receiver, but unlike them it had the bell built in to the instrument rather than housed in a separate box. It was based on a design by Ericsson of Sweden that had been in use there from 1932. In spite of fears (expressed in an article written in 1938) that there was 'a serious disadvantage in combining the bell with the telephone in residences where the bell has to be heard in all parts of the house', this new table telephone proved very popular, and remained the standard British model until 1959.

It has been remarked that the 332 Bakelite telephone has echoes of cubism in its boxy look and sharp edges, and even today many of the phone symbols used on signs and notices bear a strong resemblance to it. The 332 was undoubtedly a smart instrument – perhaps best described as the smart phone of its day.

WHO'S LISTENING IN AT **192**?

333

Geese at sunset

Near the south-east corner of Ireland is the shallow inlet of Wexford Harbour, and sheltering its northern entrance is a sand-dune system, partly planted with coniferous forest. This is the Raven Point nature reserve. It has important plants, flocks of wading birds, sometimes nesting terns – and geese.

Half the world population of Greenland white-fronted geese (*Anser albifrons flavirostris*) spend the winter in Ireland, the majority in Wexford. By day up to 10,000 geese feed on grassland here, but each evening they fly out to the safety of the sandbanks off the Raven Point to roost. Their daily commute takes them over the dunes, and on a winter evening massed ranks of geese can be seen flying low overhead against a crimson sunset.

The Convention on Wetlands of International Importance, better known as the Ramsar Convention, was signed by an initial 21 nations in the Iranian city of Ramsar in 1971. It is the only intergovernmental treaty to concentrate on a particular ecosystem, committing signatory countries to 'the conservation and wise use' of the lakes and rivers, swamps and marshes, bogs and fens, estuaries and deltas, mangroves and coral reefs, rice paddies, reservoirs, and shallow seas of the world.

Today 168 countries have signed the convention. Between them they have designated 2,181 Ramsar sites, of which Raven Point is number 333.

CHECK **191** FOR ANOTHER ENVIRONMENTAL TREATY

334

A new name for an old tower

In June 2012, Queen Elizabeth II marked 60 years on the throne with a church service in Westminster Abbey, a concert at Buckingham Palace, a visit to the Epsom Derby, and a very soggy pageant on the River Thames. In her honour, the clock tower in the Palace of Westminster was renamed the Elizabeth Tower. The tower was designed by Sir Charles Barry (1795–1860) and the foundation stone was laid on 28 September 1843, but work was not completed until 1859.

Residents of the UK (but not visitors from overseas) can climb the tower – provided they get advance permission through their own Member of Parliament. There are impressive views across London from the top, as well as views of the four clock faces (each 7 metres in diameter), and of course Big Ben himself: Big Ben is not, and has never been, the name of the tower, but is the nickname of the massive bell, weighing over 13,000 kilograms, that rings out across the city every hour.

There is no lift inside the Elizabeth Tower, so the way to the top involves a climb up 334 small, worn steps that are set in a tight, windowless spiral. For reasons unknown, the 182nd step, counting from the bottom up, is carved with its own number. But don't linger there too long: there are still 152 to go.

HEAD DOWNSTREAM TO ANOTHER LONDON LANDMARK AT **68**

335

A STAR IS BORN?

SDC335.579-0.292 – known to its friends as Spitzer Dark Cloud 335 – is the catchy name of the largest star-forming core ever discovered in the Milky Way. Images from NASA's Spitzer space telescope (launched in 2003) first hinted at its existence, and subsequent data from the Herschel telescope on the island of La Palma, together with high-resolution images from the ALMA telescope array in Chile's Atacama Desert, provided the first in-depth look at what was going on in this enormous cloud of gas and dust some 10,000 light years away from earth.

The outer regions of the cloud have a filamentary structure, with gas moving along these filaments, feeding the formation of stars in the centre. The centre itself has two areas of higher density. One of these will probably be the birthplace of a cluster of several hundred stars, resembling the star cluster which can currently be seen at the heart of the Orion Nebula. The other high-density area is massive, and researchers believe that it will ultimately form just one star with a mass many times that of our own sun.

The discovery of Spitzer Dark Cloud 335 has helped enormously in advancing astronomers' understanding of how stars form. Tracking the early stages of the process is still a major challenge, however, and the internal workings of this proto-stellar cloud remain virtually unknown.

336

WHO'S COUNTING THE DIMPLES?

The dimpled chin looks rugged on American actors John Travolta and Kirk Douglas, and beguiling on Sandra Bullock. Dimpled cheeks look cute on any baby, American or otherwise. And the dimpled golf ball is an absolute necessity for anyone striding around the golf links with a bag full of sticks, in search of a collection of holes into which to hit those dimpled balls.

Golf balls were not always dimpled. In the fourteenth century they were made of solid wood (beech or box). These were superseded by 'featheries', which were made of goose feathers (the recommended quantity was about enough to fill a top hat to the brim), which were boiled, softened, cooled, and sewn into a small leather pouch. In 1845 completely smooth balls started to be made using gutta-percha – the gum of the sapodilla tree. It was soon discovered, however, that these balls travelled further, and could be more easily controlled, if they were scuffed up and given a few extra dents.

In 1905 the first dimpled golf ball was manufactured (by Englishman William Taylor), and by 1921 all major tournaments required the use of dimpled balls of a standard weight (no more than 45.93 grams) and size (diameter no larger than 42.67 millimetres). The dimples are evenly distributed over the surface of the golf ball. And although the number of dimples can vary, the most common American ones have 336 of them. That's six more than the usual British ones – but hey, who's counting?

COUNT DIMPLES AGAIN AT **275**?

ACCOUNTING FOR THE DEAD

Many of the numbers associated with the sinking of RMS *Titanic* on the night of 14/15 April 1912 are hard to pin down. The number of people on board is variously given as between 2,201 and 2,224, and both the number rescued (706–711) and the number lost (1,490–1,517) are uncertain. But one figure that is clear is the number of bodies recovered: 337.

The rescue of passengers and crew from the freezing waters of the North Atlantic is a well-known part of the *Titanic* story, but the fate of those who perished has received less attention. RMS *Carpathia*, the ship that picked up most of the survivors, found three people dead in a lifeboat, and a fourth passenger succumbed shortly after being rescued. But the task of searching for fatalities fell mainly to the cable ship *Mackay-Bennett*, which was chartered for that purpose. In the days following the disaster, *Mackay-Bennett* and a handful of other ships retrieved 327 bodies. Over the next few weeks six further corpses were found, including three discovered in a collapsible lifeboat by *Titanic*'s sister ship *Olympic*.

Overall, then, 337 bodies were retrieved – less than a quarter of those who had died. Many were buried at sea, largely because Canada forbade the landing of a corpse unless it was embalmed, and the *Mackay-Bennett* did not have sufficient supplies of embalming fluid. Just 209 of the dead were taken to Nova Scotia, where some were claimed by their relatives. But no one came for 159 of the victims, and they now lie in the Halifax cemeteries of Fairview Lawn, Mount Olivet, and Baron de Hirsch.

THERE IS A HAPPIER ATLANTIC CROSSING AT **234**

338

A godly place for wildlife

The purpose of UNESCO's World Heritage List is to identify,
protect, and preserve the world's cultural and natural heritage.
This ambition is embodied in the 1972 Convention concerning
the Protection of the World Cultural and Natural Heritage. At the
time of writing, there are 981 sites on UNESCO's list, and 30 of
them are in India.

Manas Wildlife Sanctuary, in Assam, north-east India,
became Site number 338 in 1985. Named after the Hindu
goddess Manasa, the sanctuary covers an area of 39,100 hectares
in the foothills of the Outer Himalayas. It deserves its place on
UNESCO's list because its exceptionally diverse range of habitats
– alluvial grasslands, forested hills, and tropical evergreen forests
– supports an equally diverse fauna, including a number of species
that are IUCN Red Listed: the Asian elephant (*Elephas maximus*),
Indian rhinoceros (*Rhinoceros unicornis*), kalij pheasant (*Lophura
leucomelanos*), and sloth bear (*Ursus ursinus*). The sanctuary also
forms the core of an extensive tiger reserve.

Inclusion on the World Heritage List is not guaranteed to be
permanent. So far, two sites (Germany's Dresden Elbe Valley and
Oman's Arabian Oryx Sanctuary) have been delisted because
they failed to maintain UNESCO's strict criteria. For now,
Site number 338 is not under threat, although the future of its
Red-Listed species is still far from secure.

339

A CARIBBEAN ODDITY

The Caribbean island of Barbados is a bit of an oddity. In a region in which every other island changed hands at least once (and in some cases several times) over the centuries of colonial rule, Barbados was the only one to remain under the same colonial power for the entire time. For a period of 339 years, from 1627 until 1966, Barbados was a British colony.

After the island had apparently been cleared of its indigenous population by the Spanish and Portuguese in the sixteenth century, a permanent English settlement was established there in February 1627. Barbados was one of the earliest colonies in the New World, and quickly became one of the most important, for several decades earning more from its trade than all other English colonies combined. From the 1640s the Barbadian economy was based on sugar-cane cultivation, and thousands of slaves were imported from West Africa to work on the plantations. There were slave rebellions in 1675 and 1816, and slavery was eventually abolished in 1834. But sugar continued to be the mainstay of the economy throughout the island's 339-year colonial history – and it is only since Barbados gained its independence on 30 November 1966 that it has been supplanted by other industries, notably tourism.

Barbados is also a Caribbean oddity in that it is not actually in the Caribbean Sea. It is the easternmost of the West Indies, lying some 160 kilometres east of the Windward Islands chain, geologically distinct, and surrounded entirely by the Atlantic Ocean.

ALL THAT SUGAR WILL NEED WEIGHING – SEE **113**

340

A WALK ON THE WILD SIDE

'Climb the mountains and get their good tidings. Nature's peace will flow into you as sunshine flows into trees. The winds will blow their own freshness into you, and the storms their energy, while cares will drop away from you like the leaves of autumn.'

For many people, this sentiment rings as true today as it did over a hundred years ago when it appeared in John Muir's *Our National Parks* (1901). Muir (1838–1914) was born in Scotland and emigrated to the USA with his family when he was eleven. He was a prolific writer and he worked tirelessly to draw attention to the destruction of the country's wilderness through farming, deforestation, and the damming of rivers. He was also instrumental in the establishment of Yosemite National Park in 1890, and the Sierra Club two years later.

John Muir was a prodigious walker. He thought nothing of tramping over 1,600 kilometres from Indianapolis to Florida, or through the Yosemite wilderness, with virtually no equipment. Shortly after his death, work began on the construction of the John Muir Trail. The trail starts in Yosemite National Park and finishes at Mount Whitney. It is 340 kilometres long, give or take the odd stride here and there, and it encompasses numerous peaks, lakes, and canyons as it wends its way through some of the USA's most impressive wilderness. Today's trail walkers would surely concur with John Muir that 'the world is big and I want to have a good look at it before it gets dark'.

AMBLE BACK TO **72** FOR A GOOD WALK SPOILED

341

A GLASS OF SHERRY AND A VERSE OR TWO

In 2009, Carol Ann Duffy became the UK's first female Poet Laureate, 341 years after John Dryden's appointment as the first official laureate in 1668. Duffy took over from Andrew Motion, beating Benjamin Zephaniah, Roger McGough, Simon Armitage, and Jackie Kay in the running for the honorary post, and during her ten-year tenure she is expected to write verse that celebrates important national events.

Duffy has commented that she took on the position in recognition of the great women poets of the present century. And there have certainly been many female poets – among them Stevie Smith, Christina Rossetti, Adrienne Rich, and Elizabeth Barrett Browning – who never got a look-in during the 341 years since Dryden was appointed.

Duffy receives an honorarium of a few thousand pounds, which she donates to the Poetry Society to fund a prize for the best collection of the year. She is also rewarded with a payment of a 'butt of sack' – in modern terms, about 600 bottles of sherry. In an interview with the *Guardian* on 1 May 2009, she commented that she likes hers dry.

ANOTHER POET, WHO WAS NEVER LAUREATE, CAN BE FOUND AT **54**

342

A proper bottle

Forget the giant plastic ones, the upside-down ones that stand on their lids, and the squeezable ones with flip-up or twist-open tops. And don't even think about the awkward little sachets that spill their contents when you try to tear them open, or the abomination that is Dip and Squeeze® (yes, that's a registered trademark). The only proper way to enjoy Heinz Tomato Ketchup is out of an octagonal glass bottle with a twist-off metal cap.

Henry Heinz first served up his ketchup in 1876, seven years after the company was founded, and the familiar – sorry, the iconic – glass bottle appeared in 1890. Packaging technology has moved on, generating a range of plastic alternatives, but the old – sorry, the classic – glass bottle lives on. They tried to retire it in the 1990s, but howls of protests led to a comeback. In America today the old-fashioned – sorry, the vintage – bottle is seen mainly in restaurants, while domestic fridges are stocked with various plastic versions, but in Europe the proper – yes, the proper – bottle is still widely available, sold for domestic as well as catering use.

The traditional American Heinz Tomato Ketchup bottle holds 14 ounces (397 grams) of the red stuff, but the European equivalent contains a more modest (and for the purposes of this book more suitable) 342 grams.

Never mind what speed the ketchup comes out of the bottle. The bottle should be an octagonal glass one. Take your pick between the larger American version and the 342-gram European one. And choose your own adjective.

FOR SOMETHING ELSE THAT IS KETCHUP RED, SEE **186**

343

Adventurous cats and bulging sacks

Cats have nine lives, and they need so many because they have more than their fair share of adventures and misadventures. One pussy cat went to London to look at the Queen; another sailed over the horizon in a beautiful pea-green boat. Little Johnny Flynn dropped one down a well (and it was just as well that Tommy Stout was on hand to effect a rescue). One particularly lucky cat enjoyed a moonlit night with a cow, a laughing dog, a fiddle, and assorted cutlery and crockery.

Cats also star in the popular riddle that begins 'As I was going to St Ives, I met a man with seven wives...' And pedants can ponder to their hearts' content upon the question of 'How many were going to St Ives?' No matter: regardless of whether they were travelling towards the Cornish town or away from it, the number of cats remains the same – 343.

Even for the most committed cat lover, that is an awful lot of feline friends. And the figure of 343 doesn't even take account of the kits, for each cat had seven of them. The sacks must have been well and truly bulging.

344

FROM A POW CAMP TO A MUSEUM

During World War Two, the small town of Łambinowice (Lamsdorf) in Poland was the location of a prisoner-of-war camp. It was known as Stalag-344 (Stalag VIII-B prior to 1943) and it was one of the largest POW camps for Allied servicemen.

In total, it is estimated that more than 100,000 prisoners passed through the camp. Yet, strangely, it was renowned for its hospital – which housed operating theatres, X-ray facilities, and wards big enough to accommodate more than 100 patients. Although the hospital was controlled by the *Oberst Arzt* (Colonel Doctor), the staff were all prisoners.

At the end of the war, once the Russian army had advanced into Germany, many of the prisoners were marched westwards, in what has become known as the Death March. Conditions were so bad that many men died of exhaustion. Some of those who survived managed to walk far enough to be met, and liberated, by the Americans. But those who walked into the Soviet-occupied areas were not so lucky, for they were held for several more months, before eventually being freed at the end of 1945.

Stalag-344 is long gone, but its buildings now house one half of the Central Museum of Prisoners of War (the other half is in Opele, some 40 kilometres away), and its collections and exhibitions provide a vivid insight into Nazi-occupied Poland and the experiences of so many prisoners.

MAKE AN ESCAPE ATTEMPT AT **358**

WITH APOLOGIES TO W. S. GILBERT

This book is packed with information vegetable, animal, and mineral. At least some of the kings (and queens) of England are featured, as are several fights historical, and there are occasional references to the scientific names of beings animalculous. Mythic history is covered, too – not to mention crimes and peculiarities – and although there is no specific discussion of Raphael, Gerrit Dou, or Johann Zoffany, there is plenty of art. And music (fugues, airs, and dins). Washing bills as such do not appear, but Babylonic cuneiform is touched upon here and there. Rifles, sorties and surprises, modern gunnery (though not so many nunneries) – it's all here, along with a good sprinkling of infernal nonsense.

And although matters mathematical are covered rather skimpily, with not a whole lot o' news about binomial theorem, there is space for one or two cheerful facts about the square of the hypotenuse. The Pythagorean theorem, named after – and possibly devised by – the Greek mathematician Pythagoras of Samos (*c.*575–490 BCE), states that in a triangle in which one of the corners is a right angle, the square on the hypotenuse (the longest side, the one opposite the right angle) is equal to the sum of the squares on the other two sides. The smallest possible Pythagorean triangle based on integers (whole numbers) has sides of 3, 4, and 5 units in length, and as a result it is sometimes described as a 3-4-5 triangle.

(Apologies also to Pythagoras. And Euclid.)

PERFORM *THE PIRATES OF PENZANCE* AT **218**

346

Metres for old rope

In the Napoleonic Wars, Britain needed warships, and warships needed rope. Nelson's flagship HMS *Victory* would have required over 50 kilometres of it, for standing rigging, running rigging, and a host of other uses. And the longer the bits of rope, the better. So rope was made in a ropewalk, and the one at the naval dockyard at Chatham in Kent was long enough to make a good cable-length or two. The brick-built ropewalk building dates from the early 1790s. It still operates commercially, as well as being a tourist attraction, and internally it is 346 metres from end to end.

The rope-making process starts with hemp, which in *Victory*'s day would have been imported from Russia. The hemp fibres are hatchelled (teased out and straightened), then spun (in one direction) to form yarn, which is tarred and then twisted together (in the opposite direction) to form strands. The strands are laid out along the length of the ropewalk, drawn out and then closed (twisted together, reversing the direction of twist once again) to form a rope. This involves machinery that travels from one end of the ropewalk to the other as it twists the strands together. Some of the length of the strands is taken up in the twist, so a ropewalk of 346 metres would be capable of producing about 300 metres of best-quality rope for His Majesty's Navy.

MORE DEFENCES AGAINST NAPOLEON AT **156**

347

A PLATONIC FOOTNOTE

The British philosopher A. N. Whitehead famously described the European philosophical tradition as 'a series of footnotes to Plato'. There clearly isn't space here to discuss all the finer points of Plato's philosophy, but there is just about room for a footnote on his life, which ended in 347 BCE – and about which rather little is known for certain.

Plato, born somewhere between 428 and 423 BCE (probably), was actually named Aristocles (possibly). He is believed to have been nicknamed Plato (*platon* means 'broad') because of the breadth of his shoulders (he may – or may not – have been a wrestler in his youth), or possibly for the width of his forehead, or maybe with reference to the expansiveness of his eloquence.

Plato was a dedicated disciple of Socrates, and after the death of Socrates he probably travelled widely (for an unknown number of years), during which time he may (perhaps) have written some of his philosophical works on the nature of knowledge, belief, and (un)certainty. He then returned to Athens, where in around 385 BCE (the date is uncertain) he founded a school of learning known as the Academy. The origin of the word 'academy' is unclear – it may have been a place name, or the school may have been named after someone called Akademos, or Academus, or perhaps Hecademus.

Plato died in his sleep, or perhaps at a wedding feast. But he certainly died in the year 347 BCE. Maybe.

IF SOMETHING NOT SO PLATONIC IS MORE TO YOUR TASTE, TRY **69**

A RED ROCK AT THE HEART OF AUSTRALIA

Uluru, the huge and remarkably homogeneous sandstone inselberg at Australia's geographical heart, rises 348 metres above the surrounding desert plain. A climb to the top is a dangerous undertaking, for it is very steep and often slippery. Many people suffer heat exhaustion or panic and have to be rescued, and more than 30 have died in the attempt. But there is another reason not to climb. Uluru is a sacred site for its traditional Aboriginal owners, the Anangu, and trampling up its sides is a disrespectful activity.

Uluru's caves, cliffs, and fissures bear drawings and paintings that relate numerous stories of the Anangu ancestors and the Dreamtime; indeed, the area has been settled in some shape or form for well over 10,000 years. Yet the first sight of Uluru by a non-native person was not until October 1872, when the explorer Ernest Giles saw it from a distance. The following year, the surveyor William Gosse named it Ayers Rock, in honour of Sir Henry Ayers, the Chief Secretary of South Australia at the time. The official name today is Uluru/Ayers Rock. But whatever the name, at the start or end of the day the rock glows red in the heart of Australia.

349

A TIE-BREAKER

In the late 1960s and early 1970s, changes were afoot in Sweden. No sooner had they made everyone switch from driving on the left to driving on the right (3 September 1967) than they set about reforming the parliament, scrapping the old two-chamber system in favour of a unicameral body. The first elections to the new Swedish parliament (Sveriges Riksdag) were held in September 1970, and the parliament was formally opened in January 1971.

The new Riksdag had 350 members. But in the 1973 general election the centre-right and left-wing groups each won 175 seats, resulting in what became known as the 'lottery Riksdag', in which the results of many votes were decided by drawing lots.

Why did they not realise that this was an inherent problem with an even number? It has been suggested that a left-wing alliance of one sort or another had been comfortably in power in Sweden for so long that they failed even to consider the possibility of a tie. Be that as it may, the experience of the lottery Riksdag was enough to prompt a change in the rules, and since 1976 the Riksdag has had 349 members.

FOR ANOTHER GATHERING OF POLITICIANS (AMONG OTHERS) SEE **103**

350

An adaptive strategy

A female grey seal (*Halichoerus grypus*) gives birth once a year. On the European side of the Atlantic it generally happens between September and November; in America it's a couple of months later. When the time comes, large numbers of female seals haul out onto the beaches of their traditional breeding colonies, where the males are waiting. Each female spends three weeks ashore, and in that time she gives birth, suckles the pup, comes into oestrus, mates, and then heads back to sea, leaving the abruptly weaned pup to fend for itself.

Mating takes place just two weeks after the female has given birth, and next year's pup will be born at the same time as this year's, resulting in a gestation period of (on average) 350 days. But it only takes about eight months for the embryo to develop, so grey seals (like all other seals and sea lions, and a few other mammals) follow a strategy of delayed implantation. The fertilised egg does not immediately implant in the uterus, but spends the first several weeks in a state of dormancy.

Delayed implantation is an adaptation to ensure an annual reproductive routine no matter what the actual time taken for embryonic development. Given that grey seals do all their breeding – giving birth, suckling, mating – in one short period on shore each year, they need to delay things a bit, and 350 days is just about right.

AT **40** THERE'S A DELAY OF A DIFFERENT KIND

351

Trumpets and traffic jams

George Frideric Handel's music is catalogued in the Händel-Werke-Verzeichnis (HWV), published between 1978 and 1986, and each composition is assigned a number. HWV 351 is the ever-popular *Music for the Royal Fireworks*. In April 1749, when the piece was first rehearsed, in public, at the Vauxhall Gardens in London, a crowd of more than 12,000 turned up, blocking the surrounding roads and causing traffic chaos for several hours.

Handel (1685–1759) had been commissioned to provide suitably celebratory music to mark the signing of the Treaty of Aix-La-Chapelle at the end of the War of the Austrian Succession, which had involved most of the powers of Europe, including Britain. He wanted to create something that could be played out of doors, and notwithstanding the traffic chaos of that first public rehearsal in Vauxhall Gardens, the work was a great success, receiving its first, rather less chaotic, official performance at Green Park a few days later – although by all accounts it rained and the fireworks were a bit of a damp squib.

Handel originally wanted the *Music for the Royal Fireworks* to be on the grandest of scales – with no fewer than sixteen trumpets and sixteen horns – but in the end he had to tone things down a bit, settling for a mere nine of each. However, the cacophonous traffic jam at the first public rehearsal must have exceeded all his expectations as far as decibels were concerned.

DID YOU GET STUCK IN THE TRAFFIC JAM AT **223**?

DEMOCRACY SUSPENDED

On 26 June 1975, India's president, Fakhruddin Ali Ahmed, was asked by Prime Minister Indira Gandhi to declare a national emergency. India had just suffered a severe drought, its economy was struggling, and morale was low following the war with Pakistan. Amid strikes, demonstrations, and disorder in the cabinet, the PM feared that the country was heading towards chaos.

The national emergency was declared under Article 352 of India's constitution, which provides for the declaration of such an emergency on three possible grounds – war, external aggression, or internal disturbance – and it was the last of these that Gandhi invoked. The state of emergency gave the PM the right to suspend elections and to order a massive crackdown on civil liberties. The police were brought in, and some protesters and strike leaders were imprisoned; others went into hiding or fled the country. Gandhi herself described the state of emergency as bringing democracy 'to a grinding halt'. It lasted for 21 months until 21 March 1977, at which point Gandhi called for elections to be held once more, and all political prisoners were released. The return to democracy was seen as paramount.

Article 352 had been invoked twice before (during the 1962–1968 India–China War, and again during the Indo-Pakistan war of the early 1970s). Under the 1978 44th Amendment to the Indian constitution 'internal disturbance' was changed to 'armed rebellion', but Article 352 remains in place, although unused since 1977.

THERE'S ANOTHER CONSTITUTIONAL CRISIS AT **363**

353

THE SECOND PEARL HARBOR DISASTER

Landing Ship, Tank (LST) is the designation for those US naval vessels that supported amphibious operations during World War Two. Sometimes irreverently nicknamed 'Large Slow Targets' by their crew, they were capable of carrying a lot of soldiers, as well as vehicles and other cargo, directly onto shore.

On 21 May 1944, at Pearl Harbor US Naval Base in Hawaii, LST-353 exploded while unloading heavy ammunition at West Loch. The explosion ignited gasoline stored in drums on neighbouring ships, and very soon several other LSTs were ablaze amid clouds of billowing black smoke. Two more violent explosions soon followed, and men were blown overboard or leapt into the water to try to escape the flames. In total, 163 died, 396 were injured, and six LSTs, including LST-353, sank.

It is not known for sure what caused the initial explosion. Whatever the origin, there was a press blackout immediately after the disaster; survivors and eyewitnesses were not allowed to write about the incident in letters home, and it was classified as top secret until 1960.

In comparison to the Japanese attack on Pearl Harbor in December 1941, this second disaster is still comparatively unknown. It was not until the 1990s that the first memorial was unveiled, on the shore of West Loch. And it was not until the following decade, some sixty years after the event, that the gravestones of unidentified victims were altered from simply stating 'unknown' to 'Unknown, West Loch Disaster, May 21, 1944'.

FLOAT BACK TO **170** FOR ANOTHER BOAT WITH A LARGE CAPACITY

354

COPIES OF A COPY

In the year 354 CE, a wealthy inhabitant of Rome named Valentinus received a useful gift. It was a book, a compendium of practical information for the Roman who had everything, and it was a beautiful object, displaying the work of the foremost calligrapher of the day, Furius Dionysius Filocalus, along with several full-page illustrations. It included an almanac or calendar for the year 354, listing important events, holidays, anniversaries, astrological phenomena, and lots of other useful information.

Valentinus' book is generally called the Calendar of 354 or the Chronography of 354, but it is also referred to as the Filocalian or Philocalian Calendar. Valentinus was a Christian, and the book is notable for containing one of the earliest references to 25 December as a feast day celebrating the birth of Christ. It is also a uniquely valuable record of life in fourth-century Rome.

Unfortunately, the original Calendar of 354 does not survive. Nor does the illustrated copy that was made in the ninth century. Today, the details of this important manuscript are known almost entirely from a motley collection of Renaissance copies of a copy, none of which, on its own, contains a full representation of the original.

PUT PEN TO PAPER AGAIN AT **214**

355

SAVING LUCILLE

The Gibson ES-355 has been a favourite instrument for many guitarists, among them blues maestro B. B. King, who likes to tell the story of how one particular model of the ES-355 came to be named 'Lucille'.

In the winter of 1949, a fire broke out at a dance hall in the town of Twist, Arizona, where King was playing. A kerosene-filled barrel, which was being used to heat the hall, was knocked over, spreading fuel across the floor. The flames spread quickly, and the building was evacuated, with King among those who escaped. Realising that he had left his guitar – at that time he was playing a Gibson L-30 – inside, King rushed back into the blazing building to rescue it.

He later discovered that the barrel had been knocked over by two men who were fighting over a woman named Lucille. From then on, King has named every guitar that he has ever owned 'Lucille', and he wrote a song of the same name, to provide a permanent reminder never again to do anything as stupid as run into a burning building – or fight over a woman.

In 1980 the Gibson Guitar Corporation produced a number of ES-355 guitars with the name 'Lucille' on the headstock. Although King has played many Gibson guitars (including the L-30 which he had rescued from the flames back in 1949), he has a particular fondness for the ES-355, and, of course, for 'Lucille' – both the guitar and the song.

RUSH BACK TO **146** FOR ANOTHER BURNING BUILDING

356

THE DEATH ZONE

It is commonly stated that mountaineers refer to altitudes above 8,000 metres as the death zone, because above that altitude atmospheric pressure is below the 356-millibar threshold – the lowest that human physiology can cope with.

The term 'death zone' belongs to sensationalist books and films rather than to mountaineering, but it is true that mountains over 8,000 metres – of which there are fourteen in the world, all in the Himalayas – present a major challenge. It is also true that the deleterious effects of altitude on the human body are largely due to hypoxia (shortage of oxygen) caused by reduced atmospheric pressure. But where does 356 millibars come from?

Is there a link between 356 millibars and 8,000 metres? Standard atmospheric pressure at sea level is 1013.25 millibars, and it decreases with altitude until at about 8,000 metres it is likely to be around 350–400 millibars – but the actual value depends on temperature and humidity as well as altitude.

Is 356 millibars the pressure below which we cannot survive? It depends on who you are, of course. Even a slight reduction in pressure causes altitude sickness in some people, while others live all their lives in the rarefied atmosphere of La Rinconada, Peru (5,100 metres above sea level), and many people have survived for long periods at much higher altitudes and much lower pressures.

It turns out that 356 millibars is linked neither to a specific altitude nor to specific physiological effects. In natural systems, you cannot rely on precise numbers to reflect an untidy reality.

THERE IS AN UNUSUALLY PRECISE BIOLOGICAL NUMBER AT **302**

GO AHEAD, MAKE MY DAY

Devotees of spicy food may have come across 357 Mad Dog chilli sauce, made by the Ashley Food Company of Sudbury, Massachusetts. The connotations of 'Mad Dog' are clear enough, but why 357? The number refers to the fact that the stuff measures 357,000 on the Scoville scale, a system for measuring how hot and spicy a food is. The scale (also referred to as the Scoville organoleptic test) was devised in 1912 by the American pharmacist Wilbur L. Scoville (1865–1942). It specifies by how much a product needs to be diluted in sugar water before the heat is undetectable by taste. The heat of a chilli pepper comes from a chemical called capsaicin, which in its pure state measures about 16 million Scoville units. The very hottest peppers come in at a little over a million, and a typical chilli sauce could be anywhere between 500 and 10,000.

The manufacturers of hot sauces compete to produce the hottest, and at the outer margins of this macho (and for the most part American) market are some products that are not foodstuffs at all, but collectors' items, frequently advertised with quotations from Clint Eastwood's *Dirty Harry*. If 357 Mad Dog sounds a bit much, you should definitely stay well clear of Mad Dog's Revenge, After Death, Anal Angst, or Blair's 16 million (all readily available on both sides of the Atlantic), which have Scoville units measured in the millions. You have been warned.

FOR MORE MACHO MARKETING, TRY **314**

NO GREAT ESCAPE

Mention *The Great Escape*, and most people instantly think of Steve McQueen, a motorbike (a TT Special 650 Triumph, disguised as a wartime BMW, to be exact), and a seemingly impenetrable and permanently guarded perimeter fence around POW camp Stalag Luft III. McQueen's character, USAAF Captain Virgil Hilts (otherwise known as 'the Cooler King' because he spends so much of his time cooling down in the slammer), is best known for his daring leap over the fence on the motorbike (a stunt actually performed by McQueen's friend Bud Elkins, even though McQueen was a keen motorcyclist).

In the film, the fence was constructed of barbed wire fixed to wooden struts positioned at regular intervals. These days, however, any prison fence is more likely to be made of 358 high-density wire mesh fence, manufactured in China and apparently ideal not just for prisons but also for military sites, embassies, schools, and other secure compounds. 358 mesh fence consists of very closely spaced steel and carbon mesh, supported by tall metal struts, and it is almost impossible to climb or cut. Yet although it comes in a choice of colours – green, black, or yellow – it is hard to imagine the Cooler King making his bid for freedom over such a prosaic fence.

GALLOP ALL THE WAY BACK TO **30** FOR MORE FENCES TO JUMP

359

Formulas, algorithms, sieves, and primes

359 is the highest prime number in this book, and we have listed 71 others, starting with 2. A prime number is a positive integer greater than 1 that is divisible only by 1 and itself. An alternative definition is that a prime number is one that has exactly two factors (1 and itself). And that is why 1 is not prime: it has only one factor.

Prime numbers are easily defined but not so easy to find. There is an infinite number of them, and there is no simple formula for producing a list, or for determining whether a given number is prime. There are, however, algorithms (step-by-step processes) that can be used for both these tasks. At its simplest, you work out whether a number is prime by the process of trial division, systematically testing whether the number in question is divisible by any smaller number.

The trial-division process is semi-automated in prime-number sieves. The earliest and simplest of these is the Sieve of Eratosthenes, which works by sequentially removing composite (non-prime) numbers, starting with multiples of 2, then multiples of 3, and so on. Eratosthenes (276–194 BCE) would have done it with pencil and paper (or rather stylus and wax tablet), but these days computers are better at this sort of task.

ERATOSTHENES MAKES ANOTHER APPEARANCE AT **276**

360

BLAME IT ON BABYLON

Why is a circle divided into 360 degrees? Why not 100, or 500, or some other apparently rounder number? We could discuss pi (π, 3.141592…), and we could introduce the concept of the radian, and we could explain that a full circle is 2π radians – but instead we're just going to blame the Babylonians.

In ancient Babylon, from about 5,000 years ago, people counted not in tens but in sixties. Their mathematicians were also interested in trigonometry (the study of triangles), and having worked out that six nice neat equilateral triangles overlaid on a circle divide the circle into six nice neat equal parts, it would have been natural to divide each of those six divisions into 60. So there you have it: $6 \times 60 = 360$.

That, at least, is one theory. Alternatively, the idea of dividing the circle into 360 degrees may have sprung from the fact that a year is very close to 360 days in length. It is also worth noting that 360 is a very convenient number, as it is divisible by 2, 3, 4, 5, 6, 8, 9, 10, 12, 15, 18, 20, 30, …

We can also blame the Babylonians for the fact that an hour is divided into 60 minutes, and a minute into 60 seconds.

TURN TO **60** FOR SOMETHING THAT REALLY ISN'T THEIR FAULT

TIME IN SPACE FOR ONE OF THE ARTS

How do astronauts fill their downtime, besides eat, sleep, chat, and take a little exercise? For Daniel Barry and Koichi Wakata, who flew on NASA's STS-72 *Endeavour* mission in January 1996, the answer was simple: play Go.

The game of Go (*wéiqí* in Chinese) originated in ancient China and spread to the rest of East Asia sometime between the fifth and seventh centuries, but it didn't become popular in the West until the end of the nineteenth century. In China the game was considered to be one of the Four Cultivated Arts, together with calligraphy, painting, and playing music on a seven-stringed instrument called a *gǔqín*.

Go is a game for two, using a board with a grid of squares. Originally it was played on a 17×17 grid, and beginners still often play on smaller boards with 9×9 or 13×13 lines, but nowadays a typical board has 19×19 lines, making a total of 361 intersections or points. The players use small round pieces called stones (one set black, the other white), and the aim is to capture one's opponent's stones by surrounding them – and then removing those stones from play – and to claim as many of the 361 points as possible.

Wakata and Barry were the first astronauts to play Go in space (using a specially made board). But perhaps 8 days, 22 hours, 1 minute and 47 seconds – the duration of the mission – was just not long enough for them to cultivate their skills in the other three arts.

362

A SMALL SPARK IN A BIG REVOLUTION

In the early 1920s, cats' whiskers and crystals began to give way to wireless sets that used valves. Developments in valve technology since the invention of the thermionic valve in 1904 had paved the way for mass broadcast radio, and when the BBC started broadcasting in 1922 it really became essential to have a valve wireless. Home-built receivers were all the rage, and there was a thriving trade in components through the 1920s and 1930s. Britain was abuzz with all things wireless, and the technological advances continued apace. Triodes gave way to tetrodes, and then to pentodes. There was always something new to attract the attention of the enthusiast, and the highlight of the year was the annual National Wireless and Radio Exhibition, rebranded as Radiolympia in 1936.

Somewhere in the midst of this buzz of excitement, electricity, and radio waves was the 362 Radio Valve Company. Based in Hackney, east London, the company began manufacturing valves in 1933, competing with Mullard, Marconi, Ever Ready, Mazda, and the rest. A while later 362 moved a few kilometres north to Highbury, but the company ceased trading in 1937. And that is about all that it has been possible to discover about the elusive 362 Radio Valve Company. Why was the company called 362? Why did it go out of business? Even the resources of twenty-first-century telecommunications have failed to reveal any more about a company that played its own small part in the telecommunications revolution eighty years ago.

363

A MANIFESTO FOR THE TRICOLORE

France has had its fair share of political turmoil, and since the 1789 Revolution much of this unrest has focused on the conflict between monarchists and republicans. This was certainly the case during the Third Republic, in May 1877. President Patrice MacMahon, whose sympathies lay firmly on the side of the monarchists, was pitted against the overwhelmingly republican Chamber of Deputies, the majority of whose members favoured a parliamentary system of government.

The disagreement between president and parliament resulted in *La Crise du Seize Mai* (the 16 May Crisis), when 363 deputies passed a vote of no confidence in the president. Among the signatories of the *Manifeste des 363* (Manifesto of the 363) was Georges Clemenceau, who had taken part in the 1871 Paris Commune. Clemenceau went on to become prime minister (twice), and he was one of the principal architects of the 1919 Paris Peace Conference and the Treaty of Versailles. Among the *Manifeste*'s other signatories were Jean Casimir-Perier and Émile Loubet, who later became France's sixth and eighth presidents respectively.

In the aftermath of the crisis, parliament was dissolved, new elections returned a republican majority, MacMahon resigned, and a parliamentary system of governance, rather than a presidential one, held sway. Although France went on to encounter further tensions between parliaments and presidents, there is no sign that the *tricolore* will be replaced by the white flag or fleur-de-lis of the Ancien Régime any time soon.

364

Un-birthday presents

You only need to gather 23 people together before it is more likely than not that two of them will share a birthday – but how many people do you need before two of them share an un-birthday?

A puzzle like that would most likely have scrambled the brain of Humpty Dumpty in Lewis Carroll's *Through the Looking-Glass* (1871). After all, his maths is a little shaky, and he'd rather see Alice write it out on paper before he is completely convinced that there are 364 days in the year on which he might receive an un-birthday present. He is, however, very proud of the cravat that the White King and Queen gave him on such an occasion, and he is quite certain that it is not a belt. He is definitely on firmer ground when it comes to words and definitions, and when he says that 'glory' means 'a nice knock-down argument', that's what it means.

Given his soft-boiled approach to numbers, it would probably be best not to ask Humpty Dumpty how many presents are received in the song 'The Twelve Days of Christmas', for that involves not a simple subtraction but quite a lot of adding, and maybe even multiplication. The answer is 364 – and unless the recipient's birthday falls somewhere between 25 December and 6 January, they would all be un-birthday presents.

TO WRAP AN UN-BIRTHDAY PRESENT, YOU COULD TRY **178**

THE LURE OF A NUMBER

The 365 days of the year have long held a fascination for human beings, and measuring and marking the turning of the years has been a preoccupation ever since our Stone Age ancestors aligned their sacred sites with the winter solstice, or the summer solstice, or the equinox.

The lure of 365 has endured through the millennia. It surfaced a few hundred years ago in the building of 'calendar houses' – a small number of grand houses in various countries that had 365 rooms or 365 windows – and it is evident today all around us. Tourist brochures assure us that there are 365 islands in Clew Bay in the west of Ireland, and just the same number in Panama's San Blas archipelago. Sun worshippers on Antigua are invited to choose a different beach for every day of the year. A pub on the Isle of Wight is proud of its 365 whiskies. You can climb 365 steps to the church at Pollença, Mallorca, and many other flights of steps apparently match exactly. Back home from holiday, we encounter any number of computer programs, radio stations, websites, blogs, and businesses with 365 in their names.

The Stone Age builders were actually measuring the annual cycle, and for them a precise count mattered. But in these more recent examples it's often just a nod towards the number of days in the year – marking, but not measuring, the year. Does it matter if some of them are not strictly accurate?

And what should we make of a book that uses the number 365 in its title, but does not in fact contain precisely 365 topics?

FOR AN ACCURATE COUNT, TAKE JUST ONE FINAL STEP TO **366**

366

JUST AN APPROXIMATION

…For of course there aren't exactly 365 days in the year. It actually takes more like 365 days, 5 hours, 48 minutes, 45.216 seconds (365.24219 days) for the earth to orbit the sun – though the precise figure depends on where and when you measure it.

The fact that 365 days is only an approximation has been known since antiquity, and for a long time devisers of calendars have included periodic adjustments to keep the calendar year synchronised as closely as possible with the solar year. The Julian calendar, introduced by Julius Caesar in 46 BCE, included a leap year of 366 days every four years, thereby achieving an average calendar year of 365.25 days.

But Julius was already out of date. The Babylonians and Egyptians had long ago worked out that the solar year was slightly longer than 365 but not quite as long as 365.25 days.

As the centuries passed the difference between 365.25 and 365.24219 meant that the seasons got progressively out of sync with the calendar. By 1582 the date of the equinox had shifted about 10 days, and Pope Gregory XIII introduced the Gregorian calendar, changing the simple rule (one leap year every four years) to a more complex one, that years divisible by 100 should only be leap years if they were also divisible by 400. This is the system currently used in most of the world, and it results in an average calendar year of 365.2425 days. Not a bad approximation – and perhaps not a bad way of ending a book that covers *approximately* 365 topics.

LEAP BACK TO **179** FOR FURTHER CALENDAR CAPERS

ACKNOWLEDGEMENTS

We are very grateful to George, Caroline, Owen, and Ruth for putting up with us (and occasionally humouring us) while we wrote this.

We thank Rebecca Budgett, Paul Hoffman, and Gina Taylor for suggesting interesting topics that helped us to plug what might otherwise have been three embarrassing gaps, and Mark Avery for nagging us to get on with it.

Our agent Andrew Lownie provided invaluable advice and support, and we are also delighted with all the help and encouragement we have received from the team at Square Peg: Rosemary Davidson, Fran Barrie, Kris Potter, Alice Palmer-Brown, Minty Nicholson, Ceri Maxwell, Mary Chamberlain, Anthony Hippisley, Lindsay Nash, and Simon Rhodes.

INDEX

372